Dr. Phillip L. Hunsaker is an Associate Professor of Management and Organizational Development at the University of San Diego. He is an avid researcher and writer with a multitude of articles in both academic and professional journals. He is an author of several books, including *You Can Make it Happen: A Guide to Self-Actualization and Organizational Change*. Dr. Hunsaker is an experienced consultant and conducts professional seminars throughout the country.

Dr. Anthony J. Alessandra is a nationally recognized professional speaker, consultant, and author in the fields of sales, management, and communications. He averages 120 speeches per year to thousands of people and frequently appears on radio and TV talk shows.

He is a prolific writer of articles, author of the best-selling book *Non-Manipulative Selling*, and co-author of *The Competitive Edge in Selling* and *Build a Better You—Starting Now!* (Vol. 2).

Besides playing a lead role in the top-selling film *The Power of Listening*, Dr. Alessandra is under contract to help produce a series of sales training films with Walt Disney Productions.

THE ART OF
MANAGING
PEOPLE

Phillip L. Hunsaker
Anthony J. Alessandra

A SPECTRUM BOOK

PRENTICE-HALL, INC., *Englewood Cliffs, New Jersey 07632*

Library of Congress Cataloging in Publication Data

HUNSAKER, PHILLIP L
    The art of managing people.

    (A Spectrum Book)
    Includes bibliographies and index.
    1. Personnel management.   I. Alessandra, Anthony J.,
joint author.   II. Title.
HF5549.H876   658.3   80-12757
ISBN 0-13-047472-X
ISBN 0-13-047464-9 (pbk.)

10   9   8   7   6   5   4   3   2   1

Printed in the United States of America

Editorial/production supervision and interior design by Frank Moorman.
Cover design by Ira Shapiro
Manufacturing buyer: Barbara A. Frick

PRENTICE-HALL INTERNATIONAL, INC., *London*
PRENTICE-HALL OF AUSTRALIA PTY. LIMITED, *Sydney*
PRENTICE-HALL OF CANADA, LTD., *Toronto*
PRENTICE-HALL OF INDIA PRIVATE LIMITED, *New Delhi*
PRENTICE-HALL OF JAPAN, INC., *Tokyo*
PRENTICE-HALL OF SOUTHEAST ASIA PTE. LTD., *Singapore*
WHITEHALL BOOKS LIMITED, *Wellington, New Zealand*

Contents

v

3 Doing Unto Others, 32

4 Deciding How to Decide, 50

5 Analyzing Transactional Styles, 69

16 Developing Action Plans, 233

17 Implementing Action, 244

18 Following Through, 250

19 What Do You Do with What You've Learned?, 257

Preface

The art of managing people productively and effectively is perhaps the most challenging task facing today's managers. Numerous books have been written presenting theories, concepts, strategies, and techniques with the express purpose of helping managers "manage" others better. Many more books will be written in the future on this same topic. Why then should you spend your time reading *this* book versus all the others? How is it different? What makes it important reading material for you? And what can you expect to get out of this book once you've completed reading it?

The art of managing others is a dynamic process that is ever changing and evolving. Many of the managerial concepts proposed only a few years ago cannot and will not work in today's environment. People have changed. The business environment has changed. Government has changed. The world economy has changed. The scarcity of resources has worsened, especially the valuable resource of skilled labor. Attracting, training, motivating, and keeping employees has become much more difficult and much more expensive. It will get much worse in the future. Managing others productively and effectively becomes much more important in times such as these. It will become even more important in the future. It is to this crucial issue that this book is addressed.

This book was developed to overcome many of the traditional manager-employee relationship problems. Although its ideas are not radically new, how they are combined in establishing the manager-employee relationship makes our approach unique. It is based on the philosophy that people perform effectively and productively when the manager allows them to obtain optimum personality expression while at work. Employees need to be permitted to be more active and independent and to have more control over their own jobs and in expressing their own opinions in order to maximize their personal, professional, and organizational productivity. *The Art of Managing People* shows the manager how to develop a strong trust bond with employees in order to facilitate the development of an effective team of satisfied productive individuals, held together through healthy interpersonal relationships.

The Art of Managing People introduces you to a number of ways to diagnose, understand, and relate to different types of people. You will be able to take a close look at the different ways people prefer to learn, and you will learn how you can facilitate that process. You will also learn how to relate to different personality types effectively and productively, and you will acquire the ability to assess individual decision styles and how to apply that knowledge in the problem solving process.

In addition to the above material, you will learn numerous interactive communication skills such as questioning techniques, active listening skills, nonverbal communication skills, and feedback skills. The various questioning techniques and strategies will give you a greater ability to uncover your employees' problems and needs, while the listening skills will help you to be more sensitive, attentive, and responsive to your employees during the communication process. Your increased awareness of the nonverbal messages others send you will make you more sensitive to what those other people are really communicating and feeling. The feedback skills will close the communication loop and will help you to verify that you understand exactly what others are telling you and that they understand exactly what you are telling them.

By reading, assimilating, and using the skills guidelines and techniques that are presented in this book, you will be more able to interact with your employees and solve problems in an open, honest atmosphere of trust and helpfulness. Employee problems will be genuinely solved, and the increased support you will gain will lead to greater fulfillment of personal, professional, and organizational goals for both you and your employees. The bottom line benefit will be increased productivity for everyone involved in this unique managerial approach in the art of managing people.

Many of the ideas and concepts in this book have been "field-tested" over the last several years in the authors' seminars and speeches. The input and comments from the thousands of managers, supervisors, sales managers, and salespeople helped shape and refine the material into a practical, success-oriented book. We both would be delighted to receive reactions from readers regarding the book's content or application. We welcome opportunites to learn from your comments and to help you integrate these concepts into your own organizations.

This book evolved out of our many years of research and experience. During those years we have come in contact with numerous people, who in one way or another, directly and indirectly, contributed to this book. The list is too long and cumbersome to mention. But to all those people out there who shared their thoughts, ideas, and time with us over the years, we wish to take this opportunity to thank you. Without all of you, this book may never have come to be or may have never been written the way it actually was. We would like to offer special thanks to Phillip S. Wexler for his conceptual contributions prior to and during the writing of this book. Special thanks also go to Glend Holt, who literally transcribed, edited, and typed the manuscript day and night in order to get it finished on time. Lastly, we wish to offer a very personal thanks to our wives, Johanna and Janice, and our children, Justin, Kathy, Phillip, and Sarah, whose understanding and support during our writing allowed us to complete the manuscript and personally survive the process involved.

Tony Alessandra
920 Kline Street 100
La Jolla, Ca. 92037
(714) 459-1515

Phil Hunsaker
441 A Avenue
Coronado, Ca. 92118
(714) 293-4511

To our parents,
who provided our first experiences
in the Art of Managing People

THE ART OF MANAGING PEOPLE

1

*"Oh, wad some power the giftie gie us to see oursels
as others see us."*
Robert Burns, 1786

Building Productive Managerial Relationships

Have you ever wished that you could magically know what
other people are really thinking about you when you are
interacting with them? There are plenty of reasons why this
information could be very valuable to you as a manager. There
may also be plenty of reasons why you would rather not know.

"That incompetent SOB. He's trying to get me to do his job
again."

"Another phony smile. She doesn't really care about me."

"He makes me feel so stupid and helpless."

"She's treating me like a child. When I get the chance, I'll slip
it to her good."

"He asks questions as if doubting everything I say."

"She does all the talking. Obviously, my opinion doesn't count."

"His poker face keeps me guessing whether he understands me
or is even listening to me."

"She argues with everything I say. I'm always wrong. She's
always right."

Thousands of managers have such things said about them
every day. But because they can't get inside the heads of their

1

subordinates, peers, and superiors, they are unaware of why they are having such problems. In fact, many of them are unaware of any problems existing at all. And we're talking about some of the brightest managers with the best technical track records in industry today. In most of these cases the problem is not lack of experience, energy, intelligence, or dedication but neglect of building and maintaining productive relationships with others. In attempting to determine what managers need most to be effective, a countless number of surveys have produced a very consistent answer. More than anything else, a manager needs to be able to get along with other people. You probably aren't too surprised with this answer. Then why is it still such a monumental problem for so many managers?

One reason is that managers typically are not well trained in relating productively with others. Many managers today have advanced degrees in business administration, engineering, or the like, but such technical expertise does not magically confer equivalent expertise in managing relationships. And neither do years of successful experience in a technical area. Consequently, most managers simply are not as well equipped to deal with people problems as they are with technical ones. Even if they were, chances are that most managers would not think in terms applicable to people problems.

In the business world, management is almost always viewed in terms of productivity. Why? Because productivity is the key to the success of the organization and to your future as a manager. You evaluate your subordinates on how much they produce, because you are evaluated on how much they produce. Under this one-dimensional system of evaluation, it is easy to slip into the point of view that people are similar to such other resources as material and money, which are to be exploited as much as possible for the company's good. Today's employees will not tolerate this type of treatment without severe negative consequences for both their own well-being and their contribution to the company's goals. Successful managers realize that for employees to be most productive, they must have opportunities for satisfying their own needs built into the work environment. Consequently, managers need a thorough awareness of employees' values, needs, and reasons for behaving, as well as personal skills in communicating with and motivating employees toward the accomplishment of organizational goals in ways that will be accepted and not resented.

Getting the work out is only one side of the productivity coin. For long-term effectiveness, you must accomplish this work by being sensitive to the needs of those who work for and with you. In fact, management by definition is getting the work done through the efforts of other people. You may be able to get short-term results by exploiting and dominating people, but your effectiveness—and maybe your career—will no doubt be jeopardized in the long term. The resulting hostility and resentment that will have built up will eventually be released, either openly or secretly, to cause your failure as a manager.

An analogy often used to illustrate the two sides of the productivity coin is that of a bicycle. Technical knowledge and people knowledge can be thought of as the two wheels. Technical knowledge is the back wheel, which makes the bicycle go. It supplies the drive that you have to have to go anywhere. Obviously, *technical* management is important. The front wheel is the *people* knowledge. It steers, directs, and takes the back-wheel power where you want to go. You can have all the back-wheel expertise in the world; but if people won't cooperate or don't know where to go with it, you won't go anywhere. This is what Interactive Management is all about!

No matter how ambitious or capable you are, you cannot be an effective manager without knowing how to establish and maintain productive relationships with others. You must know how to relate so that others want to work with you and accept you rather than reject you.

Does this mean that you become mushy and other-directed, primarily concerned with servicing the needs and desires of others? Or that you should develop a master strategy that will

Technical   People
Knowledge   Knowledge

give you the breaks at the expense of others, or enable you to play up to those who can do you the most good while paying little attention to others? The answer to these questions is, of course, a resounding *no!*

It does mean, however, that you should sincerely do everything you can to develop strong, friendly, honest, and trusting relationships with all of the people you work with, including your bosses, subordinates, and fellow managers. In your position as a manager, you automatically assume two responsibilities: (1) to do the best technical job you can with the work assigned to you, and (2) to interact with all people to the best of your ability. It is with the second of these responsibilities that this book is designed to help you. The goal is to develop your skills of managing transactions with others in ways that spell success for yourself, others, and the organization as a whole.

THE INTERACTIVE APPROACH
TO MANAGING PEOPLE

Research on human personality suggests that healthy individuals need to be treated with respect and to have opportunities to feel competent and independent as they actively pursue goals to which they are committed. Unfortunately, research on technical management indicates that its directive, production-oriented characteristics tend to create situations where employees feel dependent, submissive, and passive and where they use few of their important abilities, let alone developing them. Their activities are aimed at the organization's and manager's needs rather than at their own; and they often end up frustrated, resentful, and underproductive. Under these conditions, employees will tend to adapt by leaving, manifesting defense mechanisms (such as daydreaming, aggression, or ambivalence), or rebelling openly against the manager and the system.

If employees leave or use defense mechanisms to suppress their frustrations, management may not even be aware of the problems being created. In the case of open rebellion, however, the technical manager's responses are usually in the form of "corrective actions" such as increased controls, stiffer penalties, or other actions that tend to compound the employees' frustrations. The result is an increasing distance, mistrust, and resentment on both sides. Nobody wins.

The interactive management philosophy was developed to overcome some of these manager–employee relationship problems. Although the ideas are not radically new, how they are combined in establishing the supervisor–employee relationship makes this approach unique. It is based on the philosophy that it is neither healthy nor profitable to manipulate or exploit other people. This philosophy incorporates the belief that people perform effectively because they understand and feel understood by the supervisor, not because they are forced to comply by a mandate from above. It revolves around helping people understand procedures rather than forcing them to comply. The entire process is built around trust-bond relationships that require openness and honesty. Table 1-1 points out some major differences between interactive and technically oriented management.

Company Oriented versus Employee Oriented. In technical management, the manager is predominantly interested in the task instead of the employee. Getting the job done, regardless of the human costs, is the primary motivator. Verbal and nonverbal behaviors suggest urgency, impatience, and dominance.

On the other hand, the interactive manager fills the role of a counselor, consultant, and problem solver. Helping the subordinate determine the best course of action and how to implement it takes top priority. All verbal and nonverbal behaviors project trust, confidence, patience, empathy, and helpfulness. The result in this new form of management is a close, open, trusting manager–employee relationship—a win–win relationship.

**Table 1-1 Differences between Technical
and Interactive Management**

Technical	*Interactive*
Company oriented	Employee oriented
Tells	Explains and listens
Forces compliance	Develops commitment
Task oriented	People oriented
Inflexible	Adaptable
Thwarts needs	Satisfies needs
Creates fear and tension	Establishes trust and understanding

Tells versus Explains and Listens. The technical manager dominates the conversation, asking for little verbal input from subordinates except to indicate compliance at appropriate points. Conversely, in interactive management the emphasis is on problem solving that incorporates two-way discussion and feedback. The manager is knowledgeable, competent, and confident in the verbal communication skills of questioning, listening, and feedback.

Forces Compliance versus Develops Commitment. *Power* and *authority* are key buzzwords for the technical manager. "Do it my way or else!" "Managers are the thinkers. Employees are the doers." "Management makes the decisions around here!" These are familiar phrases in technical management. Thus, the manager controls, persuades, and figuratively "browbeats" employees to do as requested *now*, whether or not they are ready. Although this technique may work in the short run, it generates dissatisfied workers who are apt to rebel subtly or quit when they get the chance.

An effective blending of short-term and long-term objectives is the trademark of interactive managers. They allow employees "breathing room" to solve their own problems in a reasonable period of time. Immediate compliance is not as important today as building an efficient and effective work team. Although this orientation may take a little longer in getting positive results from the employees, it leads to less resentment, more manager–employee trust and goodwill, better long-term morale, and greater team effectiveness.

Task Oriented versus People Oriented. Meeting production deadlines is more important to the technical manager than developing people. This orientation very often leads to frustrated employees who only give the minimum required effort.

Interactive management is people oriented. The employee's problems and/or needs are as important as the task. The interactive manager's ultimate objective is to develop relationships with employees so that they are motivated to accomplish organizational goals of their own volition.

Inflexible versus Adaptable. Technical managers typically approach and interact with different employees in the same way all the time. They are not sensitive to variations in the styles, needs, and problems of their different employees. Technical managers often are insensitive and oblivious to cues that an individual employee has unique and pressing needs at this particular time or under the present circumstances.

Flexibility is a key skill used by interactive managers. They are flexible in communicating with all different styles of employees. Their management style is adapted to each individual employee and situation. They are simultaneously perceptive of the verbal and nonverbal cues that a subordinate sends and are willing and able to change their approach and objective if necessary.

Thwarts Needs versus Satisfies Needs. When you tell someone that you know what the person's problem is and proceed to present the solution to it without getting much feedback, the person tends to become defensive, secretive, and resentful. The interaction becomes more like a battle—a win–lose situation. An employee will not freely share important information with a manager under these conditions and often will create "smoke screens" (false fronts) to throw the manager off balance. Obviously, this is not a productive relationship.

In interactive management, the supervisor is skilled in information gathering in order to help the employee openly and honestly discover personal needs and problems. With this approach, the employee perceives the relationship as a "helping" one. Trust, confidence, and openness are free flowing in this "win–win" association. In addition, the employee is totally involved in the solution process with the manager. This allows the employee to be more personally committed to the implementation of the plan.

Creates Fear and Tension versus Establishes Trust and Understanding. The six previously discussed behaviors culminate in a supervisor–subordinate relationship based either on fear and tension or on trust and understanding. In technical management, fear and defense levels are high. Both the manager and the employee play games with each other (for a detailed discussion on games, refer to Chapter 5). Management becomes more of a process of persuasion and control rather than problem solving and facilitation. The supervisor–employee relationship deteriorates as defensiveness and distrust continue to increase.

Conversely, in interactive management, trust, acceptance, and understanding are the norm. The supervisor–employee communication process is open, honest, and straightforward. Information is openly shared, and problems are genuinely resolved. Whether or not a decision is made, both supervisor and employee feel good about each other and about their interaction. Both sides win.

PRINCIPLES OF INTERACTIVE MANAGEMENT

There are four basic principles behind the interactive management philosophy. They are aimed at developing a trusting relationship between two adults. This is in contrast to technical management, which typically develops as a suspicious relationship between a naughty child and a critical parent.

1. The entire management process is built around *trust-bond* relationships that require openness and honesty on the part of both the supervisor and the employee.
2. Subordinates comply, not because they are made to, but because they feel *understood* by the manager and understand the problem.
3. People strive for the right to *make their own decisions*. They resent being manipulated, controlled, or persuaded into making a decision even if that was the decision they would ultimately have made.
4. Do not solve subordinates' problems. They will resent the solution, and if you as the manager inflict the solution, they will resent you also. Point out problems; don't solve them. Let subordinates *solve their own problems* with your help.

By following these principles, the interactive manager allows employees to obtain optimum personality expression while at work. Employees are permitted to be more active than passive, more independent than dependent, to have more control over their world, to feel accepted and respected, and to exercise many of their more important abilities. As employees experience these things with their supervisor, a trust bond is formed that facilitates the development of an effective team made up of satisfied, productive individuals held together through healthy interpersonal transactions.

We realize that it will be difficult for managers who are held responsible for results and who have been used to "keeping on top" of what subordinates are doing to drop old habits suddenly and trust that employees will automatically and immediately take the ball. In fact, they probably won't. Their experience has taught them that you are in charge and that their roles are to implement what you direct. So we're talking about a gradual process with initial risks of mistakes and failures. These must be seen as opportunities for learning and not as dangers to be avoided for fear of reprisal.

In communicating this atmosphere of growth and learning to employees, keep in mind that your actions speak louder than words. Don't attempt interactive management unless you are willing to trust your employees and give them the opportunities to adjust to your changed style and expectations.

There is a five-step process we recommend to ease the transition and aid in the establishment of effective relationships for joint problem solving. These five steps, presented in Table 1-2, enable the interactive management philosophy to be translated into action. Can you see the probable differences in employees' reactions to the two management procedures?

Trust Bond. Mutual respect and understanding are prerequisites for joint problem solving. The development of a firm trust-bond relationship with your employee is the foundation of interactive management. Employees prefer a supervisor on whom they can rely, someone who cares about them and will help fulfill their personal needs. Under these conditions, employees can let their guard down and not worry about being

Table 1-2 Technical versus Interactive Management Procedures

Technical	Interactive
Establish power base.	Establish *trust* bond.
What is your problem?	Define the problem situation.
Here is my plan for you.	Let *us* make a new action plan.
If you don't do it . . .	Commitment and implementation.
I'll be watching you!	Follow-through

exploited. They can dare to experiment and take risks conducive to personal and professional development.

The interactive manager must acquire an understanding of the subordinates and the communication skills to facilitate the building of a mutual trust relationship. This provides both an opportunity and a threat for many managers, because it requires them to be more open and complete as people in their own role as managers.

Define the Problem.   Once a strong trust bond has been established with subordinates (or even while building the trust bond), the interactive manager deepens the relationship by becoming totally involved in the problem-solving process with the employees. It is mutually determined what exactly the current situation is like for the employees. What are their personal and task goals? What are subordinates currently doing to solve their problems or satisfy their needs? This diagnostic activity relies very heavily on effective information sharing and information-gathering skills, as well as a keen understanding on the part of the manager of the "style" differences among employees.

The interactive manager determines whether the subordinate is fully satisfied with their relationship and working procedures. The employee is urged to crystallize personal goals and objectives and to match them with the company's objectives to determine if the current relationship is the most efficient and effective method of achieving the desired results for both. This situational analysis leads to the conclusive question: Can another plan of action be more productive in helping the employee and the company achieve mutual goals and objectives?

Develop New Action Plans.   Together, both the interactive manager and the employee begin planning new courses of action. The major role of the supervisor is to ask the proper questions in order to help the subordinate solve her own problems. The supervisor "actively" listens to the employee and helps direct the process toward the realization of both personal and professional goals and company objectives. Hopefully, the newly derived action plan will be mutually beneficial. However, it is important to remember that the interactive manager acts as a guide and not as a controller, manipulator, or persuader. If the employee is allowed to "discover" the solution for herself, it will have more personal meaning and value. Hence, it is more likely to be implemented—enthusiastically.

Commitment and Implementation. The commitment process in interactive management centers on "when," not "if." If subordinates are allowed to have a major role in determining goals and objectives and to design a workable plan to optimize those desired results, they become personally committed to the implementation of the plan. The manager's role is to ask the employee to commit to her own plan at some specific point in time.

Follow-Through. In step 4 of interactive management, "Commitment and Implementation," the supervisor asked the subordinate to make a commitment to the new action plan. In step 5, the supervisor makes a commitment to the employee. The supervisor must assume the responsibility and the challenge to maintain the relationship after the agreement has formally been made. The supervisor must constantly seek feedback from the subordinate to monitor the situation and the results. The supervisor must react to situations before they become problems rather than waiting for something to happen that requires "fixing up." In the final analysis, it is follow-through that determines the future relationship with an employee. The interactive manager develops a thorough follow-through strategy for each employee that firmly cements their long-term professional and personal relationship. The follow-through is a sensitive, constructive process as opposed to the traditional suspicious overseer's approach.

These steps of Interactive Management, which are covered in detail in the last part of this book, are transformed into action through the use of specific skills that are covered in the first two parts. Part I, "Understanding People," explores the unique differences in how people learn, interact with others, and make decisions. Part II, "Interactive Communication Skills," covers in detail the verbal, vocal, and observable communication processes. Let's look a little closer at these two crucial parts and how their chapters unfold.

UNDERSTANDING PEOPLE

Learning How to Learn. Successful managers today can be distinguished, not so much by their particular knowledge or skills, but by their ability to adapt and master changing job and career demands. All of us have unique ways of learning with both strong and weak points. It is important for managers to be aware of their own and subordinates' learning styles and the alternatives made available. Personal and team development can then proceed in the most efficient and effective manner.

Doing Unto Others. People with different behavioral styles inherently create tension between themselves simply by being near each other. As this tension increases, the probability of their establishing a trust bond decreases. In order to increase the chances of establishing trust with others, you must be able to keep tension at a minimum level. This requires knowing how to identify the different behavioral styles and how to relate to each style effectively and productively. In order to relate effectively and differentially, the interactive manager must (1) learn about the behavioral characteristics of each behavioral style, (2) be able to identify the behavioral style of the person with whom he or she is dealing, and (3) acquire skills in behavioral flexibility in order to treat people the way they want to be treated.

Deciding How to Decide. Different people perceive and process information in different ways. The interactive manager must be able to perceive these differences and adapt to them in order to utilize employees' abilities most effectively. It is important to have methods for assessing your own and others' decision styles and to know how to apply this knowledge in fruitful information exchange for effective goal setting, decision making, and implementation.

Analyzing Transactional Styles. In transactional analysis (TA), the emphasis is on examining manager–subordinate styles of relating. Our focus on TA is to introduce supervisors to a simple and effective technique for improving their understanding of how and why people relate to others as they do. This should lead to an increased effectiveness in interpersonal communications, which will aid the supervisor in securing genuine cooperation and respect from subordinates.

INTERACTIVE COMMUNICATION SKILLS

The Art of Questioning. This chapter covers the various types of questions, when to use them, how to use them, and with whom to use them; the art of getting the other person to "open up"; and how to ask the proper questions to allow subordinates to discover things for themselves.

The Power of Listening. This type of listening involves hearing your employee's words, processing that information in your mind, and using that information to help structure your relationship. It also involves verbally and nonverbally projecting to your subordinate that you are really listening. There are numerous learnable skills for "actively" listening to other people. This is one of the best ways to establish trust relationships with others.

Projecting the Appropriate Image. How you "come across" to others very often determines how they will treat you. · If you project a good image—professional, authoritative, knowledgeable, successful, enthusiastic, and so on—your employees are much more likely to trust you, believe you, and accept your leadership and guidance. If your image is inappropriate, the opposite is likely to happen. This chapter explores various ways for you to project appropriate images of yourself to others.

Communicating through Voice Tones. When it comes to choosing between the meaning of what is said versus how it is said, people most often choose the latter. The same exact words said with a different vocal emphasis can have significantly different meanings. Effective communication requires an awareness not only of the way you say things but also of the vocal intonations of your employees in order to gather more information, meaning, and feeling from the words spoken.

Using Body Language Effectively. This is regarded by

many experts as the most important element of nonverbal communication, if not the most important factor of communication *in general*. You not only receive positive and negative vibrations from others in the form of body language; you also send them. Therefore, an important communication aspect of interactive management is an awareness of the silent messages you send to your subordinates and of the body language they project to you.

Spatial Arrangements Say Things. The way we use time, space, and things "says" things to other people. When people are kept waiting or you don't have enough time to spend with them, negative feelings are created. When you intrude too closely on your subordinates' personal space or territory, you'll notice that they become uncomfortable and uneasy. Space violations of this nature can block the trust-building and communication processes without your ever knowing why. The nature of your relationship may also be affected by your use of things to communicate, consciously or unconsciously, relative status and images.

Making Sure with Feedback. Feedback is necessary to verify that you understand exactly what others are communicating to you. More subtly, feedback is a way of showing sensitivity to the nonverbal messages that your employees are communicating to you.

CONSTRUCTIVE MANIPULATION

Manipulation is a nasty word to most of us; yet if it is looked at in a constructive way, it is an integral part of interactive management. Actually, we all try to control the attitudes and behavior of others, and they are working just as hard to manipulate us. We start trying to manipulate others in infancy and continue until death. Those of us who are managers, supervisors, or teachers are paid to be manipulators. Rather than try to deny reality, let's take a closer look at the process. If we substitute the word *lead*, *motivate*, *manage*, or some other polite name, it may make the idea more palatable. Better yet, look at manipulation with respect to its outcome. If the outcome is destructive, manipulation will cause resentment, anger, and defensive reactions. On the other hand, if the outcome is constructive and helps others to obtain their objectives, it produces mutual respect and trust. For example, threatening someone is a manipulative technique that does not work. But positive reinforcement, another manipulative technique, does work, because it builds the other person's self-esteem. It's not necessarily *what* you do that counts; it's *how* you do it!

Parenting, teaching, counseling, and managing are all manipulative roles in which we try to get others to do what they "ought" to do. Constructive manipulation is often essential to helping people overcome self-defeating behaviors that interfere with effective performance or their own personal growth. Some of us are better at constructive manipulation than others. Some ground rules that may help follow.

1. **Modeling.**—*Perhaps the most powerful method of manipulating is your personal example. If you obey rules and set high standards for yourself, your employees will take the lead from you.*

2. **Give feedback.**—*Keep your door open. Encourage employees to talk to you about their problems. Listen. Then give employees as much information as you can. Also provide information about competition, productivity, costs, and other factors that affect their jobs. Most importantly, give feedback on good job performance. This can be as simple as a comment of "Good work" or a notice on the bulletin board.*

3. **Confront.**—*Explain to employees why mistakes or poor performance are important and costly to the company. This kind of feedback, given in a understanding way, is essential if problems are to be solved and avoided in the future.*

4. **Value others.**—*Although employees may have hang-ups and problems you don't have, remember that they do have the same human needs you do—to be accepted and to feel valued and worthwhile, to themselves and others. Providing satisfaction of these needs for recognition is the cornerstone of building productive relationships.*

5. **Set high expectations.**—*People do better with praise, encouragement, and expressed confidence than they do with humiliation, impatience, and indifference. A long list of studies have demonstrated that if we communicate our expectations that a person will do well, the outcome will probably be high performance, and vice versa. This concept of self-fulfilling prophecies is a powerful management tool. If employees are perceived as potentials rather than problems, possessing strengths rather than weaknesses, they will be more productive and grow to their capabilities.*

6. **Positive stroking.**—*This is perhaps the most direct way of acknowledging the value of others. Positive strokes are compliments relating to the other person's behavior in a particular situation. Examples are: "You sure are a pleasure to work with" or "I really appreciate the tact you used in handling that angry customer."*

WHAT TO EXPECT

The finest stroke you can give anyone is your active attention and listening without judging or criticizing what that person has to say. Also, people are willing to listen and take action on suggestions only when they trust the person who gives those suggestions. Consequently, the primary theme of this book is creating trust bonds leading to constructive positive relationships with others as a means to personal, professional, and organizational effectiveness. To do this, it is essential to understand ourselves and others, to be effective in communicating this understanding, and to be able to facilitate the achievement by others of mutually acceptable goals.

A major portion of this book focuses on helping you learn ways to build the trust bond. It explains tension-reducing communication techniques to foster mutual understanding and respect. Frameworks for diagnosing and understanding different personality styles are presented, so that you will know how to relate to different types of employees in the most effective ways. Finally, the interactive management process is explained as it applies to helping you achieve greater personal and organizational productivity through the effective management of others.

To sum up the philosophy of this book: We can be more effective managers by increasing both our understanding of others and our skills for communicating effectively in order to build more productive interpersonal relationships with employees. By becoming more interpersonally effective, we can make our employees and the organization more effective. *Everybody can win!*

ADJUSTING EFFECTIVELY TO PERSONAL STYLE DIFFERENCES

Interactive management is a process of dealing with people as individuals in order to build trust, openness, and honesty in the manager–employee relationship, thereby improving productivity in the organizational setup. To treat your employees as unique individuals, you as the manager must understand what makes them different from one another. With this knowledge, you can go about managing your employees as unique individuals with unique personalities, problems, and needs. This "custom-tailored" approach to managing employees in an organizational setting is one of the major thrusts of interactive management.

The following chapters on learning styles, behavioral styles, decision styles, and transactional styles will provide you with increased knowledge and specific skills to manage your employees as unique individuals. They will, more than likely, repay your increased managerial sensitivity with increased trust and belief in you as a manager and with increased productivity in their personal lives, professional roles, and within the organizational setting.

2

Learning
How to Learn

Successful managers in today's rapidly changing world are distinguished not so much by a set of technical skills as by their ability to *learn* and adapt to the fluctuating demands of their careers. Continuing success requires the ability to explore new opportunities and to learn from past successes and failures.

This chapter presents a model of the learning process developed by David A. Kolb at M.I.T.* to enhance the ability to learn of managers and organizations. It describes how the learning process and individual learning styles affect both manager and employee effectiveness. Knowledge of these learning concepts can aid the interactive manager when called upon to teach employees new concepts and skills. The results of proper application can be more productive and satisfied employees and more effective organizations.

---

*The two primary references are: David A. Kolb, Irwin M. Rubin, and James M. McIntyre, Chapter 2, "Learning and Problem Solving," *Organizational Psychology: An Experiential Approach*, 3rd ed. (Englewood Cliffs, N.J.: Prentice-Hall, 1979), pp. 27–54; and David A. Kolb, "On Management and the Learning Process," *Organizational Psychology: A Book of Readings*, 2nd ed. (Englewood Cliffs, N.J.: Prentice-Hall, 1974), pp. 27–42.

One purpose for studying the learning process is to understand how people go about generating concepts, rules, and principles from their experiences as guides for their future behavior, and how they modify these concepts to improve their effectiveness in new situations. Consequently, the learning process is both active and passive, concrete and abstract. Kolb conceives it as the four-stage cycle diagramed in Figure 2-1: (1) Concrete experience is followed by (2) observation and reflection, which leads to (3) formation of abstract concepts and generalizations, which can be developed into (4) hypotheses to be tested in the future, which lead to new experiences.

If an individual is to be an effective learner, skills are necessary in all four learning areas: concrete experience (CE), reflective observation (RO), abstract conceptualization (AC), and active experimentation (AE). Effective learners must be open to learning from new experiences (CE), reflect upon what they observe in these experiences (RO), integrate their conclusions into workable theories (AC), and apply their theories in new situations (AE). The learning process is continuously recurring. People repeatedly test concepts in new experiences and modify them as a result of observation and analysis of the outcomes.

How concepts are modified and what experiences an individual chooses to engage in are a function of the individual's personal goals and objectives. Consequently, different people will be interested in different experiences, will use different concepts to analyze them, and will draw different conclusions as a result. Learning will vary for people with varying objectives. An implication for managers is to make sure that learning objectives are clear and consistent. Otherwise, subordinates

Figure 2-1 The Learning Model

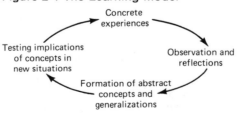

may learn things other than what is intended, and the learning process will be inefficient.

DIMENSIONS OF LEARNING

Even if goals are clear and consistent, effective learning is difficult to achieve. The four-stage learning model indicates that the learner must constantly shift among abilities that are polar opposites of each other. These abilities can be integrated into the two primary dimensions illustrated in Figure 2-2. The first dimension is concrete–abstract, and the second is active–passive.

Because of different life experiences and psychological makeup, as well as variations in current environments, different people are comfortable with different learning dimensions. Some people thrive on working with figures and assimilating information into logical theories, but they fear and avoid letting themselves go in experiencing the emotions of the moment. Others prefer to react spontaneously, "by the seat of their pants," and are bored if they are asked to reflect and think things out. A planner may place heavy emphasis on abstract concepts as opposed to a skilled artisan, who values concrete experience more highly. Managers are primarily concerned with the active application of concepts, whereas time-and-motion people are more involved in using observational and reflective skills.

As a result of these differences in individual abilities and preferences, and the demands of different occupations and situations, people develop different learning styles. Knowledge of these variations can help the interactive manager create

Figure 2-2 Learning Dimensions

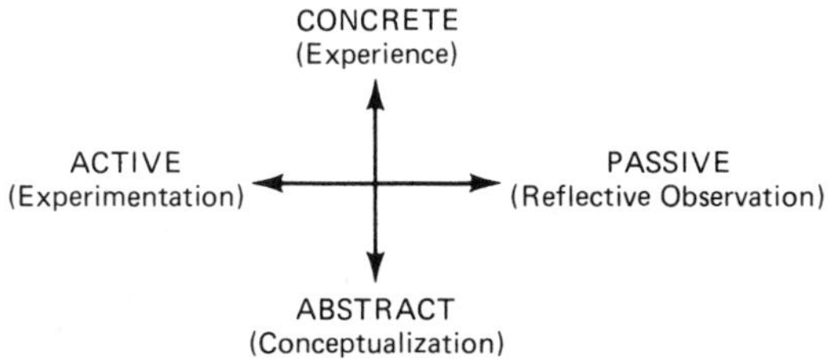

```
              CONCRETE
             (Experience)
                  ↑
                  |
   ACTIVE         |         PASSIVE
(Experimentation)←+→  (Reflective Observation)
                  |
                  ↓
              ABSTRACT
          (Conceptualization)
```

better learning situations for subordinates. The net result will be higher employee productivity and job satisfaction.

INDIVIDUAL LEARNING STYLES

The four learning modes—concrete experience, reflective observation, abstract conceptualization, and active experimentation—represent the four stages of the learning cycle. Consequently, they are all important components of the learning process, and no individual mode is better or worse than any other. A totally balanced use of the four learning modes is not necessarily the best, however. The key to effective learning is being aware of, and able to utilize, each mode when it is appropriate.

Because of our unique abilities and past experiences, most of us tend to be more comfortable with, and therefore to emphasize, some learning modes rather than others. The overemphasis of some modes and avoidance of others may at times be effective if these are the skills necessary in our particular situation. Most often, however, we are involved in a variety of situations requiring different learning modes. Also, most situations change over time, making shifts in learning styles more appropriate. Consequently, although it is good that we have strengths in certain learning modes, it is important that we recognize the importance of all four, when they are appropriate, and how they can be used most effectively.

It is also important to be able to recognize your own predominant learning style and those of others. This awareness may allow you to take advantage of learning strengths and to avoid weaknesses when, for example, you are putting together a task team or making other work assignments. The objective is to use this knowledge to facilitate effective learning and compatible work groups.

LEARNING MODES

The learning modes that reflect each of the learning stages—CE, RO, AC, and AE—are *feeling*, *watching*, *thinking*, and *doing*, respectively. These learning modes are matched to the respective learning-cycle stages in Figure 2-3.

Figure 2-3 Learning Modes

Feelers are individuals who learn best by involving themselves in experiences. They rely on intuition and feelings to make decisions in each situation, which they treat as unique. Feelers learn best from specific examples and are not receptive to abstract theories or universal values and procedures from authorities. They are "people oriented," making them empathic of others and open to feedback and discussions with CE peers.

Thinkers are most comfortable with abstract conceptualization. They rely on rational logic when making decisions. Thinkers learn best in impersonal learning situations directed by authorities who emphasize theory and abstract analysis. They are oriented more to things and ideas than to people and feelings. They are often frustrated by the unstructured, "mushy" feelers, who, in turn, see them as cold and aloof.

Doers learn best through active experimentation and use the results of their tests to make future decisions. They are extroverts who thrive on doing and learn best when actively involved in projects or discussion groups, as opposed to passively receiving instructions or listening to lectures.

Watchers take a reflective, tentative, uninvolved approach to learning. Their decisions are based on careful observation and analysis. Watchers tend to be introverts who prefer learning situations such as lectures or films, where they can be detached, passive, and impartial.

LEARNING-STYLE TYPES

After reading the characteristics of individuals representing each pure learning style, you probably saw yourself in more than one learning mode. This is to be expected, because each person's learning style in real life is some combination of the four basic learning modes. To determine an individual's learning-mode combination, or learning-style type, we can plot our perception of that person on the two primary learning-dimension continua—concrete–abstract and active–passive. The characteristics of each dimension can now be combined from the previous descriptions of the learning model and learning modes. They are illustrated in Figure 2-4.

Identifying Learning-Style Types.   As a rough estimate of learning style, we can rate any particular individual as being more concrete or abstract and more active or passive. If the person is an extrovert who is always involved in what's happening, as opposed to someone who generally sits back and doesn't say or do much, place an X toward the active end of the scale. How close to the center or to the end of the scale you place the X will depend on how extreme the person is relative to others. Then rate the same person as being more concrete or abstract in the same manner. The results of these two ratings will place the person in one of the four learning-style quadrants. Someone who is concrete and active is called an *Accommodator.* Someone who is concrete and passive is a *Diverger.* Someone who is abstract and active is called a *Converger.* Finally, a person who is abstract and passive is called an *Assimilator.* The four learning-style types are illustrated in Figure 2-5.

If a person is only slightly more concrete than abstract, and only slightly more active than passive, he or she would fall in the Accommodator quadrant, but the ratings on the concrete and active dimensions would be very low. If we were to mark

Figure 2-4 Characteristics of Learning-Mode Dimensions

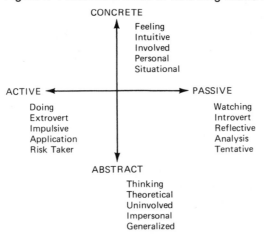

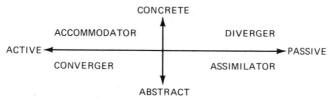

Figure 2-5 Learning-Style Types

Xs on each scale and plot their point of interception in the Accommodator quadrant, the lines would cross very close to the intersection of the primary learning-dimension axes. Consequently, this person would actually have a relatively balanced learning style. This is in contrast to someone rated as extremely more concrete than abstract and extremely more active than passive. The second person probably relies very heavily on the accommodation learning style. The same can be said about extreme or balanced individuals in any of the remaining learning-style quadrants. The differences in learning-style extreme versus balance are illustrated in Figure 2-6.

CHARACTERISTICS OF LEARNING-STYLE TYPES

Based on both empirical research and clinical observation, the following characteristics have been determined for the four learning-style types.

Figure 2-6 Extreme versus Balanced Learning Styles

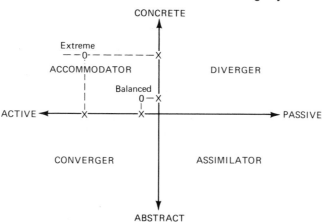

The *Accommodator*'s dominant learning abilities are in the areas of concrete experience and active experimentation. Accommodators are doers and feelers. They are risk takers who quickly discard plans or theories that do not fit their own experience. They rely on intuition and trial-and-error problem-solving methods and prefer to go with other people's opinions rather than do their own analyses. Although they are at ease with people, Accommodators are sometimes seen as impatient and pushy. Accommodators are so named because they excel in rapidly adapting to specific circumstances. They usually have educational backgrounds in practical technical fields (e.g., business administration) and take action-oriented jobs in such fields as management or sales.

The *Assimilator* has learning strengths opposite those of the Accommodator. Assimilators are best at abstract conceptualization and reflective observation. Assimilators are watchers and thinkers. They are good at creating theoretical models and excel in inductive reasoning, where they assimilate disparate observations into an integrated explanation. They are more concerned with abstract concepts than with other people's feelings or opinions. If a logical and precise theory does not fit the facts experienced, the Assimilator is likely to disregard or reexamine the facts, as opposed to the Accommodator, who will probably disregard the theory. Assimilators usually have educational backgrounds in the basic sciences or mathematics and can be found in research and planning departments.

The *Converger* is best at learning through abstract conceptualization and active experimentation. Convergers are thinkers and doers. They are good at the practical application of ideas, especially to specific problems with a single correct solution, where they utilize hypothetical-deductive reasoning. Convergers are relatively unemotional and prefer to work with things rather than people. Their educational backgrounds are usually in more technical areas in the physical sciences, and their typical job choice is engineering.

Divergers have learning strengths opposite those of convergers. They are best at concrete experience and reflective observation. Divergers are watcher-feelers with strong imaginative abilities. They can see a situation from many perspectives and generate a multitude of divergent ideas. Divergers are interested in people and are emotional, though in a more controlled and understanding manner than Accommodators.

They usually have broad cultural educations in the humanities or social sciences and tend to be found in jobs such as counseling, personnel, or organizational development. The characteristics of each learning-style type are illustrated in Figure 2-7.

The compatibility of any two individuals in a learning situation depends a great deal on the similarities and differences in their predominant learning styles. Groups of same-style individuals tend to learn best together, followed by mixed groups who have at least one learning dimension in common. Heterogeneous learning groups with extremely opposite styles will probably experience considerable inefficiency and conflict. The compatibility of learning-style group compositions is illustrated in Figure 2-8.

LEARNING STYLES AND PROBLEM SOLVING

Although individuals with different learning styles experience tension and may have difficulty communicating with one another, the various strengths of all four styles are necessary for successful problem solving. Each learning style contains characteristics necessary for efficacy in a different stage of the

Figure 2-7 Characteristics of Learning-Style Types

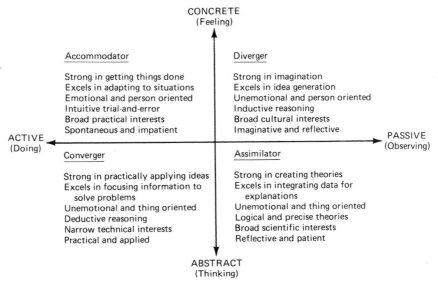

CONCRETE
(Feeling)

Accommodator

Strong in getting things done
Excels in adapting to situations
Emotional and person oriented
Intuitive trial-and-error
Broad practical interests
Spontaneous and impatient

Diverger

Strong in imagination
Excels in idea generation
Unemotional and person oriented
Inductive reasoning
Broad cultural interests
Imaginative and reflective

ACTIVE
(Doing)

PASSIVE
(Observing)

Converger

Strong in practically applying ideas
Excels in focusing information to
    solve problems
Unemotional and thing oriented
Deductive reasoning
Narrow technical interests
Practical and applied

Assimilator

Strong in creating theories
Excels in integrating data for
    explanations
Unemotional and thing oriented
Logical and precise theories
Broad scientific interests
Reflective and patient

ABSTRACT
(Thinking)

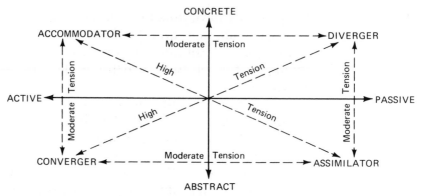

Figure 2-8 Relative Incompatibility of Learning Styles

problem-solving process. Figure 2-9 overlays the problem-solving process on the learning cycle to demonstrate which learning dimensions match up with different problem-solving activities.

As can be seen in Figure 2-9, the stages of the problem-solving process correspond with learning-style types. Initiating

Figure 2-9 Comparison of Learning Dimensions and Problem-Solving Processes

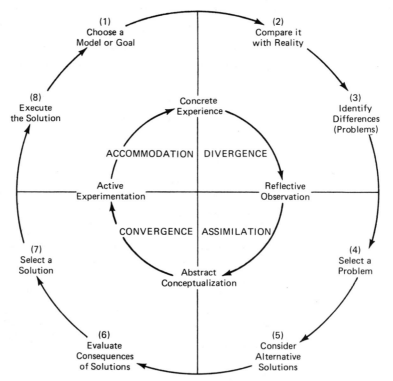

problem finding based on some goal or model of how things should be is a strength of the Accommodator, who also excels at executing specific solutions. The Diverger is good at comparing the objectives or ideal models with reality and then identifying the differences or problems that exist. The Assimilator excels in determining priorities so that a problem can be selected and then formulating models for solving it. Finally, the Converger is strong at evaluating the consequences of the various solutions suggested and then picking the best solutions, which the Accommodator is best at implementing.

The problem-solving process can be facilitated by utilizing the strengths of people with different learning styles in a sequential manner. When solving a complex problem, the interactive manager can use the following guide to assign activities to individuals with different learning styles. Use *Accommodators* for the following:

— Commitment to goals
— Initiating the problem-solving process
— Dealing with the people involved
— Exploring opportunities
— Implementing plans, trying things out
— Accomplishing tasks

Use *Divergers* for the following:

— Collecting information
— Sensing values and feelings
— Identifying problems and opportunities
— Creative thinking
— Generating ideas and alternatives

Use *Assimilators* for the following:

— Defining the problem
— Quantitative analysis
— Using theory and formulating models
— Planning implementation
— Establishing evaluation criteria

Use *Convergers* for the following:

— Setting priorities
— Designing experiments
— Measuring and evaluating
— Interpreting data
— Making decisions

GUIDELINES FOR MANAGING
THE LEARNING PROCESS

Awareness of the learning model and differences in individual learning styles can be very helpful in facilitating the learning of managers and subordinates. It can also be used to improve the problem-solving process and to enhance individual productivity. The following suggestions are intended as further guidelines for effectively managing the learning process to enhance productivity and satisfaction.

First, try to assign individuals with appropriate learning styles to the demands of specific situations. Research has demonstrated that people choose occupations that are consistent with their learning styles if they can. Also, once people are in a particular situation, they are shaped to fit the existing learning norms. If there is a mismatch between the individual's learning style and the job situation's learning norms, the individual will be more prone to resign or get out of the situation than to change learning style.

Second, learning from experience should be emphasized as an important and legitimate goal for all organization members. Managers should budget time specifically to critique and learn from experiences such as meetings and important decision-making activities.

Third, the importance of all aspects of the learning process and the strengths and needs of each different learning style should be emphasized. Opposing perspectives, action and reflection, concrete involvement and analytical detachment are all important for effective learning and problem solving. Differences in perspective should not only be tolerated but encouraged.

Finally, a flexible manager who can adapt easily and identify with individuals with different learning styles should be charged with the responsibility for integrating and coordinating the activities of people and departments with different learning styles and requirements. This includes resolving conflict and managing tensions inherent in the varying learning styles so that the organization maintains a balanced learning style overall. This is essential if the organization is to maintain its effectiveness in problem solving and adapting to changing organizational demands and opportunities. It is essential to interactive management.

Learning-style differences are just one dimension of understanding and managing differences among your employees. Employees also exhibit differences in their social behavior, their decision making, and their dominant mode of interpersonal transactions. These are covered in subsequent chapters. Armed with this additional information and skill, the interactive manager is well on the way toward increased flexibility with employees—with the resulting increased trust, faith, and productivity that go along with it.

3

Doing
Unto Others

"Do unto others as you would have them do unto you." At first
glance, this verse seems sensible and humane, an effective rule
to live by. However, as incredible as it may seem, you stand a
greater chance of productively relating to others when you
break this rule.

If you interpret the golden rule literally, you will find that
it is based on the assumption that others wish to be treated the
same way you do. This assumption is not necessarily true. In
fact, according to the concept of behavioral styles, this is rarely
the case. Furthermore, if you dutifully follow the golden rule,
the odds of relating effectively to others can be significantly
against you.

Behavioral style advocates suggest breaking the golden rule
and replacing it with another—the *platinum rule*. This is simply:
Do unto others as they would have you do unto them; or *Treat
others as they wish to be treated*. This new rule implies that
others may not wish to be treated the same way you may favor.
In short, it allows for individual differences and preferences.
This "new" way of viewing human interaction actually began in
1924 with Carl Jung's research on psychological types. The four
types were as follows:

1. Thinker: organized, structured, accurate, research oriented.
2. Sensor: goal oriented, active, concerned with results.
3. Intuitor: imaginative, impetuous, stimulating.
4. Feeler: emotional, spontaneous, introspective.

Acceptance of the behavioral styles concept hinges on the acknowledgment that human beings are not totally unpredictable. In fact, based upon repetition of the same kinds of activities and situations, people develop habitual ways of dealing with their environment. When we are children, we choose random behaviors to satisfy our needs. Those behaviors that work become habitual reinforcements. Hence, people are somewhat predictable because they behave habitually.

When people act and react in social situations, they exhibit observable behaviors that help to define their social, or behavioral, styles. These behavioral styles can be identified according to two primary characteristics: assertiveness and responsiveness. Behavior indicative of these characteristics is readily recognizable within the context of others' verbal, vocal, and visual behaviors.

In the behavior style model,* *assertiveness* is defined as the amount of control one person tries to exert over other people and the situation. It is the forcefulness a person uses to express his or her thoughts, feelings, and emotions to other people. Assertive behavior is divided into high assertiveness and low assertiveness. Selected descriptions of the behavior of each of the assertive styles are given in Table 3-1.

The other major dimension of behavioral styles, *responsiveness*, refers to the readiness with which a person expresses emotions and develops relationships. Responsive behavior is divided into high responsiveness and low responsiveness. Selected descriptions of the behavior of each of the responsive styles appear in Table 3-2.

If we displayed the two assertiveness extremes on a horizontal axis, it would look like Figure 3-1. Any specific person may rank high, low, or somewhere in between. The graphic

---

*In addition to the work of Carl Jung and others, much of our work on behavioral styles was an outgrowth of the work done by Dr. David W. Merrill of Reid, Merrill, Brunson and Associates, Denver, Colorado. Dr. Merrill has been developing and refining his social style model for well over fifteen years and provides business and industry with a questionnaire that measures social (behavioral) style.

Table 3-1   Assertiveness Descriptions

Low Assertiveness	High Assertiveness
Quiet	Verbose
Mild opinions	Strong opinions
Avoids risks	Takes risks
Meditative decisions	Swift decisions
Pleasing first impression	Powerful first impression
Shy	Active
Reserved	Confident
Supportive	Confronting
Easygoing	Impatient
Slow actions	Fast actions
Listens	Talks

exhibition of the responsiveness extremes is shown on the vertical axis in Figure 3-2. As with assertiveness, any particular individual may rank anywhere on the responsiveness scale. Responsiveness and assertiveness levels vary across individuals. Any particular person may be high on both, low on both, high on one and low on the other, or somewhere in between on one or both scales.

When the two scales are combined, as in Figure 3-3, they form four quadrants that divide assertive and responsive behavior into four different patterns referred to as behavioral styles. The name of each style, *amiable, expressive, analytical,* and *driving,* represents its general characteristics. These styles are

Table 3-2   Responsiveness Descriptions

Low Responsiveness	High Responsiveness
Aloof	Personable
Formal and proper	Relaxed and warm
Fact oriented	Opinion oriented
Guarded	Open
Controlled	Dramatic
Disciplined	Flexible
Task oriented	Relationship oriented
Hides personal feelings	Shares personal feelings
Thinking oriented	Feeling oriented

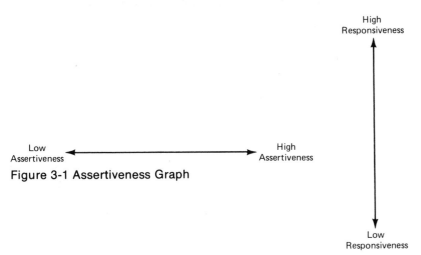

Figure 3-1 Assertiveness Graph

Figure 3-2 Responsiveness Graph

similar to Jung's Feeler, Intuitor, Thinker, and Sensor, respectively. A person's behavioral style is not a complete profile of personality or character, but it is effective in describing the way that person interacts with others in social and work situations when able to do things his or her own way. Knowledge of the four behavioral styles can help you understand better why people behave as they do, which in turn will allow you to interact more effectively with them to build productive relationships.

Each of the four styles has its own unique behaviors when dealing with others in interpersonal relationships. The predominant characteristics of each style are shown in Figure 3-4. Each quadrant represents unique combinations of responsive-

Figure 3-3 Four Behavioral Styles

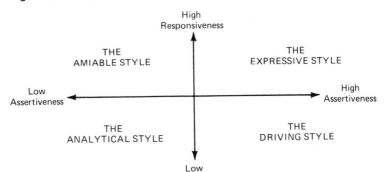

ness and assertiveness levels, resulting in unique ways of behaving.

After reviewing Figure 3-4, you may have concluded that one or more of the behavioral styles is better than others. This is not true. There is no "best" style. Figure 3-5 presents some of the more common adjectives that are used to describe the unique strengths and weaknesses of each behavioral style. There are successful people, as well as failures, in each style group. Be content with your style. Keep in mind that if others perceive your actions as appropriate and comfortable for them, they'll probably use the positive adjectives in describing you. If your behavior causes tension for others, more than likely they will use the negative adjectives to describe you. The most

Figure 3-4 Predominant Characteristics of Each Behavioral Style

HIGH RESPONSIVENESS

AMIABLE STYLE	EXPRESSIVE STYLE
Slow at taking action and making decisions	Spontaneous actions and decisions
Likes close, personal relationships	Likes involvement
Dislikes interpersonal conflict	Dislikes being alone
Supports and "actively" listens to others	Exaggerates and generalizes
Weak at goal setting and self-direction	Tends to dream and get others caught up in his dream
Has excellent ability to gain support from others	Jumps from one activity to another
Works slowly and cohesively with others	Works quickly and excitingly with others
Seeks security and belongingness	Seeks esteem and belongingness
Good counseling skills	Good persuasive skills

LOW ASSERTIVENESS ← → HIGH ASSERTIVENESS

ANALYTICAL STYLE	DRIVER STYLE
Cautious actions and decisions	Firm actions and decisions
Likes organization and structure	Likes control
Dislikes involvement with others	Dislikes inaction
Asks many questions about specific details	Prefers maximum freedom to manage himself and others
Prefers objective, task-oriented, intellectual work environment	Cool and independent; competitive with others
Wants to be right and therefore relies too much on data collection	Low tolerance for feelings, attitudes, and advice of others
Works slowly and precisely alone	Works quickly and impressively by himself
Seeks security and self-actualization	Seeks esteem and self-actualization
Good problem-solving skills	Good administrative skills

LOW RESPONSIVENESS

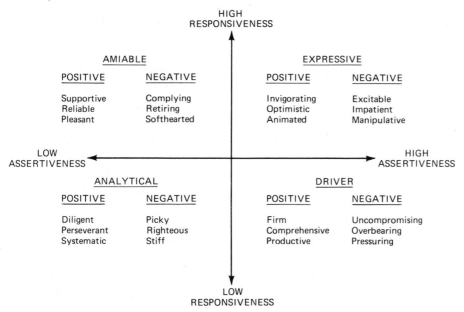

Figure 3-5 Positive-Negative Descriptions of Each Behavioral Style

important thing is to learn how to use your style effectively during interactions with others. Understanding where people are coming from can help you to be more at ease with them and to adjust your own behavior in ways that will make them feel more comfortable with you.

In reviewing Figures 3-4 and 3-5, you may have personally identified with some of the characteristics of all four styles. That's natural. Each of us possesses some traits from all four styles but in varying degrees. Most people, however, have a dominant behavioral style. It is like a theme that runs through your life similar to a theme in a musical composition. It does not describe all actions, but it is a recurring and predictable component. Just as music has many variations around the main theme, so does your behavior. The main behavioral theme in your life is your dominant style.

BEHAVIORAL STYLES AND INTERPERSONAL PROBLEMS

Although it is important to be aware of the characteristics of each behavioral style, it is even more useful to understand how people with different styles relate to each other. When individuals with two different styles interact, they usually behave according to the characteristics of their own style. Because of inherent pace and priority differences, there is a good chance that tension will result from their transaction. This tension leads to distrust, low credibility, and eventually to an unproductive relationship. A typical example is that of the Expressive personnel manager—complete with warm, open handshakes, first names, and questions about personal interests—who complains about the narrow-mindedness of the production manager. The production manager is clearly Analytical—quiet, somewhat remote (generally keeping her desk between herself and others), stone-faced, and fact-oriented. You can almost imagine the encounters these two have. As the personnel manager is involved in building a friendly relationship and dealing in general opinions and feelings, the production manager, anxious to get down to business, is pressing for details. As a result of their disastrous contacts, the personnel manager thinks the production manager picky and aloof, interested in neither him nor his services. The production manager thinks the personnel manager uncertain of his points and intrusive in concerns that have no bearing on the business. The tension between the two is obvious, and both have justifiable reasons for the lack of ease, none of which have anything to do with the product involved.

Each behavioral style has its own unique set of priorities as to what is most important to do and its own pace in terms of how fast things should be done. For some, it is "I want it yesterday"; for others, "sooner or later" is acceptable. When the pace and priorities of two styles are not compatible, "toxic" or tension-producing relationships develop. As you can see from Figure 3-6, the Driver/Expressive and Amiable/Analytical interactions result in priority problems. Whereas the Driver and the Analytical want to have facts and accomplish tasks to reach goals and objectives, the Expressive and the Amiable want to cultivate personal relationships. The Driver and the Analytical, given a choice, would begin a task without much concern for, or acknowledgment of, personal relationships. The Expressive and the Amiable, given the same choice, won't start a task until they develop the personal relationships to their satisfaction. These two will still be getting to know each other while the Analytical and the Driver are already headlong into the task.

Let's look at a few examples of typical problems a Driver encounters. When the Driver interacts with an Amiable, they

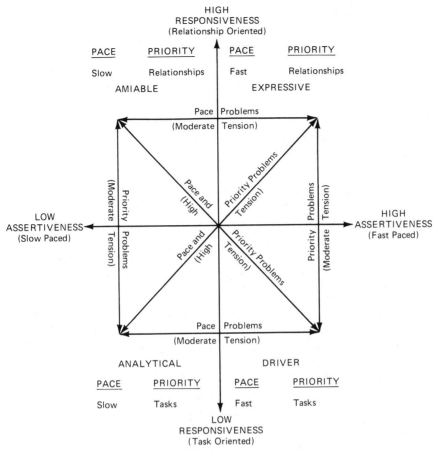

Figure 3-6 Toxic Relationships of Behavioral Styles (Pace and Priority Problems)

have two major problems. They have a pace problem because the Driver moves fast, whereas the Amiable moves slowly. Also, they have a priority problem because the Driver places tasks over relationships, and the Amiable places relationships over tasks. These two styles have a high probability of a tense relationship.

When the Driver relates with the Expressive, they have one thing in common—they are both fast paced. However, they have a priority problem. The Expressive places more emphasis on personal relationships than on tasks, whereas the Driver begins tasks with little concern for personal relationships. These two styles have a moderate degree of tension in their relationships.

The Driver and the Analytical also have one thing in common—their priorities. They both place the task at hand before the personal relationship. However, the Driver is fast paced, takes risks, and makes quick decisions. The Analytical gets "uptight" when he or she has to make decisions without the opportunity to analyze all the alternatives fully to avoid any chance of making a wrong decision. This pace problem leads to a moderate degree of tension in the Driver–Analytical relationship. Similar problems develop between the other styles.

Although it may seem like a hopeless case when two different behavioral styles interact, this is not necessarily so. There is a way for two different styles to interact productively while reducing tension and increasing trust and credibility. This occurs when one or both styles "bend" to meet the needs of the other, when they exercise *behavioral flexibility*. The solution revolves around treating others the way they want to be treated—practicing the platinum rule.

When these toxic pairings do occur, one or both must adjust behavioral style to avoid increasing tension in each other. Ideally, both would move partway. For example, in the Driver/ Expressive interaction, the Driver should try to show some concern for people rather than appearing to treat them as only a resource. The Expressive, on the other hand, should try to show more concern for completing the task even if the personal relationships have to be put temporarily to the side. In a manager–employee situation, of course, the manager may have to make most, if not all, of that temporary adjustment.

UNPRODUCTIVE BEHAVIOR

What happens to others when you do not adjust your behavior to meet their style needs? Think of the personnel and production managers whose styles brought them to tension and distrust in the previous example. The Expressive personnel manager saw the production manager's questions as a personal challenge, an attack from which he had to save face. His response was to talk more and move faster, pushing the Analytical production manager into still greater tension. Eventually, the personnel manager reached the stage of attacking the production manager personally. The production manager reacted by refusing to have further meetings with the personnel manager and refusing even to talk with him over the telephone.

With each individual, there is a point at which tension increases until it results in stress. People undergoing stress seek to reduce that stress in any way possible. Unfortunately, this is usually unproductive. Stress is often "dumped" on another person, either verbally or psychologically. Each behavioral style has its own characteristic manner of "dumping" stress in unproductive behavior. The Expressive attacks, the Driver dictates, the Analytical withdraws, and the Amiable submits.

As a rule, an Expressive (like the personnel manager in our example) resorts to unproductive behavior by verbally attacking the person who causes the stress. Most people react to attack from an Expressive with increased tension of their own, which at some point can push them into stress, too. At this point, the relationship can be severely damaged.

The Driver under stress tends to become overbearing, pushy, uncompromising, and dictatorial. It's an outgrowth of the Driver style: If you're hopping mad, tend to desire control, and think the facts support you, others will see you at your worst. When a Driver is acting unproductively, he or she tends to control anyone or anything that gets in the way. Others usually experience considerable tension and react by shifting into their unproductive styles.

The Amiable who resorts to unproductive behavior generally gives in or submits. The purpose is to avoid conflict at all costs. Although the Amiable's unproductive behavior may appear to be a "go-along" attitude on the surface, it is certainly not that. Resentment builds and is stored up. Subsequent interactions are likely to be full of distrust and tension.

Like the production manager in our example, the Analytical's unproductive behavior is withdrawal from the other person or the situation. Being less assertive in nature, an Analytical would rather flee from the unpleasant relationship than deal with it directly. Thus, the Analytical typically seeks more and more information and wants to think it over as a means of avoiding the other person and the unpleasant situation.

This behavior is an unproductive method of relieving tension. Technical management alone often leads to tension and distrust in the supervisor–subordinate relationship. This increased tension on the part of the subordinate may exhibit itself in the form of unproductive behavior. Similarly, regardless of the type of management, if the supervisor acts in a way that reduces his or her own tension and disregards the style needs of the subordinate, increased tension and unproductive behavior by the subordinate will probably result. In either case, the supervisory relationship becomes sour, and no cooperation is achieved regardless of the needs of the subordinate or the demands of the situation.

To avoid unproductive behavior in your subordinates, peers, and superiors, you must be able to meet their behavioral style needs. In essence, you must treat them the way they want to be treated. Not your way, but their way. This means that you must be flexible in your behavior with all four behavioral styles. For example, if she moves fast, you move fast. If he likes to take his time and get to know people, allow more time for the meeting. Move at the pace and priority of the individual involved. When you meet someone's behavioral style needs, a climate of mutual trust begins to develop. That person will not get into a contest with you, and you will have a more productive relationship. And as you develop a better personal interaction, you will also feel better about yourself.

You need to identify a person's behavioral style accurately within a relatively brief time if you are to react positively and appropriately. The following two sections of this chapter deal with verbal and nonverbal clues useful in identifying different behavioral styles and with specific skills to enhance your flexibility in dealing with them.

IDENTIFYING BEHAVIORAL STYLES

You now have some knowledge of the four types of behavioral styles, and you know how important it is to interact appropriately with a person's particular style. The next step is how to identify, accurately and rapidly, which of those styles another person represents. To identify someone's style, you must *observe what that person does*.

Observation. In order to assure accuracy in observing a person in action, you need to observe a wide range of verbal and nonverbal behaviors. This may require you to stimulate more behaviors by asking questions (probes) and by "actively" listening.

Next, you must analyze the observed behaviors so that you can place the person on both the responsiveness scale and the assertiveness scale. To help you accomplish that, the behavioral style characteristics have been translated into a list of *observable* behaviors in Figures 3-7 and 3-8. *Behavior* refers to actions you can *see*, not value judgments. For example, if you see a person hopping up and down, is she doing so because she is hop-stomping mad, stepped on a nail, has a foot that is asleep, or is extremely happy and excited? You can't tell by looking. All you can do is say she is jumping up and down. To find out *why* she is jumping requires additional verbal and nonverbal communication skills.

To identify the behavioral style using the responsive–assertive scales, first locate the person's position on the *responsiveness* dimension. It is easier to classify responsiveness behaviors quickly because they are more readily visible. Then determine the level of assertiveness demonstrated. The result is placement of the person into one of the four behavioral style quadrants through the process of elimination. For instance, if you determine that a person is exhibiting higher than average responsiveness, you are automatically eliminating the styles with low responsive behavior—Drivers and Analyticals. Likewise, if you determine that the person is also high in assertiveness, you automatically eliminate the remaining style with low assertiveness—the Amiables. Therefore, by the process of elimination, you are left with the Expressive style.

Figure 3-7 Observable Responsive Behavior

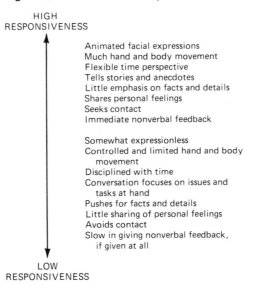

HIGH
RESPONSIVENESS

Animated facial expressions
Much hand and body movement
Flexible time perspective
Tells stories and anecdotes
Little emphasis on facts and details
Shares personal feelings
Seeks contact
Immediate nonverbal feedback

Somewhat expressionless
Controlled and limited hand and body
    movement
Disciplined with time
Conversation focuses on issues and
    tasks at hand
Pushes for facts and details
Little sharing of personal feelings
Avoids contact
Slow in giving nonverbal feedback,
    if given at all

LOW
RESPONSIVENESS

LOW ASSERTIVENESS ◄─────────► HIGH ASSERTIVENESS

Soft handshake	Firm handshake
Intermittent eye contact	Steady eye contact
Little verbal communication	Much verbal communication
Questions tend to clarify, support, inform	Questions tend to be rhetorical, emphasize points, challenge information
Makes tentative statements	Makes emphatic statements
Few gestures to support conversation	Gestures to emphasize points
Low voice volume	High voice volume
Slow voice speed	Fast voice speed
Little variation in vocal intonation	Emphasizes points by changing voice intonation
Communicates hesitantly	Communicates readily
Slow moving	Fast moving

Figure 3-8 Observable Assertive Behavior

Confirmation. After identifying another's style based on observable behavior, you should use *behavioral confirmation* to corroborate your choice. Behavioral confirmation is simply looking for behaviors that are characteristic of the style you believe a person represents. In other words, your observations lead you to label the person. Now check this against the characteristics of the various styles. If you determined that the person is a Driver, look for specific characteristics that you expect from a Driver—competitive, impatient, efficient, decisive, fact-oriented, dominant, goal-oriented, and so on. If the person exhibits these types of characteristics, you have verified your choice. You can now feel comfortable in interacting with that person as a Driver. Use the same behavioral confirmation process with the other three styles. Always test and validate your initial style choice. The price for being wrong is much greater than the amount of time spent in confirming an initial guesstimate.

Some of the more readily identifiable characteristics that help confirm each style are displayed in Figure 3-9. Although the list has different words from those you saw originally in Figure 3-4, it suggests the same kind of characteristics and gives you a broader way of looking at the styles. Compare these descriptions with what you observe in order to confirm an identified behavioral style.

You've now observed and labeled the behavioral style of the other person and confirmed your observation. You have identified the individual as a Driver, and you need to develop trust. What do you do now? You cannot expect the other person to adapt to you. *You* must adapt to him. You're ready to learn behavioral flexibility skills to help you *use* this information effectively. You're ready to practice the platinum rule!

BEHAVIORAL FLEXIBILITY

After you have correctly identified the style of the person with whom you are dealing, you then must plan ways of interacting effectively with that individual. The ability to be changeable and adapt in different interpersonal situations is called *behavioral flexibility*. It is something you do to yourself, not to others. The flexible manager controls only her part of the relationship in order to make the subordinate feel more at ease.

The flexible manager tries to meet the style needs of her subordinates as well as her own. She negotiates the relationships

Figure 3-9 Corroborative Behavior for Each Style

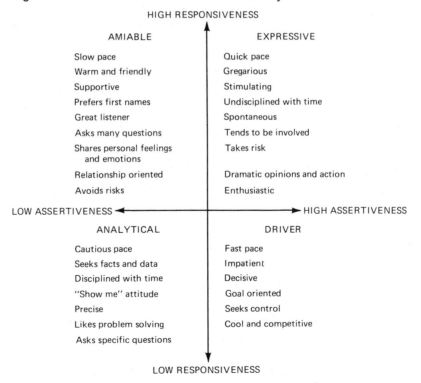

HIGH RESPONSIVENESS

AMIABLE	EXPRESSIVE
Slow pace	Quick pace
Warm and friendly	Gregarious
Supportive	Stimulating
Prefers first names	Undisciplined with time
Great listener	Spontaneous
Asks many questions	Tends to be involved
Shares personal feelings and emotions	Takes risk
Relationship oriented	Dramatic opinions and action
Avoids risks	Enthusiastic

LOW ASSERTIVENESS ← → HIGH ASSERTIVENESS

ANALYTICAL	DRIVER
Cautious pace	Fast pace
Seeks facts and data	Impatient
Disciplined with time	Decisive
"Show me" attitude	Goal oriented
Precise	Seeks control
Likes problem solving	Cool and competitive
Asks specific questions	

LOW RESPONSIVENESS

and displays tact. Because she often steps out of her own style preference and "comfort zone" in trying to meet others' needs, she often raises her own tension level temporarily in order to make it easier for subordinates to relate to her. To meet subordinates' behavioral style needs best, therefore, you will often have to alter actions natural to your style. This is what is meant by behavioral flexibility.

Behavioral flexibility is independent of behavioral style. It varies greatly across people, even of one style. No style is "naturally" more flexible than another. You can choose to be flexible with a person today and inflexible with that person tomorrow. It is an individual decision to "manage" your own style so as to meet another's style needs and thus reduce the possibility of his experiencing tension.

Your flexibility level with others very often determines their perceptions of you. Raise your flexibility level, and they will perceive you more positively; lower it, and they will perceive you less favorably. It is much like a smoker refraining from smoking in a room full of nonsmokers. Behavioral flexibility is controlling your own behavior when doing so makes other people more comfortable.

As with any good thing, however, too much or too little behavioral flexibility can be negative. A person with too little flexibility will more than likely be viewed by others as solely or predominantly concerned with his own needs. Because he consistently acts according to *his* pace and priorities, he will be seen as blunt, single-minded, rigid, and uncompromising. On the opposite end of the flexibility scale, the highly flexible person runs into two kinds of problems. Because his pace and priority needs are constantly set aside for those of others, he may be viewed as unpredictable or wishy-washy by some who see him interact with different people. Also, a person operating in a behavioral style that is not his own will experience tension. Usually, the tension is temporary and worth the increased rapport. However, a person who maintains high flexibility in all interactions may not be able to avoid stress and inefficiency. The effectively flexible person compromises, giving in to the speed and interests of others, but not totally. He also saves this flexibility for certain special situations or where interaction would not otherwise go well and relaxes from it in many other encounters. This person meets both another's needs and his own. He negotiates relationships and shares so that everybody wins. He is seen as tactful, reasonable, and understanding—the appropriate image for the manager of people.

Table 3-3 presents guidelines for implementing behavioral flexibility as you communicate with each of the four behavioral styles.

BEHAVIORAL STYLES AND INTERACTIVE MANAGEMENT

The bottom line in applying the platinum rule is establishing trust, rapport and credibility with others. This can only be accomplished in an open, honest, tension-free relationship. When you treat others inappropriately, it makes them feel uncomfortable with you and raises their tension level. This is counterproductive to the relationship-building process.

Table 3-3   Behavioral Flexibility Guidelines

Expressives	Drivers	Analyticals	Amiables
Get Expressives to talk about opinions, ideas, and dreams, and try to support them.	Try to support the Driver's goals and objectives.	Try to support the Analytical's organized, thoughtful approach. Any contributions you can make toward her objectives should be demonstrated through actions rather than words (send literature, brochures, charts, etc.).	Try to support the Amiable's feelings.
Don't hurry the discussion. Try to develop mutually stimulating ideas together.	Ask questions that allow the Driver to discover things rather than being told.	Be systematic, exact, organized, and prepared with the Analytical.	Project that you are interested in him as a person.
The Expressive does not like to lose arguments, so try not to argue. Instead, explore alternative solutions you both can share with enthusiasm.	Keep your relationship businesslike. Do not attempt to establish a personal relationship unless that is one of the Driver's specific objectives.	List advantages and disadvantages of any plan you propose, and have viable alternatives for dealing effectively with the disadvantages.	Take time to effectively get the Amiable to spell out personal objectives. Make sure you get him to differentiate what he wants from what he thinks you want to hear.

Table 3-3 continued.

Expressives	Drivers	Analyticals	Amiables
When you reach agreement, iron out the specific details concerning what, when, who, and how. Be sure you both agree on the specifics.	If you disagree with the Driver, argue the facts, not personal feelings.	Give the Analytical time to verify your words and actions (because she *will* take the time).	When you disagree with the Amiable, do not debate facts and logic. Discuss personal opinions and feelings.
Summarize in writing what you both agreed upon, even though it may not appear necessary (don't ask permission—just do it).	Give recognition to the Driver's ideas, not to the Driver personally.	The Analytical likes things in writing, so follow up your personal contacts with a letter.	If you and the Amiable quickly establish an objective and come to a fast decision, explore potential areas for future misunderstanding or dissatisfaction.
Be entertaining and fast moving.	To influence the decisions of the Driver, you should provide alternative actions with probabilities of their success (backed by facts, if available).	Provide solid, tangible, factual evidence (not someone's opinion) that what you say is true and accurate.	Be agreeable with the Amiable by casually moving along in an informal, slow manner.
Make sure you both are in full agreement concerning when actions must be performed (specification).	Be precise, efficient, time disciplined, and well organized with the Driver.	Do not rush the decision-making process.	Show the Amiable that you are "actively" listening and you are "open" in your discussions.
The Expressive's decisions are positively affected if you use testimonials from important people or companies with which he can identify.		An Analytical likes guarantees that her actions can't backfire.	The Amiable likes guarantees that actions will involve a minimum of risk. Offer personal assurances of support. However, do not overstate your guarantees, or you will lose his trust.
		Avoid gimmicks that you believe might help you in getting a fast decision (the Analytical will think something is wrong with your plan).	

Accepting and understanding the fact that people are different and therefore need to be treated as such is integral to the concept of behavioral styles and interactive management. If you are able to go one step further and acquire a competence in identifying these differences in people, you can then treat them the way they want to be treated. Practicing the platinum rule will lead to less tension in your interpersonal relationships, along with higher levels of trust and credibility. The result is greater productivity and satisfaction in *all* your managerial relationships. Isn't that a powerful payoff for breaking the golden rule!

REFERENCES

ENGLESMAN, RALPH G., "Sizing Up Social Style," *Real Estate Today* (August 1975).

ENGLESMAN, RALPH G., "Unscrambling Nonverbal Signals," *Best's Review—Life/Health Insurance Edition* (April 1974).

HOMANS, GEORGE CASPAR, *Social Behavior: Its Elementary Form* (New York: Harcourt Brace Jovanovich, 1961).

HARVEY, JOHN H., and SMITH, WILLIAM P., *Social Psychology: An Attributional Approach* (St. Louis, Mo.: C.V. Mosby, 1977).

JABUBOWSKI, PATRICIA, and LANGE, ARTHUR, *Responsible Assertive Behavior* (Champaign, Ill.: Research Press, 1976).

JUNG, C. G., *Psychological Types* (London: Pantheon Books, 1923).

KILDAHL, JOHN P., and WOLBERG, LEWIS, *The Dynamics of Personality* (New York: Grune & Stratton, 1970).

MEHRABIAN, ALBERT, *Silent Messages* (Belmont Calif.: Wadsworth, 1971).

NOVAK, ALYS, "Mirror, Mirror on the Wall, Who's the Most Successful Executive of All," *Executive West* (March 1974).

ROSE, ARNOLD, *Human Behavior and Social Process* (Boston: Houghton Mifflin, 1962).

TAGIURI, RENATO, and PETRULLO, LUIGI, *Person Perception and Interpersonal Behavior* (Stanford, Calif.: Stanford University Press, 1958).

VERDERBER, RUDOLPH, *Communicate* (Belmont: Wadsworth, 1975).

Deciding
How to Decide

Although there are many different roles that managers are called upon to play in their various specific situations, all managers must be decision makers. Decision making is one of the most important parts of any manager's job, and how effective you are has direct application to organizational performance and the success of your career. As with learning (learning styles) and interacting with others (behavioral styles), individuals differ in the manner with which they typically go about making decisions. Different *decision styles** have different strengths and weaknesses and are more or less appropriate in various situations. Being aware of decision-style theory and knowing how to apply it can help you understand employees better and facilitate their performance by assigning appropriate decision-making responsibilities. It can also strengthen your own decision-making abilities and possibly enhance your career.

---

* Although the concept has earlier origins, the major developments and research in Decision Style theory have been carried out by Dr. Michael J. Driver at the University of Southern California. The key references to his work are listed at the end of this chapter.

THE DIMENSIONS OF DECISION STYLE

A decision style is a learned way of processing information and making decisions. It is a habit acquired through past experiences, similar to our characteristic ways of learning or relating to others. Although each of us has some unique thinking habits, research has identified certain common thought patterns used in information processing and decision making that can be used to distinguish between different decision styles.

Decision making differs among people in two key dimensions: (1) how much information is used or how *complex* it is, and (2) the degree of *focus* or number of alternative solutions generated from the information. A person's decision process increases in complexity to the degree that more information is utilized and more solution alternatives are generated. A comparison between a simple and a complex decision process is illustrated in Figure 4-1. The six points, called "variables," represent the amount of information—like facts, opinions, or statistics—that a person is aware of. The points below the variables represent conclusions such as alternatives or solutions. Person A uses less information than is available (i.e., three variables of six available) to generate one solution, whereas Person B utilizes much more information (i.e., five or six variables) to generate several alternatives or solutions. Person A is less complex and more focused than Person B.

You can probably think of people who match these different patterns, from "Let's make a quick, satisfactory decision and get on with it" to someone else who prefers to "look at all the possible data, figure out all the possible solutions, and not do anything hasty." With respect to complexity, Robert S. McNamara, Secretary of Defense for President John F. Ken-

Figure 4-1 Dimensions of Decision Making

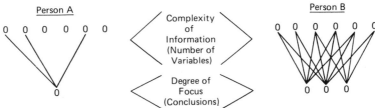

nedy, used a lot of complex information when presenting his ideas. Senators were overwhelmed with statistics, computer printouts, charts, and reams of data. McNamara's method of processing information was in stark contrast to many high-speed executives who prefer to have only the salient facts, so that they can make quick decisions and move on to the next problem. President Dwight D. Eisenhower, for example, preferred to see only brief, summarized reports from experts, which he used as the basis for his decisions.

General George Patton was a good example of a person who seemed to concentrate all of his energy on but one real focus in life—war. His library was almost entirely made up of books on war, and all his reading and studying were done in this area. It has been reported that even his honeymoon was spent at the beaches of former military battles in France. Thomas Edison, on the other hand, was interested in everything. While working on one project, he was always relating his experiences to other possible projects. Edison invented all sorts of things—from light bulbs to cameras—and founded several different kinds of businesses.

Extremes in either complexity or focus are often undesirable. Too much information can be overwhelming and lead to confusion and chaos. Too little information may not be sufficient for adequate decisions to be made at all. An extreme single focus can lead to obsession, which thwarts overall performance. Extreme multiple focus can lead to problems of overanalysis, where so many conclusions are considered that none are executed. There are some situations, however, where extremes in either complexity or focus are useful. Examples are situations requiring rapid, programmed decisions on the minimal end of the scales, and situations requiring creative adaptability on the other.

FOUR BASIC DECISION STYLES

The dimensions of complexity and focus can be combined, as in Figure 4-2, to make a matrix for identifying the four decision styles. A *Decisive* style is one that uses a minimal amount of data to arrive at one "satisfactory" decision. The *Flexible* style also relies on minimal information but shifts focus repeatedly over time, reinterpreting data and continually generating dif-

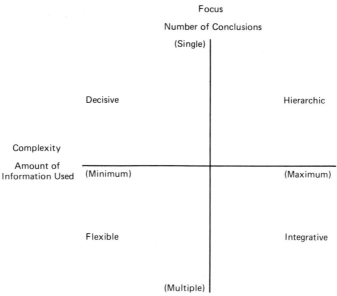

Figure 4-2 Decision Styles

ferent conclusions. The *Hierarchic* style is the opposite of the Flexible. Large amounts of data are carefully analyzed to generate one optimum decision. The *Integrative* style is similar to the Hierarchic in that maximum data are used, but instead of focusing on one best decision, the Integrative, like the Flexible, generates several different feasible conclusions.

BACK-UP STYLES

Although there may be times when you can remember making decisions according to more than one specific style, most people develop one dominant decision style that they normally use under usual conditions. When there is an abnormal oversupply or undersupply of information available for processing for a decision, or if there are severe time pressures, most people shift to a simpler *back-up* style. The back-up style will usually be either Decisive or Flexible, because these styles use less information and are faster. With respect to information processing, the Decisive style is simplest (single conclusion, minimal information), followed by the Flexible (multiple conclusions, minimal information), the Hierarchic (single conclusion, maximum information), and finally, the most complex, the Integrative (multiple conclusions, maximum information). Consequently, under adverse decision-making conditions, the Integrative has three back-up options that will be simpler and faster: Hierarchic, Flexible, and Decisive. The Hierarchic has two feasible back-up options: Flexible and Decisive. The Flexible can only shift to a Decisive style, and the Decisive can only become more decisive.

MIXED STYLES

As with behavioral styles, some people use one style predominantly when making decisions, but others frequently shift among several styles. If people's decision-making styles were plotted on the axis in Figure 4-2, *mixed* styles would be those rated moderate on both or one of the two dimensions. The most *adaptable* of the mixed styles would be that which is moderate in both focus and complexity. This adaptable style is close to the intersection of the two dimensions and could just as easily take on the characteristics of any of the four dominant styles, depending on the situation, but would not react in such an extreme fashion.

Another very common mixed style is the Integrative–Hierarchic mix. This style uses the maximum amount of information, as is characteristic of both of these pure styles, but then generates a multitude of alternatives as the Integrative does and also arrives at a single best solution as does the Hierarchic. This mix is the most complex of all styles and occurs often enough to be labeled the *Complex* style.

CHARACTERISTICS OF EACH
DECISION STYLE

Professor Michael J. Driver and his colleagues have determined that in addition to differences in the amount of information they use and how many alternatives they consider when making decisions, people also vary in how they perform other management-related functions. Figure 4-3 illustrates some of these differences with respect to values, planning, goals, organization, communication, and leadership.

DECISION STYLE CHARACTERISTICS*

	Decisive	Flexible	Hierarchic	Integrative
Values	Action Efficiency Speed Consistency Results	Action Adaptability Speed Variety Security	Control Quality Rigorous Method System Perfection	Results Information Creativity Variety Exploration
Planning	Low Data Base Short Range Tight Controls For Results	Low Data Base Short Range Intuitive and Reactive	High Data Base Long Range Tight Control of Method and Results	High Data Base Long Range Adaptative
Goals	One Organization Focus External Origin Accepted as Given	Many Self Focus External Origin Changing	Few Self Focus Internal Origin	Many Self and Organization Focus Internal and External Origins
Organization	Short Span of Control Rules Hierarchial Organization High Structure: Orderly High Delegation	Control by Confusion Loose High Delegation Minor Things Flexible Rules and Authority	Wide Span of Control Elaborate Procedures Automation Low Delegation High Structure	Team Process Matrix Organization High Delegation Flexible Structure
Communication	Short Summaries Results Focus One Solution To and Through Leader	Short Summaries Variety Several Solutions Everyone Talking To Everyone	Long, Elaborate Problem Solving Methods and Data Analysis Give "Best Conclusion"	Long, Elaborate Problem analysis from many views Multiple Solution
Leadership	Based on Position Motivation – Reward/Punishment Power and Orders Unilateral Decisions	Based on Liking and Charm Motivation – Positive Incentives Feelings and Needs Participation	Based on Competence Motivate with Information Logic and Analysis Consultative	Based on Trust and Information Motivation – Mutual Understanding and Cooperation Feelings and Facts Participation

*Adapted from Driver, M.J. and Mock, T.J. "Human Information Processing, Decision Style Theory, and Accounting Information Systems," The Accounting Review, Vol. 1, No. 3 (July 1975), pp. 490-508.

Figure 4-3 Decision-Style Characteristics

Decisive.   Individuals using this decision style use a minimum amount of information to arrive at one firm conclusion. Decisives are concerned with speed, efficiency, and consistency. They are action and results oriented. They use a minimal data base to develop tightly controlled and organized plans. Plans are short-range only, and deadlines are critical. Only one or two goals, set from above and by another authority, are pursued. These have a single focus, usually on organizational objectives. Decisives prefer hierarchical organizational structures with a short, clear span of control and clear-cut rules. Communications must be brief and to the point. Then all must pass through the manager. Written reports must be in summary format and focus on results and recommended action. A Decisive likes to receive only one solution, and long, detailed reports are often sent back, ignored, or turned over to someone else to summarize. Decisives accept authority based on position in the organization. They motivate through a rigid reward–punishment system. Decisions are unilateral, and subordinates are ordered to carry them out.

A good example of the Decisive style is one of our great military leaders and President of the United States, Dwight Eisenhower. With respect to values, Eisenhower was dedicated to truth and integrity. He was concerned with action, not ideas. Concrete results were crucial, and he did not refer to any comprehensive economic ideology. Eisenhower made minimal use of data and had his staff screen out superfluous information and provide summarized reports. He established a tight and orderly, military-type organization based on loyalty. He saw his job as acting as chairman of the board and making the important decisions himself after his subordinates had thrashed it out and offered their opinions. Although many intellectual critics (probably Hierarchics or Integratives) deplored his low use of data, his integrity and honesty won him the respect of the people.

Flexible.   This type of decision maker also uses minimal data but sees them as having different meanings at different times. Flexibles value action, speed, adaptability, and variety, which all give them security. They prefer not to plan at all and use their intuition to "play it by ear" on a reaction basis. Flexibles pursue many self-oriented goals one after another, but their objectives are what they think others want, so they change frequently depending on who is present. They prefer loose, fluid organizations with little structure or rules. They are comfortable with the resulting confusion, which gives them ultimate control because of their own creativity and adaptability. Flexibles, like the Decisives, prefer brief, to-the-point communications and reports. However, they prefer a wide variety of briefly stated solutions from which they can choose, as opposed to the Decisive's preference for the one "best" solution. They also like a lot of interaction between people on a spontaneous basis. Decisions are made on a participative basis, considering both the needs and feelings of those involved. Leadership is based on liking and charm, which is supported by using only positive incentives to activate.

William C. Durant established a large number of enterprises including General Motors. In terms of values, Durant displayed extreme Flexible patterns. His goals and plans were in a constant state of change. He was excessively concerned with sales volume, a short-term measure of results, as compared to the longer-term reports on profits. Durant made decisions through intuition and flashes of insight that were often in error because of his hasty and inadequate data analysis. Impressive surface appearance, as opposed to solid quality, which takes longer to get, are preferred by Flexibles. This may have contributed to the relatively low quality but high quantity of cars GM produced during the Durant leadership. Durant did not formally plan. He carried his ideas and strategies around in his head. Durant was even less concerned with controlling than with planning. He did not see how accounting could help production and was opposed to inventory control, which was seen as too constraining. Durant ran a loose organization and delegated extensively, but he kept the final decision-making power to himself.

Hierarchic. In contrast to the Decisives and Flexibles, people possessing the Hierarchical style utilize large masses of information that they carefully analyze to arrive at one best conclusion. Decisives value perfectionism, precision, and thoroughness. Consequently, they like to be in control of what is going on. They like thorough planning of a long-range nature, which will ensure control of both the method used and the outcomes. They are concerned with a few personal, self-generated goals that they hope to attain with a few elaborate strategies. They prefer intricate, hierarchical organizational structures with a broad span of control and elaborate policies and procedures. Hierarchics like long, detailed communications. Reports should be formal and thorough, with detailed statements of the problem, the method, and the one "best" conclusion. Brief or summarized reports are viewed as inadequate and are usually sent back for additional data analysis. Hierarchics motivate through information use and influence others through logic and analysis. Leadership is based on competence. Decisions are made unilaterally, but subordinates are consulted for additional information and opinions.

Although he is not usually thought of in this manner, Richard Nixon's decision style generally represents the Hierarchic pattern. He has always valued taking in information and using it exhaustively to support his one conclusion. Nixon decides his own goals and focuses intently on their accomplishment. He decided at age twelve that he was going to be a lawyer and consistently pursued the longer-term goal of increased power. His life appears largely to be a series of well-planned campaigns, starting with his early pursuit of a law degree, followed by his Young Republican activities, leading to a seat in Congress, and culminating with the presidency, for which he began planning as early as 1952 (i.e., the 1960 nomination). He likes schedules, orderly habits, and deadlines. Most things are well thought out before action is taken, extensive preparation is a habit. Unfortunately Mr. Nixon also provides an example of how a Hierarchic's single goal of internal origin can sometimes prevent him from considering other concerns and outcomes. Examples of Nixon's problems in this area are Watergate and his problems in purchasing a suitable residence in New York.

Integrative. Like Hierarchics, people with this decision style utilize large masses of information, but they generate a multitude of possible solutions. Integratives produce these varied interpretations simultaneously, as opposed to Flexibles, who also generate a variety of conclusions but do so sequentially. Integratives value exploring, getting all the sources of information, and doing a variety of creative things with it. They generate long-range plans based on detailed data analysis, but plans are constantly being altered and improved. Integratives are concerned with a multitude of both personal and organizational goals that they try to make compatible. They do not like being constrained in rigid hierarchical organizations and prefer loose, fluid organizations that can be adapted to the demands of various circumstances. Communications are long and elaborate, with quite involved discussions. Brief reports are shunned in favor of complex analyses from many points of view that generate a multitude of possible conclusions. They have influence because of their information-processing skills and the trust others have in them. They allow all concerned to participate in decisions, which are based on feelings, facts, and opinions. Others are motivated to contribute because of the Integrative's empathy, understanding, and sense of fairness.

Benjamin Franklin is a good example of the Integrative decision style. He valued information and variety, as evidenced by his reading every book from A to Z in his local library. Franklin was truly interested in everything. Much of his creativity was generated from his need to explore the unknown as evidenced in his famous kite flying experience and the discovery of electricity. He was very influential not only because of his vast breadth of knowledge and reasoning ability but also because he valued the feelings and ideas of others, leading them to trust and admire him.

You have probably noticed things that you like and dislike in each of the four decision styles. Some of the common ways of describing the characteristics of each style are presented in Figure 4-4. Whether you personally would attach a positive or negative value would depend largely on your own style and its

Figure 4-4 Positive-Negative Descriptions of Each Decision Style

DECISIVE		HIERARCHIC	
POSITIVE	NEGATIVE	POSITIVE	NEGATIVE
Reliable	Rigid	Rigorous	Dogmatic
Consistent	Simplistic	Precise	Overcontrolling
Fast	Shallow	Thorough	Nitpicking

FLEXIBLE		INTEGRATIVE	
POSITIVE	NEGATIVE	POSITIVE	NEGATIVE
Intuitive	Shallow	Inventive	Complicated
Adaptable	Indecisive	Empathetic	Nosy
Congenial	Fickle	Cooperative	Wishy-washy

compatibility with the others. We talk about getting along with different styles in a later section of this chapter. The main thing to keep in mind is not your immediate feelings toward people with different decision-style characteristics but how their unique strengths can be used and their weaknesses avoided in specific decision-making situations.

IS THERE A "BEST" DECISION STYLE?

There is no "best" decision style that fits all jobs or situations. Any given style, however, performs better when there is an appropriate match between the job and the individual. Highly programmed jobs requiring speed and consistent behaviors according to given procedures, for example, would be performed best by an individual with a Decisive style. In jobs such as claims adjusting, which require speed but also need ingenuity and adaptability—as opposed to consistency and reliability—the Flexible style would be more effective. In highly complex and rapidly changing situations, such as aerospace research, the Integrative style would be more successful. Project managers in charge of such endeavors as a moon landing, which require the analysis of a large array of data to accomplish a single purpose, usually do a better job if they have Hierarchic decision styles.

The important point in all the foregoing examples is that in order to determine the best individual decision maker, both the person's decision style and the characteristics of the situation must be analyzed so that an appropriate match can be achieved. In determining the optimum person–job match, the following procedure is suggested:

1. Determine the job demands:
   a. Amount and complexity of the data that must be used.
   b. Time pressure.
   c. Need for diffuse multiple focuses.
   d. Amount of responsibility.
   e. Social complexity (type of influence needed, type of people supervised, etc.).

    2. Determine the person's basic decision style:
      a. Decisive
      b. Flexible
      c. Hierarchic
      d. Integrative
    3. Select the combination that best matches the individual to the situation.

Determining an appropriate match is dependent on accurate assessments of the job requirements and the individual's decision style. This means that an in-depth job analysis must be undertaken using the variables listed. It is not enough to rely on written job descriptions that may not even refer to the relevant variables. Next, decision styles must be accurately assessed. This can be done by checking the characteristics of individuals being considered against those listed in the Decision-Style Characteristics chart in Figure 4-3. You should appraise individuals in as many situations as possible to make sure that your evaluation is not overly influenced by unusual factors in a unique circumstance.

The illustrations of well-known business and political leaders presented in the section on characteristics of each decision style are brief examples of how these appraisals can be made. To fine-tune your first approximation of matches, it is also useful to look at unique advantages and problems of each style.

ADVANTAGES OF EACH STYLE

As mentioned earlier, a specific decision style may be evaluated as either positive or negative, depending upon the style of the specific evaluator. There are distinct advantages and disadvantages to each style, however, and the previous section has explained how they can be matched to specific job characteristics to increase the chances of effective performance. In addition to studying how style characteristics have advantages for different jobs, one can highlight their strong points by visualizing which styles would be most appropriate at typical stages of a business development, which proceeds through creativity, start-up, production, and expansion.

The Integrative style is highly creative and would be best suited to the idea-generation and planning phase. Flexibles have a fluid, exploitive nature and are well suited to entrepreneurial activities needed in the start-up stage. During the small-scale production stage, the Decisive's efficiency and consistency would definitely be advantageous. As the scale of production increases and becomes more complex, the Hierarchic would probably be the best type of manager because of the associated strengths of quality, control, and information processing.

The general conclusion is, however, that each decision style has unique characteristics that can be either advantageous or disadvantageous depending upon the specific situation. The critical dimensions of each situation must be determined as it is encountered, perhaps using the foregoing procedure. Some of the strengths of each decision style that can then be considered are provided in Figure 4-5.

PROBLEMS OF EACH STYLE

Just as each decision style has certain characteristics that are advantageous, each also has particular problems. These special problems are illustrated in Figure 4-6.

Figure 4-5 Advantages of Each Decision Style

(Single Focus)

DECISIVE	HIERARCHIC
Fast	High quality
Consistent	Complete
Reliable	Rigorous
Loyal	Controlled
Orderly	Logical
Obedient	Thorough

(Minimum Information)   (Maximum Information)

FLEXIBLE	INTEGRATIVE
Intuitive	Creative
Adaptable	Empathic
Likable	Cooperative
Fast	Informed
Spontaneous	Open
Exploitive	Wide-ranging

(Multiple Focus)

(Single Focus)

DECISIVE	HIERARCHIC
Rigid	Suppressive or tyrannical
Avoids introspection	Perfectionist
Low self-concept	Unable to delegate
Avoids change	Argumentative
Unreceptive to complex data	Does not share credit

(Minimum Information) (Maximum Information)

FLEXIBLE	INTEGRATIVE
Shallow	Indecisive
Unable to concentrate	Unable to meet deadlines
Too fascinated with variety	Avoids detail
Unwilling to accept structure	Passive
Poor planner	Overemphasizes process versus results
Appears flippant	Too intellectual

(Multiple Focus)

Figure 4-6 Problems of Each Decision Style

Decisive. Decisives are often perceived as being rigid and too quick on the draw. They are uncomfortable with introspection and consequently avoid many avenues of self-development. They often have negative feelings toward themselves and are uncomfortable with change. Finally, their tendency to close off complex information in their press for action contributes to suboptimal decisions.

Managers can help Decisives cope with their special problems by helping them find appropriate jobs in the organization. By supplying an abundance of positive strokes and feedback, the manager can foster a positive self-image. Also, by avoiding asking Decisives to create new procedures and by having staff experts analyze complex data for them, the manager can eliminate a lot of the stress that could bog down the otherwise efficient Decisive.

Flexible. Flexibles are often perceived by others as being shallow and spineless. They suffer from an inability to concentrate and are too fascinated with variety to focus on completing what they start. They are poor planners and are unwilling to accept structure and discipline. Consequently, they are very often not taken seriously by others.

As with all styles, the manager can help Flexibles by assigning them to jobs that fit their style. Staff experts should be assigned to handle long-range planning and research activities, and the manager should avoid assigning Flexibles any long-term projects requiring concentrated efforts.

Hierarchic.   Hierarchics are often perceived by others as being tyrannical, suppressive, and overcautious. They have an excessive fascination with detail and are committed to perfectionism. They feel contempt for incompetence and have an inability to delegate. They do not give others credit and usurp other's ideas as their own. They are very aggressive and argumentative and are very often seen as threatening by their immediate supervisors.

The manager can avoid some of the Hierarchic's problems by keeping them from line management jobs and assigning them to staff positions. It might help to assign them to team projects where they may learn to respect the competence of others and to give them the recognition deserved.

Integrative.   Integratives are perceived as indecisive, wishy-washy, overly intellectual, and confused. They are often too interested in the process and not enough in the results. They are usually rather passive and depend too much on others. Integratives lack interest in detail and suffer from an inability to meet deadlines.

Integratives can be helped by keeping them out of control positions because of their indecisiveness. They should be assigned staff support for working with detail and enforcing deadlines. If possible, set up a team approach for Integratives, and utilize their creative potential.

COPING PRODUCTIVELY WITH OTHER STYLES

In decision-making situations, it is important to keep the respect of others and to avoid unnecessary tension and conflict that can lead to mistrust and hostility. As with behavioral styles, the key concept here is *flexibility*. You must be able to "bend" as much as possible to accommodate the other's decision style so that a good relationship can be maintained. Then the other style will concentrate on using strengths instead of weaknesses during the decision process. Figure 4-7 summarizes several things you can do to maximize the productivity of your interactions with the various decision styles.

Decisive. When coping with Decisives, always present conclusions first, and provide details only if asked. Be positive, and avoid personal criticism. Avoid the appearance of uncertainty; be firm in your position. Be on time, and keep things impersonal and businesslike. Do not expect interpersonal warmth; impress with the volume of production. Never go over a Decisive's head if you value your relationship and your job.

Figure 4-7 Coping Productively with Other Styles

(Single Focus)

DECISIVE	HIERARCHIC
Present action conclusions first	Respect his control values
Avoid detail	Relate suggestions to his preferred method
Be positive and avoid criticism	Present both your data and conclusions
Be firm and appear certain	Expect him to "correct" your proposals
Be on time	Never "win" an argument
Produce results	Don't make quick replies
Don't expect friendliness	Try for zero defects
Keep things impersonal	Make informed comments
Never go over his head	Listen well

(Minimum Information)   (Maximum Information)

FLEXIBLE	INTEGRATIVE
Show initiative	Present problems
Suggest new ideas	Refrain from offering solutions
Be fast	Have a variety of data sources
Don't overkill a topic	Avoid absolutes
Don't be too personal	Try to cooperate
Keep out detail	Communicate hunches
Stay loose	Do your own control
Keep an open mind	Be ready to shift topics
Don't ask for long-term commitment	Be open

(Multiple Focus)

Flexible.   When interacting with a Flexible, keep a lookout for new ideas to suggest. Show initiative, and move fast because action is what counts. Do not overkill a topic or make it too complex. Keep conversations moving, and keep interactions pleasant but not too personal. Build results through new ventures, and never ask for close guidance. Stay loose; keep detail out of conversations, and keep open to new suggestions.

Hierarchic.   When dealing with a Hierarchic, try to learn rapidly his central values and preferred methods for doing things. Then try to relate your suggestions to these values and methods. Present both your data analysis and conclusions. Expect the Hierarchic to redo or "correct" your proposals, and do not argue excessively, especially not enough to "win," and never in public. Think through your answers, and avoid quick replies. Establish respect by listening well and trying for zero defects.

Integrative.   It is best to deal with an Integrative by presenting problems as opposed to solutions. Your data analysis should be thorough and based on many sources. Keep away from absolutes, and be prepared for long, wandering discussions. Avoid being competitive, and strive for cooperation. Accept and communicate hunches, and plan on doing your own control. Be aware of the Integrative's interest in you, and be open and honest.

APPLICATIONS TO INTERACTIVE MANAGEMENT

Being able to diagnose subordinates' decision styles and knowing how to adjust to each style appropriately can aid the manager in assigning administrative responsibilities, designing decision-making procedures, and determining the composition and method of various task teams. Knowledge of each decision style's strengths and weaknesses can facilitate proper task matches and result in better productivity and satisfaction. Finally, knowing how to cope effectively with other decision styles can contribute to more trust, liking, and productivity in your interpersonal relationships. Some specific applications of decision-style theory follow. You can probably think of several that apply to your own specific situations.

Make job assignments involving tasks that match the employee's decision style. It would be unproductive, for example, to assign a task involving complex information processing and generation of alternatives to a Decisive. If you discover a person already in such a dilemma, remove him before he collapses under the pressure, try to reduce the load by assigning staff assistants, or redefine the position.

It would be just as disastrous to assign an Integrative to a task that required only simple and routine behavior. If the Integrative overcame the boredom and dissatisfaction pushing her to quit, she might withdraw internally by daydreaming, which would lead to decreases in performance. Another possible behavior would be to attempt to complicate the assignment, which could also impair performance and lead to other organizational strains. Again, if you should encounter a subordinate already in such an incongruent position, you should take some action to provide a better match. In this case, assigning additional responsibilities, making the job more complex, or transferring the individual to a more demanding position would help.

Knowledge of decision styles and situational demands can also provide useful information to help the manager decide how much participation is needed and whom to include in a specific decision situation. As you can tell from the characteristics described earlier, you would want different people involved in committees formed to handle recurring, standardized problems than you would select to staff committees formed to brainstorm a variety of creative solutions or analyze a novel, complex problem in depth.

As has been seen in the last three chapters—on learning styles, behavioral styles, and decision styles—the interactive manager must be knowledgeable of the unique differences in employees. Furthermore, this information must be utilized to "adjust" personal and managerial approaches to these diverse styles. The payoffs are indeed powerful—higher employee productivity, greater employee self-respect, increased respect for you both personally and as a manager, increased employee morale and satisfaction, lower turnover, and a host of other equally favorable outcomes. These are the payoffs awaiting the interactive manager.

REFERENCES

DRIVER, M.J., "Career Concepts and Career Management in Organizations," in C. Cooper (ed.), *Behavioral Problems in Organizations* (London: Prentice-Hall International, in press).

DRIVER, M.J., and LINTOTT, J., *Managerial Decision Diagnostics: A Key to Integrating Man, Organization, and Environment in a Productive System*, working paper, Graduate School of Business Administration, University of Southern California, 1972.

DRIVER, M.J., and MOCK, T.J., "Human Information Processing, Decision Style Theory and Accounting Information Systems," *Accounting Review*, Vol. 50, No. 3 (July 1975), pp. 490–508.

DRIVER, M.J., and ROWE, A., "Decision Making Styles: A New Approach to Solving Management Decision Making," in C. Cooper (ed.), *Behavioral Problems in Organizations* (London: Prentice-Hall International, 1979).

DRIVER, M.J., and STREUFERT, S., "Integrative Complexity: An Approach to Individuals and Groups as Information-Processing Systems," *Administrative Science Quarterly*, Vol. 14, No. 2 (June 1969), pp. 272–285.

Analyzing
Transactional Styles

Whenever you communicate or interact with another person, you are entering into a transaction. Transactions are moves that people make when dealing with others. Transactional analysis (TA) is a practical approach to understanding personality and analyzing interactions between people. TA is designed to help us focus on the roles we play when interacting with others and the needs and habits that influence our exchanges. Understanding TA concepts and knowing how to apply them in our interactions with superiors, subordinates, and peers can enhance our interpersonal effectiveness. Just as important, it can also help us help others feel and function better.

TA provides managers with a simple and pragmatic framework for analyzing transactions with subordinates as they are progressing. It also provides the tools to keep these transactions on a productive track.

EGO STATES

Imagine a supervisor angrily scolding an employee who has arrived very late with the materials needed for her task group to begin work for the day. The supervisor's face is red and scowling, her voice is loud and shrill, her body tense and animated. Suddenly the telephone rings, and the supervisor hears a friend's voice. The supervisor's posture relaxes, her voice softens, and a smile comes over her face. In TA terms, the supervisor has changed ego states.

Everyone has three ego states or perceptions of the world: *the Parent*, *the Adult*, and *the Child*. They are separate and distinct sources of behavior. All three ego states are normal and necessary for the interpersonal coping of any fully functioning human being.

From your Child comes intuition, creativity, spontaneous drive, and enjoyment. The Adult processes data and computes probabilities of options. Your Adult also regulates and acts as go-between for your Parent and Child. Your Parent incorporates the attitudes and feelings, both critical and nurturing, that you learned from your parents. The Parent provides you with rules for how you ought to behave and the activities that are deemed acceptable. Your Parent makes many of your minor decisions automatic, because "That's the way it's done." This frees the Adult for more important decisions.

All three aspects of personality have a great living value. Only when one or the other disturbs the *healthy balance* is there any reason for concern. Otherwise, each aspect—Parent, Adult, and Child—is entitled to equal respect and has an important place in your life. These three ego states are depicted in Figure 5–1.

The *Parent* begins developing at birth and is fairly well matured by the time you reach the age of five. This ego state consists of recordings of all the things you saw and heard from all the authority figures you knew (especially your parents or substitute parents) in your early years. The Parent ego state

Figure 5-1 Ego States

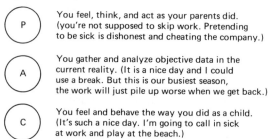

P — You feel, think, and act as your parents did. (you're not supposed to skip work. Pretending to be sick is dishonest and cheating the company.)

A — You gather and analyze objective data in the current reality. (It is a nice day and I could use a break. But this is our busiest season, the work will just pile up worse when we get back.)

C — You feel and behave the way you did as a child. (It's such a nice day. I'm going to call in sick at work and play at the beach.)

within you behaves and feels similarly to your early childhood authority figures. Recordings of all the rules and regulations that you heard as a child are stored in your Parent ego state, and they are communicated by you to others both verbally and nonverbally. The Parent in you is the one who says things like "You should," "You should not," "You must," "Don't," "This is right," "That is wrong." Slogans such as "An eye for an eye," "Boys will be boys," and "You can't change a leopard's spots" also reflect Parent recordings. Your Parent can be critical, or supportive, or both.

The *Child* ego state is what you were when you were very young. The Child ego state within you has feelings and behavior similar to those you had when you were a child. This ego state consists of all your emotions and feelings, your creativity, impulses, curiosity, risk taking, love, and even your fears, guilt, shame, revenge, and dependence. These emotions are often contradictory to the way the child is "taught" he or she should feel by authority figures. Your Child may say things like "Wow," "Gee whiz," "I want it now," "I dare you," and so forth. Your Child can be "Free," "Adaptive," or a "Little Professor." The *Free* Child acts independently in an uninhibited manner, doing things because they bring pleasure. Free Child behavior is not under the direction of your Parent ego state. It simply does what comes "naturally." It can be affectionate, sensuous, and giving or fearful, self-indulgent, and aggressive. The Free Child emerges in such roles as the joker who is always instigating horseplay or the supervisor who always demands that things be done her way when she wants. The key is knowing how to express the Free Child appropriately. Your Child can also be *Adaptive* and do things because they make others happy rather than making you happy. The Adaptive Child is under the influence of your internal Parent ego state and is amiable, polite, obedient, unassuming, and controlled. An example of the Adaptive Child role is the employee who always says "please" and "thank you," never comes in late or leaves early, and has a perfect attendance record. The *Little Professor* is the Child's intuition. It is the ability to interpet the meaning of the supervisor's scowl or the employee's hand gesture. The Little Professor is also the Child's ability to manipulate adults. Examples are the teary-eyed secretary telling her male supervisor how hard she tries to keep up with her work in spite of the continuous distractions from the stock boys. Or it may be the supervisor trying to gain sympathy from the secretary as he asks her out for a drink to discuss how his wife doesn't understand him. A final example is a young male management trainee trying to ingratiate himself with the supervisor by telling her she doesn't look old enough to be such an expert in her field.

The *Adult* ego state starts developing slightly before one year of age, when the child begins to think and test the soundness of the concepts that are being taught. This ego state is that part of you that thinks logically and objectively gathers information. It figures things out by looking at the facts. It is your "computer" that stores information and processes it to make rational decisions and solve problems. Your Adult ego state gathers its information from three sources—the Parent, the Child, and the Adult ego states. The Adult can then separate fact from fiction, reality from fantasy, and truth from lies in order to make a reasonable, unemotional, practical decision. The Adult typically asks many questions, makes decisions, sees them through, and moves to the next problem.

Very often your Parent and Child come into conflict with each other, and tensions get high. An important function of the Adult is serving as the arbitrator between the other two ego states. Figure 5–2 depicts the interrelationships of the three ego states. It is your Adult's job to help meet the Child's needs without getting into trouble, which is the main concern of the Parent. As long as the Adult is doing its job appropriately, a healthy, balanced personality results. Overemphasis of the Parent or Child can lead to emotional and/or social problems.

Figure 5-2 Interrelationships of Ego States

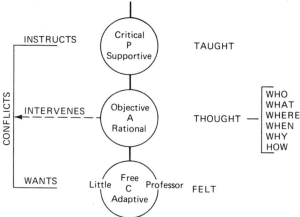

How can you tell which part of you is in control? Four ways of checking are listed next.

Analyze Your Behavior. Here you should be concerned with your posture, gestures, voice, and the words you use. Different ego states are indicated by a tall, straight stance; broad waving gestures; a booming voice; and words like *correct, right*, and *should* versus a slouched body; a downward gaze with little eye contact; a weak, whiny voice; and words like *can't, won't*, and *gee*.

Analyze How You Get Along with People. If you are bossy and think you know it all, people will tend to become cautious and guarded around you. If you are fun loving and happy, others will respond to you differently than if you are manipulative or demanding. If you behave as an Adult, there is a good chance that others will be Adult toward you also.

Analyze Your Childhood. Try to remember how you spoke when you were a child and how your parents talked. You may notice that sometimes you still talk the same way you used to when you were a child. Other times, you will hear yourself speaking exactly as your parents did.

Analyze Your Feelings. Awareness and sensitivity to your own feelings can give you the best clue of what ego state you are currently operating from. You can actually feel that part of you (i.e., Parent, Adult or Child) that is active in you at any given moment.

TRANSACTIONS

A transaction is an exchange of meaning between two people. Although the most commonly thought of transactions are verbal, they may also consist of nonverbal exchanges (e.g., facial expressions, physical actions, tone of voice, etc.). All conversations are a series of transactions between two people, each of whom may be initiating and responding from any one of the three ego states. Consequently, exchanges can be of any nine ego-state combinations: (1) Parent to Parent, (2) Adult to Adult, (3) Child to Child, (4) Parent to Child, (5) Parent to

Adult, (6) Adult to Child, (7) Adult to Parent, (8) Child to Parent, and (9) Child to Adult. These possible combinations are depicted in Figure 5–3. In this and the following diagrams, the person initiating the transaction (i.e., the sender or stimulus) is always on the left, and the person responding to the transaction (i.e., the responder) is always on the right. The arrows show the direction of the communication.

All transactions fall in one of three categories: complementary, crossed, and ulterior. When the transactional stimulus generates the expected transactional response, the resulting transaction is *complementary*. All of the ego-state transaction combinations in Figure 5–4 are complementary. Notice that the lines of communication are parallel (uncrossed). These parallel lines denote that the lines of communication are open and have a good chance of remaining that way indefinitely. Examples of complementary exchanges or stimulus–responses sets of Parent–Parent, Parent–Child, Adult–Adult, and Child–Adult are illustrated in Figure 5–4 between a subordinate and a manager.

There are times when the transaction lines become *crossed*. This results in a communication breakdown and a nonproductive relationship between manager and subordinate. Crossed transactions occur when the response from the second person is unexpected or not appropriate. Figure 5–5 illustrates this phenomenon between a manager and a subordinate. The communication about scheduling overtime will probably break down, and a defensive transaction will ensue regarding prejudice. Crossed transactions stop the original communication and cause tension and distrust in a relationship.

Figure 5-3 Ego-State Transaction Combinations

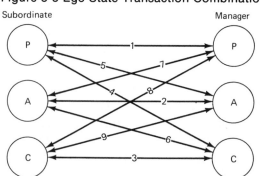

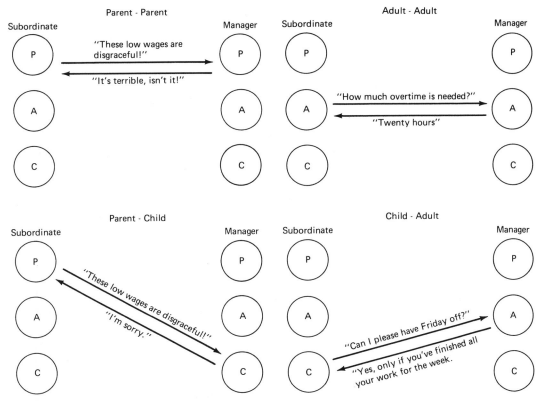

Figure 5-4 Complementary Transactions

The most complex type of transactions are those with hidden messages in them. These *ulterior* transactions involve more than two ego states. Usually they are initiated by a seemingly Adult–Adult transaction, but they have a Child–Child or Parent–Child ulterior meaning. Ulterior transactions can be

Figure 5-5 A Crossed Transaction

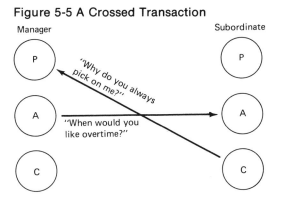

angular—which involves three ego states—or *double*—which involves four ego states. Figure 5–6 gives an illustration of an angular ulterior transaction where a manager successfully "hooks the Child" of the subordinate.

Figure 5–7 gives an example of a double transaction between a male manager and a female subordinate. A naive bystander might only overhear a straightforward Adult-to-Adult exchange of words about working overtime. Between the direct transaction participants, however, tone of voice and facial expressions would indicate a secret Child-to-Child exchange.

One difference between the two types of ulterior transactions is the amount of control the initiator imposes on the responder. One reason the double transaction is so useful in flirting is that it allows the respondent to ignore the hidden message and respond only to the spoken words. This freedom is not a part of the angular transaction in which the initiator tries to gain control over the receiver's response by "hooking" the Parent or Child. This is generally a negative form of manipulation, usually resulting in a win–lose outcome. It should be avoided by an interactive manager because when it is detected, it will immediately or eventually erode the supervisor–subordinate trust bond.

The goal of interactive management is to put your Adult in charge of your transactions. This is the ability to switch responses from Parent and Child ego states to the Adult when appropriate and knowing when to let the automatic responses of the Parent and Child operate. *Appropriate* is the key word, and it applies to the requirements of the situation and the needs of others with whom we are interacting. It requires awareness of your own ego states and how they affect your transactions with others.

Figure 5-6 An Angular Ulterior Transaction

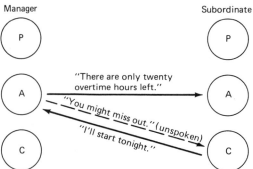

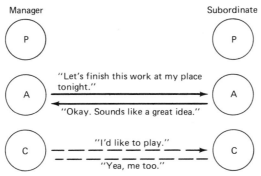

Figure 5-7 A Double Ulterior Transaction

Analyzing the four areas referred to earlier (i.e., behavior, interactions, childhood, and feelings) can help you get in touch with yourself. Knowing the appropriate ego state also requires the ability to acquire and accurately process data about the adult requirements of the reality in which you are interacting. This aspect was discussed in Chapter 4, "Decision Styles." Finally, awareness of the current ego state of the person you are interacting with is necessary if you are to adapt appropriately to avoid crossed, tension-producing relationships. The verbal and nonverbal clues listed in Figure 5–8 should be useful in aiding you assess the Parent, Adult, and Child ego states of others. Although we strive for complementary Adult–Adult transactions in interactive management, they are not always the most appropriate kind. When discussing the safety features of a new, automated production system, it may be best to appeal to the Parent. Appealing to the Child ego state, on the other hand, may be most appropriate when covering the "fun" or social aspects of a job and work group. However, it is important to keep in mind that "reality testing" happens in the Adult ego state. This occurs when you pause to think about what is actually happening, what your options are, and what the consequences are of each action, as opposed to simply "reacting" to a stimulus. It is with reality testing that productive communication is achieved.

STROKES

Strokes are recognition and acknowledgment such as a smile, pat on the back, or praise. Even a sneer or slap in the face is some recognition and better than being ignored. Strokes are so

	VOCAL AND VISUAL	VERBAL
P A R E N T	Finger pointing, head shaking, hand-wringing, arms folded across the chest, patting a person on head or shoulder, foot-tapping, wrinkled brow, pursed lips sigh, impatient snort, grunts. A comforting touch, consoling sounds, holding and rocking.	Always; never; remember; you ought to know better; you should do better; don't. Poor thing; dear; sonny; honey; there, there. Now what; naughty; stupid; disgusting; how dare you; shocking; asinine; absurd; ridiculous; horrid. If I were you; cute; you're all wet. Unthinking, evaluate reactions of all types.
A D U L T	Lively facial expressions; listening; appropriate responses to what the other person is saying. Concerned; interested appearance and posture. Relaxed calm when appropriate; vigorous "body english" when appropriate.	Why; what; where; when; who; how. Alternates; possible; probably; relatively. Identification of opinion as opinion (not fact). Restating what the other person said and identifying it as a restatement to check understanding.
C H I L D	Tears, pouting; temper tantrums; high-pitched whining voice; quivering lips. No answer; sullen silence. Downcast eyes; nail-biting, nose-thumbing; shrugging shoulders. Giggling; squirming; raising hand for permission to speak; teasing; taunting; needling.	Baby talk; best; I don't care; I hope; I wish; I want; mine; I dunno. Look at me! Didn't I do good? Nobody loves me. Back-biting after the other person has left the room. Mine's bigger than yours. Wow! Gee Whiz!

Figure 5-8 Verbal and Nonverbal Clues to Ego States

important and necessary that a teenager would rather be admonished than completely ignored. Everyone needs strokes. They are necessary for physical and psychological health. They say, in essence, "I know you are there and care enough to acknowledge it."

A *positive* stroke is one that makes you feel good about yourself and your situation. Examples are a pat on the back, a compliment, or a friendly smile. Conversely, a stroke that makes you feel bad about yourself is a *negative* stroke. Examples are a kick in the pants or an insult.

A *conditional* stroke is one given for what you *do* rather than for who you *are*. Some managers only stroke their employees if they do outstanding work. For example: "I really think your attitude is better when you do exactly as you're told." Unfortunately, this leads to unproductive behavior and game playing. People prefer strokes for "being" rather than strokes for "doing." When you stroke an employee for who she is rather than for what she does, your stroke is *unconditional*. It has no strings attached. You are telling the employee that she is respected and liked as a person per se. Unconditional positive stroking creates feelings of mutual good will and develops trust relationships.

Again there is a need for flexibility in ego states to be effective in stroking. Stroking from the Adult is effective in conditional stroking when the facts support a job well done. The more important unconditional stroking, however, is usually done by the Nurturing Parent or Free Child. When an employee is feeling depressed and things are going badly, he needs unconditional stroking most. This is when the Nurturing Parent can stroke in the most appropriate way. Strokes from the Free Child based on spontaneous feelings can only contribute to good feelings for both parties involved and usually to a more trusting and productive relationship.

LIFE POSITIONS

Depending on the type of strokes you were used to getting as a child, you arrived at one of four basic life positions. These life positions are ways you feel about yourself and about others. The basic position you came to also dictates how you give and get strokes. This circular behavior tends only to reinforce your life position. The four positions follow.

I'm OK–You're OK. This is the healthiest position. Both you and others can solve problems constructively and feel good. Both parties "get on with it" and win.

I'm OK–You're Not OK. These people blame others for their problems. They distrust others and would like to "get rid of" them. At the extreme, they become paranoid.

I'm Not OK–You're OK. This is the position of someone who feels unworthy or "one-down." He is disappointed in himself and wants to "get away from" life (e.g., in withdrawal or avoidance).

I'm Not OK–You're Not OK.   A person in this position has essentially lost interest in living productively. This is the "get nowhere" position, which can result in extreme withdrawal, hostility, murder, or suicide.

These four life positions are depicted in Figure 5–9. If your Child is coming from a "Not OK" position (i.e., the Sulk or the Loser), you have probably come to settle for more negative than positive strokes. You may turn down positive strokes because you feel you don't deserve them or even go out of your way to collect negative strokes.

If you are in an "OK" life position (i.e., the Winner or the Paranoid), you probably are open to positive strokes. Winners have stored up a reserve of positive strokes to help them feel good about themselves; consequently they can allow and help others to feel good about themselves also.

If you don't feel that you are acting or feeling like a Winner, there are some things you can do about it. Unfortunately, you cannot completely erase the old tapes from your childhood containing not-OK messages. But you can turn down their volume and update them by reality testing with your Adult. When tuned in, your Adult can recognize Child and Parent put-downs within yourself and from others. Armed with this awareness, the Adult can then choose not to respond (i.e., get hooked) to old feelings but to respond as an Adult.

With respect to management styles, the traditional or technical manager assumes that subordinates are Not OK children who are basically dependent, irresponsible, and pleas-

Figure 5-9 Four Basic Life Positions

ure seeking. Consequently, technical managers initiate and respond with Parent behavior such as tight controls, carrot-and-stick reinforcers, and use of authority. When the Nurturing Parent comes into control, the manager may actually be sheltering and protecting subordinates, which fosters their dependence and supports the Not OK position. If the Critical Parent takes charge, on the other hand, the manager assumes the role of the tough autocrat who actively drives home subordinates' Not OK feelings.

The interactive manager strives to operate from the Winner quadrant. Both the manager and the subordinate are perceived as being unconditionally OK. Interactive managers believe their subordinates are basically responsible, independent, and industrious, just like they are. These assumptions produce complementary Adult-to-Adult transactions between OK individuals, resulting in winning relationships with high trust and mutual respect.

TRADING STAMPS

Collecting stamps means internalizing your feelings (pent-up emotions) until you've saved enough to cash them in for a "prize." The concept is similar to collecting trading stamps when you buy something at a store. Once you've accumulated enough trading stamps, you can redeem them for a "free" gift. *Free* means that you don't feel guilty or that you now have a right to do something you don't ordinarily do.

A person who seeks negative strokes is called a *brown stamp* collector. Whenever you end a transaction without expressing your feelings (*venting*), you collect one or more brown stamps (depending on the severity of the incident). For instance, when a person forgets to thank you for something, that may be worth one brown stamp (bad feeling) to you. An insult may be worth ten brown stamps. You accumulate these brown stamps until you feel you have enough to trade them in for an argument with someone, a punch in the nose, or quitting your job.

Unfortunately, a subordinate may cash in his book of brown stamps on a manager even though the manager has only contributed a small percentage of stamps to that subordinate's book. The most common method that subordinates use to cash in their brown stamp book(s) on managers is refusing to do a quality job or even sabotaging work efforts. This often occurs even though subordinates need and want the bonus associated with a quality product. With this in mind, it is important for the interactive manager to remember two things:

1. Don't intentionally give your subordinate brown stamps.
2. Allow your subordinate to get rid of the brown stamps already collected constructively.

One of the best and easiest ways to avoid giving someone brown stamps is to know how to give positive strokes sincerely. In addition, knowing how to get your subordinate to vent (constructively cash in brown stamps a little at a time) is another crucial skill of the interactive manager. Several ways to accomplish these things are discussed in the remaining chapters of this book.

When a person is stuck in the I'm Not OK position, however, if you try to give her positive strokes, she may not accept them. She may even go out of her way to provoke negative strokes. Try not to give them. Remember—everyone needs strokes, and if some people are into stamp collecting, giving predominantly gold ones (positive strokes) should be the most effective strategy in helping them move from being Losers to Winners and in establishing more productive relationships.

Winners (people in the I'm OK, You're OK position) don't have to collect stamps to feel good about themselves or to use as excuses for what they feel or do. Winners also don't accept brown stamps from others, no matter who is trying to hand them out. Instead, they try to understand why the person is feeling like he does and then determine how to solve the problem. A secretary receiving a condemnation for three typing errors on the front page of a sales report (Parent–Child) might—instead of apologizing and feeling guilty (Child–Parent)—think and say: "Mr. Jones, I can tell you're pretty upset over these errors. If you wait for just one minute, I'll correct them and bring them to the meeting [Adult–Adult]."

USE OF TIME

Structuring time is a basic human need. If time is not structured, we suffer boredom and are often unable to get the strokes we desire. There are six basic ways of structuring time with other people in ways to give and receive strokes. Which ways you spend most of your time depends to a great extent on your basic life (OK, Not OK) position.

Intimacy. When both parties in a transaction are coming from I'm OK, You're OK positions, they can accept each other unconditionally and spend their time together in an open and caring relationship. Because we can't be intimate with everyone, and because we don't always feel OK (worthy of love from others) ourselves, the majority of most people's time is spent in one of the other five ways of structuring time.

Withdrawal. It is possible to be with people physically but not psychologically. Withdrawal is a nontransaction. If the conversation is boring or seems irrelevant to an individual, for example, he may withdraw by daydreaming or fantasizing. This is a way of getting somewhere in your head where the strokes are better for you.

Rituals. Rituals are fixed ways of behaving toward others where the outcomes are safe and known. A set of transactions that all of us use are greeting rituals like: "Hello, how are you?" "Fine, how are you?" Each phrase is a stroke of recognition, and a return stroke is expected. If it does not materialize, the other person is judged to be rude or unfriendly.

Activities. Activities are engaged in to accomplish tasks. Examples are work, studying, and planning. When done with others, they do not require intimacy but provide ways of receiving strokes.

Pastimes. Pastimes are socially enjoyable ways of exchanging strokes with others. Examples are comparing the performances of different cars, discussing sporting events, exchanging party stories, and talking about fashions. For some, pastimes are pleasant ways to meet people, try out new roles, and develop new relationships. For others, however, they are used as a means of warding off intimacy.

Games. When you are not being up-front with another person in a transaction, you are playing a game. Your message has a hidden purpose, like making another person feel inferior or angry, although the surface transaction may appear to be perfectly acceptable. An example from a manager to a secretary might be: "Here, let me proofread the report myself this time. We can't afford any more mistakes with these clients." When people play games, they do things that can have very negative consequences for the organization, such as failing to come through, passing the buck, making mistakes, and catching others having difficulties. Consequently, games are a powerful force in preventing people and organizations from becoming Winners.

GAMES

Although psychological games have rules, strategies, winners, and losers like Monopoly or chess, they usually are not "played" for fun or enjoyment, and there may be no lack of seriousness. Anyone who has "played" the stock market or "played" serious poker can testify to how it feels to be a loser. A game is a series of repetitious, superficially plausible, complementary transactions with an expected ulterior outcome or playoff. The concealed motivation makes the game basically dishonest and manipulative. It is usually a way to get strokes for yourself at another person's expense. The transactions in any game are as follows:

1. The players appear to have an honest reason for the transaction (e.g., to ensure the quality of reports).
2. They also exchange secret messages (e.g., "If it weren't for you!" and "Kick me, kick me!").
3. They experience a payoff; one feels superior, and the other feels put down. Both collect their stamps.
4. The Adults of both players are usually unaware that they are in a game.

Games can be recognized by the payoffs. If an encounter with another person results in a bad feeling on your part, but you realize that you asked for it, you have probably been involved in a game. Likewise, if you feel you've "won" but feel a little guilty about it, you have probably manipulated someone unfairly.

Game players may also be identified through the three

general roles they play: *Victim*, *Persecutor*, and *Rescuer*. Players may switch roles within the same game. For example, a manager (Persecutor) may feel superior after severely criticizing a subordinate (Victim) but then feel guilty and try to rescue him. The subordinate (Victim) might then switch to Persecutor by angrily telling the manager (Rescuer) that he doesn't need this kind of help, making the Rescuer the Victim.

Managers and subordinates play games for a variety of reasons. They may play games to avoid legitimate trust relationships, to receive strokes, to relieve tension, or to regain autonomy. If your subordinates are playing games with you, it may be a result of your ineffective utilization of interactive management skills.

If your subordinates play games to receive strokes from you, it may be that you do not stroke them effectively with your verbal and nonverbal communication skills. If they are playing games to relieve tension, it may be that you misread their "styles" and are not effectively interacting with them according to their needs. You may also be applying too much pressure. When your subordinates play games to regain autonomy, you may be trying to control them and their decisions too much. Finally, when your subordinates try to avoid trust relationships with you through game playing, it may be for any of the foregoing reasons or simply because they have found a negative stereotype of you. Your image (handshake, voice intonation, clothing, body language, depth and breadth of knowledge, etc.) may have partially or totally turned them off to you and your influence.

Games may also be encouraged and supported by the expectations the manager establishes for subordinates. Blaming (Victim–Persecutor) games are frequent when heavy punishments are standard for lack of performance. Games that catch people at their mistakes or one-upmanship games (Persecutor–Victim) are common when a strong sense of competitiveness is encouraged. If managers perceive themselves as Rescuers, employees may feel compelled to stay entrenched in Victim games so that the manager can continue to get her strokes.

Following is a list of games commonly played by managers and subordinates. Although managers are equally responsible for games, the following are illustrated as if motivated by a subordinate. Additional games are described in Eric Berne's best-selling book *Games People Play*.

1. **If It Weren't for You.**—*A subordinate playing this game blames someone else—either the manager or the worker—for his problems. This "buck-passing" behavior might go something like, "If I had a better product to sell, my record would be much better."*

2. **See What You Made Me Do**—*is another blaming game in which the subordinate admits that she made a mistake but blames it on the manager. "Your watching me type this letter is making me make mistakes."*

3. **Now I've Got You, You S.O.B.**—*is a game in which the subordinate attempts to "catch" the manager making mistakes. The subordinate feels superior or gets even by "zapping" the supervisor. "I checked with engineering and found that you were wrong about that machine setting. I guess managers can't know everything."*

4. **Blemish**—*players are experts in finding and pointing out tiny mistakes or flaws. "I noticed that you left for lunch five minutes early today. You said you would always be here until lunchtime if we had problems."*

5. **Bear Trapper**—*is a game in which the subordinate gets you to accept the bait, and then you realize that you have been trapped into an awkward situation. After you agree to let one employee off Friday for a special boat race she has entered, she informs you that there are five more employees in her yacht club who will also want to attend.*

6. **Let's You and Him Fight.**—*In this game a subordinate manipulates the superior into fighting with another supervisor or employee over something that will only reward the subordinate. It's a setup in which the subordinate will win something (e.g., overtime, job assignment, vacation period, etc.) after one of the two combatants loses.*

7. **Yes, But**—*is one of the most commonly played games by line and staff individuals and by subordinates and managers. Players appear to look for solutions to their problems but reject any advice they receive as a way of putting down the manager or staff person.*

8. **Corner**—*is being played when a subordinate maneuvers you into a situation in which there is no way you can come out looking good, no matter what you do. Your subordinates may complain that you don't give them enough latitude regarding how to do their work; then when you do and they make mistakes, they complain that you didn't give them enough direction. The Corner Victim's feeling is, "I'm damned if I do and damned if I don't."*

9. **Uproar**—*starts with a critical remark implying an ulterior You're Not OK message. Although the usual response is a defense, the Persecutor continues until both parties are engaged in a shouting match ending with hard feelings and considerable distance between the participants.*

10. **Rapo**—*is a seduction followed by a rejection and a put-down as soon as someone takes the bait. A typical example is a secretary posing provocatively and batting her eyelashes as she opens the door for her boss after they have been working late one evening. When he asks her out for a drink, however, she calls him a dirty old man and slams the door in his face. Although most Rapo games have sexual connotations, the same outcome would take place in situations like a subordinate openly agreeing with a supervisor's decision all during a conference and then refusing to cooperate in implementing it later, even though the supervisor thinks she has a commitment.*

11. **Courtroom**—*is often played by a person who has learned in childhood how to get a parent or authority figure to side with him and against his opponent. A subordinate (plaintiff) might come to his supervisor (judge) to plead his case against another co-worker (defendant). It is essentially the process of manipulating someone else into putting down your opponent.*

12. **Kick Me**—*players provoke a put-down from others in the form of a verbal or nonverbal kick. An extreme form of Kick Me is a subordinate provoking a supervisor to fire her.*

13. **Poor Me**—*games are those in which subordinates see themselves as helpless to do anything about improving things. For example, employees who do a lot of griping but never do anything to change their situation are playing a Poor Me game.*

14. **Harried Executive**—*players structure their time with work. As long as they are busy, they feel OK about themselves. This is a game often reinforced by supervisors and organizations because of the productivity payoffs. Too often, the negative payoffs of Harried Executive are not recognized until the player's psyche or body has suffered irreparable damage. The serious nature of Harried Executive is currently being recognized in stress reduction training in which players are retrained to balance their lives with time for others, themselves, and relaxation, as well as for work.*

Games have negative ramifications for organizations and the people in them. They focus energy on negative self-concepts or feelings about others gained in the past, waste time seeking or giving negative strokes, and utilize ulterior and devious behaviors rather than honest and trusting ones.

When games are given up, people can be more honest and open with each other, and the resulting trust can allow them to concentrate on solving legitimate organizational problems instead of protecting themselves from negative interpersonal games. These benefits can easily be transformed into time and money savings for the organization and, for those within it, better feelings about themselves and others.

STOPPING GAMES

Games can be stopped simply by refusing to play them. If you are the initiator, refuse to take your payoff. If the other person initiates, don't get "hooked," or don't provide the expected payoff. In addition, there are specific interventions or techniques you can use to stop others from playing games.

1. **Unexpected reaction.**—*Doing something unexpected, like not taking or giving the negative payoff, or simply refusing to play, are the classic ways of stopping games. This doesn't mean that the other person will stop playing games altogether, but if there is no payoff, she will probably stop playing with you and look for her negative strokes elsewhere.*

2. **Get out of role.**—*When talking about ego states earlier in this chapter, we suggested four ways of determining which part was usually in control. These were analyzing your behavior, your relationships with others, your childhood, and your feelings. The same type of analysis can be profitably utilized to determine if you are unconsciously playing a game role that encourages others to interact with you with certain games. This analysis can give you insights into any behaviors or feelings that encourage others to react to you as a Victim, Persecutor, or Rescuer. If you find that you do tend to slip naturally into one of these three roles, use your awareness of the process to resist, and continue to behave on an Adult level.*

3. **Stop discounting.**—*Games involve putting someone down— either yourself or someone else. Simply stopping from emphasizing other people's shortcomings or refraining from putting them down can end the majority of games. Most of the remainder can be stopped by not exaggerating your own personal shortcomings and quitting the collection of brown stamps. Instead of letting others give you excuses for collecting feelings of inadequacy, anger, guilt, or depression, perceive their negative response as their problem, and try to diagnose the game they're initiating.*

4. **Give and accept positive strokes.**—*Stopping games means experiencing a void in the strokes previously received through them. One way of creating additional positive strokes for yourself and others is to engage in more rituals and pastimes. Talking about favorite places to eat, sports, and hobbies can help, but you must determine in each situation when too much becomes inappropriate.*

Increased time investment in activities aimed at increasing productivity can reward the participants with more effective strokes, especially if the activities involve creative new developments that allow individuals to enhance their human potential.

Finally, giving more positive strokes to others for a job well done or, better yet, just because you care can result in a more direct and productive relationship. If your positive strokes are reciprocated, and they almost always are, positive feelings develop along with increased trust and a more productive relationship.

INTERVENTIONS

Interventions originate in your Adult ego state. They are techniques for breaking game patterns and proceeding to more productive Adult transactions. Some of the more useful interventions follow.

1. **Leveling.**—*Leveling is being honest with another person about your feelings and about what you perceive to be going on between the two of you. The feelings can be either positive or negative and can concern either productive or destructive behaviors. In the former case, leveling often leads to increased intimacy. In the latter case, it can clear the air and stop unproductive games.*

2. **Open questions.**—*Questions that allow the other person to respond in an appropriate Adult manner can sometimes contribute to a new and constructive perspective. For example, instead of answering with a "hooked" response, you might ask: "What is your major concern in this matter?" or "What ideas do you have for solving this problem?"*

3. **Paraphrasing.**—*Restating in your own words what you heard the other person say allows the other to listen and to hear what her statements sound like from your perspective. It is a nongame response that sometimes makes the game player aware of what is going on and gives her the option of rephrasing her words in a more productive manner.*

4. **Asking for confirmation.**—*Asking the other person to tell you how he interprets what you have just said also circumvents game responses. At the minimum it provides feedback on whether or not you have been heard correctly and gives you a chance to clarify further if you haven't. It also forces the respondent to think in his Adult ego state, which can discourage many impulsive Child responses.*

5. **Confrontation.**—*Pointing out a game player's inconsistencies or deceptions can be useful only if previously volunteered and specified information is used and if there are enough data to prove the point without question. This is a risky technique that can backfire if poorly worded or timed. Often, telling a relevant anecdote or story immediately following a successful confrontation can soften its effect and keep*

the other person from falling into defensive behavior originating from her Child or Parent ego state.

TA AND INTERACTIVE MANAGEMENT

The ideal relationship the interactive manager can strive to achieve with his subordinate is an Adult–Adult relationship. This is a complementary transaction and is game-free. It involves sincere positive stroking and little chance of brown-stamp collecting. Both the subordinate and the manager feel "I'm OK, You're OK" about each other. They both feel safe, accepted, and trusted. Each can openly and honestly communicate without fear or tension. Both benefit from their relationship. Both sides win.

Although the intricacies of transactional analysis can be interesting and enlightening, it is not necessary, or particularly useful, to become an "expert" in them. However, an understanding of the existence and value of our three selves (Parent, Adult, Child) can be very useful in getting a clearer view of our own feelings and actions and those of others.

A better understanding of what is going on between you and others and of some of the whys behind the behaviors is helpful but not enough. You also need to put this understanding into practice when managing others. To do this, review from time to time the procedures suggested earlier for recognizing ego states, deciding on appropriate transactions, obtaining and maintaining an OK life position, dealing positively with trading-stamp rackets, and stopping games. Some general guidelines for successfully incorporating TA into your interactive management style are given next.

1. Develop your own set of up-to-date values, and internalize them so that you can automatically respond to situations in ways that you and others perceive as ethical. This is really a job of reeducating your Parent.
2. Delay your responses to behaviors that tempt your Child or Parent into unthinking reactions. This gives your Adult time to sort out reality from the feelings of your Parent and Child.
3. Be sensitive to the Child in others. It is especially important to help the Not OK Child in others to carry its burden.

Recognize its need for support, and supply the necessary positive strokes.

4. Be sensitive to the Parent in others, and deal with it in a manner that is appropriate from its point of view. This is usually from an Adult or Child response.

5. Accept and appreciate the Child within yourself. Let your creative and fun-loving Child have free rein when appropriate. Recognize when your angry and spiteful Child is taking over, and try to temper negative behaviors with positive internal strokes.

6. Learn to recognize your Parent. Check out its admonitions and bias with your Adult. Learn to use your Nurturing Parent when appropriate.

7. When in doubt—stroke! Make your subordinates feel important. Ask yourself: "Am I being understanding, caring, and sharing?"

8. Strive for productive relationships with others. Help them build a healthy Adult. Relate primarily in an Adult-to-Adult manner—open, trusting, caring, and appropriate to the situation.

9. Strive to be aware, perceptive, and receptive to both others and yourself.

Although the remainder of this book contains valuable additional techniques for helping you become more precise in managing effective relationships with others, your background in TA and "style" differences is enough to get you started right now.

REFERENCES

BERNE, E., *Transactional Analysis in Psychotherapy* (New York: Grove Press, 1961).

BERNE, E., *Games People Play* (New York: Grove Press, 1964).

BERNE, E., *What Do You Say After You Say Hello?* (New York: Grove Press, 1972).

CAMPOS, L., and McCORMICK, P., *Introduce Yourself to Transactional Analysis* (Berkeley, Calif.: Transactional Pubs., 1972).

HARRIS, T., *I'm OK—You're OK: A Practical Guide to Transactional Analysis* (New York: Harper & Row, 1969).

JAMES, M., *The OK Boss* (Reading, Mass.: Addison-Wesley, 1975).

JAMES, M., and JONGEWARD, D., *Born to Win.* (Reading, Mass.: Addison-Wesley, 1971).

JONGEWARD, D., *Everybody Wins: Transactional Analysis Applied to Organizations* (Reading, Mass.: Addison-Wesley, 1973).

INTERACTIVE COMMUNICATION SKILLS

How well do you communicate with others? If you had to rate yourself on a scale from one (highly ineffective) to ten (highly effective), how would you rate your communication effectiveness? Better yet, how would those people with whom you communicate rate you on that scale? Do you believe you can be an effective manager without being an effective communicator? No! Remember that the definition of managing is getting things done through other people. If you cannot accurately communicate what needs to be done, how do you expect to get it accomplished? In addition, even if you can accurately communicate directives, you may do so in such a way that it causes hard feelings or "turns off" other people. In either case, the job may not get done at all, may not get done on time, may not get done correctly, or may be subtly sabotaged. Is accurate, effective, open communication important in managing others? You bet it is!

Have you ever had a breakdown in communications whereby you were misunderstood by another person or you misunderstood the other person's message? Have you ever used words or phrases that were misinterpreted by other people? Do others ever "mistrust" what you say? Have you ever discounted somebody's words because of the way he or she said them or the manner in which the words were delivered? If you answered yes to any or all of the foregoing, do not fret. It has happened to all of us at one time or another. However, the important thing to keep in mind is that these problems happen much more frequently and with much greater severity to poor communicators than to good communicators. Even if you now believe that you are not a very good communicator, this part of the book will provide you with skills crucial to becoming a much better communicator. That even goes for those of you who are already pretty effective at communications. You'll get better. Read on.

"Would you tell me, please, which way I ought to go from here?"
"That depends a good deal on where you want to get to," said the Cat.
"I don't much care where—" said Alice.
"Then it doesn't matter which way you go," said the Cat.

Alice in Wonderland, *Lewis Carroll*

The Art of Questioning

As the above quote so aptly demonstrates, if a person doesn't explicitly understand where he is going or what problems or roadblocks he may be facing along the way, he may never get there. In fact, he may never even try to get there until somebody comes along and guides him to his ultimate destination. Your role as manager is that of a guide to your employees. You guide them to their ultimate destination—the fulfillment of their personal and professional goals. One of the most critical and valuable tools in the manager's arsenal of communication skills is her art of questioning. The ability of the manager to ask the right questions at the right time to help her employees best is an essential and integral part of interactive management. Skillful questioning simplifies the manager's job because it gets employees to "open up." The employee feels free to reveal inner feelings, motives, needs, current situations, goals, and desires. With this knowledge, the manager is in a much better position to guide the employee to the ultimate achievement of personal, professional, and organizational goals. This "Socratic" approach allows the employees to self-discover goals and objectives, potential problems and roadblocks, and new plans of action. This self-discovery by the employee leads to much greater personal commitment to the implementation of the new plans that are necessary to accomplish personal, professional, and organizational goals. The bottom-line benefit of this approach by the interactive manager is greater cooperation, understanding, teamwork, and higher productivity on the part of all employees.

Questioning as a skill is seldom taught. Even though questioning is an essential tool for managers, there are few courses that deal with the fundamental principles of good questioning. Law schools may instruct students on productive ways to use questions within the courtroom where a witness has sworn to tell the truth. But these courses have little bearing on or pertinence to other situations. Outside the courtroom, where people are not obliged to answer questions, a person must learn to obtain valid and useful information through skillful questioning.

Effective questioning is a skill that all business people should develop. For a manager, however, it is an essential and integral part of the job. The ability to ask the right questions to elicit crucial information will greatly simplify your job as a manager and help you maximize your effectiveness as well as that of your employees. The most successful managers use questions to get their employees to "open up." When your employee can vent feelings about a problem, you have a better idea of how you can help provide things that the person needs to be more effective. When you and your employee more clearly understand his current situation and goals and objectives, you can both actively look for viable solutions that will satisfy his needs as well as those of the company. You also have a better chance of suggesting solutions that will enhance your mutual objectives.

No matter who or what you are concerned with, you must know what kind of questions to ask in order to obtain the information you seek. This is really the most difficult part. It takes skill to know the right questions to ask. In addition to the actual information being sought, other important aspects of questioning are how to ask questions (especially if they are personal), when to ask questions, and who to ask questions in order to get the most accurate information.

This chapter consists of three major sections. The first section examines why people ask questions. This will give you a better feel for how to use questions in different situations.

The second section examines the different types of questions that can be asked. The last section deals with strategies and techniques. These are the specific "how-to's" of questioning. After reading and implementing the ideas presented in this chapter, you will be much more skilled at gathering important information from other people, and, at the same time, they will feel good about the whole process.

WHY PEOPLE ASK QUESTIONS

The first and foremost function of a question is to motivate communication. By asking a question, you open the channels of communication and begin a verbal interaction. Once the questioning begins and a line of communication is open, the function of your questions may change. You will continue to motivate communication, but you may also use questions as tools to gain other ends. Some common uses of questions are discussed next.

Questioning to Gain Information. Questions are used regularly to ascertain facts about a number of things—the employee, her personal and professional goals, her personal and professional problems, her motivations, her performance levels, etc. In particular, it is often helpful for the manager to ask information-gathering questions about all these situations. By having your employees state their needs, goals, objectives, problems, and current situation, you get a more reliable view of their sources of satisfaction and dissatisfaction. By asking them direct questions relating to their needs, you can evaluate their situation and gear your suggestions to focus on specific employee needs and solutions.

Questioning to Uncover Motives and Gain Insight. By skillfully using questions, you can determine your employees' frame of reference. Knowing and understanding your employees' perspective can aid you in determining the best way to present your suggestions. It is imperative to understand the goals and motives underlying your employees' perspective. If you are perceptive and attentive, you will perceive these and, in doing so, be able to assist your employees in forming ideas based on their motives and goals. In effect, your job is to acquire insight through questioning and then to formulate, or help your employees formulate, suggestions that will fulfill their needs as well as those of the organization.

Questioning to Give Information.   When you ask a question like "Did you know that we have an education reimbursement program?" you are in effect giving information. You want your employees to know a fact, and you thus transmit it in question form. This type of question is unique in that the answer, if any, is inconsequential. Furthermore, you are attempting to inform your employee of more than your company's benefits. Underlying the transmission of that fact (that the company has an education reimbursement program) is an attempt to convey the company's caring and goodwill toward its employees. This type of question is helpful in emphasizing certain aspects of a situation. However, beware of insulting an employee's intelligence by making these information-giving questions seem manipulative. Avoid broad, unsubstantiated claims that attempt to placate employees.

Questioning to Obtain Employee Participation.   Occasionally, you come across employees who seem uncommunicative and withdrawn. It is necessary to draw them out and get them to participate in the conversation for you to understand properly and completely their goals, objectives, and current situation. Asking closed questions will probably be unsuccessful or, at the very least, time-consuming, because you will have to waste time guessing the proper questions to ask to get the needed information. Open questions are helpful in this situation, but the topic that will get the employee talking is often hard to find. In this situation, the experience and insight of a good interactive manager come into play. Effective managers have a feeling for the way they should proceed based on past experiences at work. Once the barrier is broken and a trust bond between you and the employee is established, you may continue to seek participation in the problem-solving process. You do so to ensure that the employee understands but also because greater participation leads to greater commitment by the employee to follow through with any potential solutions that you mutually discover. By getting your employees talking and volunteering information, you allow them to build their own convictions and approach the commitment without feeling that they are responding solely to your demands.

Questioning to Check Understanding and Interest. Questions provide the critical feedback necessary to make sure that the two-way communication is on track. This feedback allows you to verify that you have captured the true essence of your employee's message—the feeling as well as the content. In addition, it allows you to evaluate the employee's feelings and understanding about your suggestions and message. You should periodically use feedback questions to make sure that you are understanding your employee's message. Feedback questions typically begin with, "Let me see if I can summarize your major concerns." Or, "I understand you to say . . ."; and end with, "Was my interpretation on target?" or, "Does that accurately summarize your objectives?" By doing this, you are communicating a number of very important things to your employee. First, you are showing that you are making a concerted effort to listen. Second, you are proving with your actions that the employee's message is important. Third, you are confirming the message, so that there is less likelihood of misunderstanding and bad feelings. On the other hand, you should periodically check your employee's understanding of your message to make sure you have made yourself perfectly clear. Simply asking, "Have I explained that to your satisfaction?" is a good way of allowing the employee to voice any doubts or questions he or she may have at that time. Checking employee interest is also essential. You may say, "How does that look to you?" You will know from your employee's response how and where you stand and may choose to move to another area if interest is waning or nonexistent. By occasionally monitoring your employees' reactions through the use of appropriate questions, you will avoid boring them on any particular point, thus jeopardizing understanding, respect, and commitment. Often managers will continue emphasizing a point even when the employee has agreed with it. In these cases, the manager failed to check the employee's response and assumed the reaction was unfavorable when, in reality, it may have been completely favorable.

Questioning to Start an Employee Thinking. Questions that ask for opinions and suggestions serve to get the employee thinking, hopefully in terms of your suggestions and recommendations. When you ask an employee's opinion, you acknowledge her ability to contribute something meaningful and valuable. This isn't necessarily a subtle form of flattery, as you may truly accept and appreciate your employee's contributions and knowledge. It does seem reasonable that the employee would have the detailed knowledge required to operate her area of the business successfully. In view of this, you hope to take advantage of her expertise to develop useful and acceptable suggestions. You need not always try to avoid areas where you have little experience, because your employee may give you the needed insight based on her own experience. These are the very best situations: You and your employee have developed a strong trust relationship in which the two of you work together to accomplish mutual goals and objectives. The employee has the knowledge required to understand her area of the business, and your knowledge in increased by the information flow between you; both of you contribute to promote a successful, productive relationship.

Questioning to Reach Agreement.   By asking if your employee agrees with you, you can judge where you stand with him. It is useless to proceed with a subject if your employee refuses to see your point of view. Rather than proceeding with the subject, which will more than likely lead to a dead end, it is necessary to explore the areas of agreement and disagreement before you continue with that topic. When you say, "Does that coincide with your experience?" you should allow your employee time to reflect and decide if he is in agreement with you. Manipulative practices that try to promote agreement through rapid-fire questioning tactics are undesirable. Even if such tactics prompt an on-the-spot agreement, the employee may later regret his actions and try to withdraw from the commitment or even sabotage it. If you use such underhanded tricks to gain agreement, there can never be a trust bond between you and your employee, and the relationship will continually deteriorate to the point of no return. Many managers suggest that questions should be asked that will get an employee in the habit of saying yes, so that when it comes time to ask for a commitment, the employee will be used to agreeing and will go along with you. Such tactics are blatantly manipulative and can cause a complete breakdown of trust. Sophisticated employees do not like to be maneuvered and will quickly tune out of an interview if they suspect such tactics. The interactive manager does not indulge in these tactics.

Questioning to Bring Attention Back to the Subject.   If

you should fail to hold your employee's attention, a question might serve to bring her concentration back to the subject. Such a wandering of attention may be only momentary and thus may be cured by asking almost any type of question. However, if your employee's inattention and boredom are obvious and prolonged, you should consider concluding your talk as quickly as possible. Everyone has bad days, and you may return to the subject at a time that is more convenient and when the employee is more receptive.

Questioning to Give Positive Strokes and Build Trust. Asking somebody for his opinion is a tried and true form of flattery. It acknowledges his opinion, confirms his value, and requests his participation. A truly powerful positive stroke! While your employee is talking, you can exhibit your interactive listening skills, which serve as another powerful positive stroke for your employee. Together, the questioning and listening process quickly and solidly build a bond of trust between the two of you.

Questioning and Psychological Reciprocity. In plain English, psychological reciprocity means: If you scratch my back, I'll scratch yours. Applying this concept to the questioning, listening, and communications process means that if you question and listen to the contributions and comments of your employees, they will do the same for you when it is your turn to speak. Both sides win by opening up their ears and eyes and minds and hearts to communication process. Likewise, if you do all the talking and do very little listening to your employees, you will develop a habit within them to tune you out. The irony of this concept is that the more you speak, the less you'll be heard. And the more you question and listen, the more likely it will be that you will be heard by your employees.

Questioning to Discover the Tension Differential. The *tension differential* is the gap between what a person is presently doing and what they would like to be doing—their goals and objectives in relationship to their current situation. When a person's goals and objectives are currently being satisfied by her present actions, there is little tension in the person to change her behavior or actions, because they are appropriately working for her. On the other hand, if where a person is now and where she would like to be are far apart, there is greater tension in that person to modify her actions to bring her closer to her goals and objectives. As the difference between where a person is now (current situation) and where that person would like to be (goals and objectives) increases, the tension to act and change behavior increases within that person. Through skillful questioning, the interactive manager can get a keen fix on the size of that gap for each and every employee. In fact, through skillful questioning, you can even widen the gap by asking the proper questions to allow the employee to upgrade his goals and objectives or to find some displeasure with his current situation. This skill should not be confused with manipulation. Unfortunately, many people live in a state of ignorant bliss, thinking at the conscious level that they are in fact happy or satisfied when, in fact, they are not at the subconscious level. Your skills in questioning, probing, and listening will allow an employee truly to come to grips with his goals and objectives and present situation. With a clear perspective and insight, the employee can then choose a new course of action if it is warranted by examination of the tension differential.

Questioning to Determine "Style."   In earlier chapters, we discussed the unique differences in people in terms of their behavior, learning, decisions, and transactions. We suggested that the effective interactive manager must keep these differences in mind in tailoring her management style in accordance with the unique needs of her employees. One of the best ways to determine your employees' style is by asking appropriate questions that will give them the opportunity to project verbal, vocal, and visual clues that you can use to determine their style. Questions revolving around the employees' goals, hobbies, biggest job-related achievement, greatest personal achievement, likes and dislikes, and strengths and weaknesses allow employees to respond naturally and improve the chances of revealing their style. This style-revealing behavior by the employee is created through the effective use of questions by you.

TYPES OF QUESTIONS

During the course of a problem-solving interview session, you will ask many types of questions. You begin with the questions that precede most interpersonal conversations, either business or social. These include "How are you?" and similar courtesies. After the preliminaries have been taken care of, the real business begins. Next are some types of questions that are included in most interactive interviews. By properly selecting and phrasing a question, you can significantly increase your chances of getting the desired information in addition to improving your relationship with your employee. After we present the various types of questions, we move on to the numerous strategies and techniques for actually using them in an interview.

Although there are many types of questions, there are only two basic forms: open questions, which are nondirective, and closed questions, which are directive. Let's examine these two basic types more closely.

Open Questions. Open questions are generally used to draw out a wide range of responses on a broad topic. This type of question comes in many different forms and is the most widely used type by the interactive manager. They attempt to involve your employees by asking for knowledge of a subject or opinions about a topic. Open questions usually

- Cannot be answered by a simple yes or no.
- Begin with what, how, or why.
- Do not lead the employee in a specific direction.
- Increase dialogue by drawing out the employee's feelings and opinions.
- Can be used to encourage your employee to elaborate on objectives, needs, wants, problems, and current situation.
- Help the employee to discover things for himself.
- Can be used to stimulate the employee to think about your ideas.
- Allow your employees to exhibit their "style" much more readily and accurately than any other type of question.

Some examples of open questions are as follows:

"How do you feel about your present job performance?"

"What are the ways that you feel this should be handled?"

"Why do you feel this has been happening so frequently and for so long?"

"What do *you* think about it?"

"What other objectives do you think you should be pursuing at this time?"

"What do you feel is most important right now in terms of your present job description?"

"What do you like least about your present situation?"

"Who else is involved in that problem?"

"How important is that solution to you?"

"What do you think would happen if we implemented this solution?"

Closed Questions.   Closed questions require narrow answers to specific queries. The answers to these questions are typically yes, no, or some other very brief answer. Questions of this nature usually

- Allow specific facts to be obtained.
- Require little thought by the person answering.
- Are useful in the feedback process.
- Are used to gain commitment to a definite position.
- Can be used to reinforce positive statements.
- Can be used to direct a conversation to a particular desired area.

Some typical examples of closed questions are as follows:

"How many hours did you work last week?"

"Isn't that the way it happened?"

"Do you think it could be done better?"

"Is that your primary concern?"

"Do you think it should be changed?"

"Do you really want a job transfer?"

"What percentage of your quota did you produce last month?"

"When did you first discover this happening?"

"Do you agree with my analysis of the situation?"

All the other types of questions generally belong to a subcategory of either open questions or closed questions. Depending on your information needs and the situation surrounding the interview, some are more useful than others. Two of these subcategories of questions are particularly valuable—fact-finding questions and feeling-finding questions. Let's explore these two subcategories a little further.

Fact-Finding Questions. These factual questions usually take the form of closed questions. They give you important specific information on the current situation, goals and objectives, and any other areas of information that are important in managing and motivating your employees. Typically, these questions are rather easy for employees to answer, and they allow the person being questioned to enter the conversation easily and gradually. If your fact-finding questions aren't insensitive, too threatening, or too challenging, they will actually help you build trust and cooperation with the employee. When used in this manner, these questions actually serve as ideal entrées into the more personal feeling-finding questions.

When asking fact-finding questions, it is imperative that you only gather that information that is necessary to the present interview. In addition, it is critical that the information you receive from your employee be heard and recorded accurately by you. In this regard, you should take notes freely, based on the facts you are receiving, and feed them back for employee verification at the conclusion of the fact-finding phase of the interview.

Some examples of fact-finding questions are listed below.

"What is your present salary level?"
"Which company benefits did you specifically take advantage of last year?"
"How many children do you have?"
"Exactly how long does it take you to perform this aspect of your job?"
"How many people do you interface with in your department?"
"When are you planning to take your two-week vacation this year?"
"What job position are you planning to pursue next?"
"Are you interested in joining the company car pool?"

Feeling-Finding Questions. This type of question generally takes the form of an open-ended question. Such questions are used to probe deeper into the employee's mind for feelings, attitudes, convictions, motivations, and feelings. Feeling-find-

ing questions at times are personal and can be in sensitive areas
for the employee. Thus it is important for you to keep in mind
that a strong rapport and trust bond must be established before
pursuing this line of questioning.

Great personal insight can be brought to the employee as
a result of your asking him feeling-finding questions. Used
properly, they allow the employee to dig deeper into mind and
soul about why he feels or behaves the way he does. They help
the employee discover for himself what makes him tick. He is
allowed to discover problems for himself and internal motivations for his behavior. With this added insight, he is much more
willing to change his behavior if it is warranted. Employees are
usually extremely grateful for those managers who have the
unique ability to ask feeling-finding questions. Keep in mind
that it is critically important that, when asking these questions,
the manager truly exhibit active listening skills. We discuss
these specific listening techniques in a later chapter.

Feeling-finding questions usually take the following forms:

"How did you come to feel this way about your job?"

"To what extent do you feel your personal and professional goals
and objectives are being met by your present job classification?"

"Why do you feel that this is the best approach?"

"What do you feel are the least effective/most effective ways of
accomplishing your present job?"

"How do you feel this situation came about?"

"What do you like least/most about the way this problem has
been handled to date?"

"What's your opinion?"

"How many other people do you feel are in a similar situation?"

"What's your opinion on how this can best be handled?"

"How do you feel the problem should be approached?"

"What would your feelings be if we implemented this new
policy?"

In addition to fact-finding and feeling-finding questions,
there are several other subcategories of open and closed questions. Some of the more generally used types are discussed
next.

Clarifying Questions.   Structurally, these questions are a paraphrasing of the employee's remarks. Paraphrasing is restating in your own words what you heard an employee say. Be careful not to tell the employee what she meant; only feed back what you understood her to say. Clarifying questions seek verification of the content and/or feeling of your employee's message. Although this concept of feedback is dealt with in more detail in both the listening chapter and the feedback chapter, it usually takes the form of a question and thus is dealt with here. Clarifying questions may be used to

- Interpret in different words what you interpreted the speaker to mean.
- Invite the employee to expand and/or clarify an idea she has previously expressed.
- Ensure that you and the employee are "speaking the same language."
- Help clarify ambiguities and broad generalizations.
- Uncover what is really on the mind of your employee.

Some examples are as follows:

"If I'm hearing you correctly, it appears that your major concerns are. . . . Is that so?"

"Are you referring to the personnel department or the training department?"

"It seems to me that your major concern is with seniority. Is that accurate?"

"From what you're telling me about this situation, I get the impression that you're very frustrated. Or am I misreading your feelings?"

"Now are you referring to two or three other people?"

Developmental Questions. This type of question is designed to draw out a broad response on a narrow topic. They can help you

- Ask for additional information in a more detailed format.
- Encourage the employee to expand and/or elaborate upon a topic he has already introduced.

Some examples are as follows:

"Can you give me an example of what you mean by that?"

"Then what?"

"Would you please elaborate on that point?"

"Can you tell me more about it?"

"Do you recall what other types of problems you were confronted with in that situation?"

"What other things do you like to do in your spare time?"

Echo Questions.   Echo questions try to accomplish the same objectives as clarifying questions and developmental questions. They not only ask for additional information in a more detailed form by encouraging the employee to expand and elaborate on a particular subject; they also ask the employee to express in different words what he meant by his previous message. This type of question is simply a reiteration of a key word or group of words within your employee's previous sentence. For instance, the employee may have previously said to you, "Well, I would do it if I only had the proper support." In this situation you can choose to use a clarifying question to determine exactly what your employee meant by this statement. On the other hand, you could use a developmental question to have your employee elaborate further. However, in specific situations such as this, you can just as easily use an echo question and accomplish both of the previous objectives. In relationship to the employee's statement, an echo question would simply take the following form: "Proper support?" As you can see from this example, all you have done is echo back in question form the key words of the employee's statement. If done with the proper vocal intonation and quizzical facial expression, there is a great likelihood that your employee will elaborate and clarify his previous statement. However, if the echo question does not bring you the additional information you seek, you can always revert to using a clarifying and/or developmental question.

Directive Questions.   These questions are usually closed-ended questions and aid in directing the conversation to specific areas of concern. They are most useful when

- You want to change the conversation from one topic to another.

- You want to give specific direction to the reply of your employee.
- You want to guide your employee into a better specific understanding of her own needs, problems, and goals.

Some typical examples of directive questions are as follows:

"What was the other issue you wanted to discuss with me at this time?"

"Couldn't you do it the old way for one more week?"

"Why don't we go back and discuss a little further your previously mentioned goals and objectives?"

"Can you send a letter tomorrow?"

"As I see it, there are three more problems we need to solve."

Assumptive Questions. This type of question incorporates an assumption by the manager in question form and is directed at the employee. "Do you want to work overtime on Saturday or Sunday?" is a question that assumes that the employee wants the overtime and needs only to decide on a day. This type of question must be used carefully, since you must be able to judge your employee's state of mind accurately to use this type of question successfully. You risk the scorn of the employee and a lost commitment if you ask the question at the wrong time. You may even insult the intelligence of your employee by thinking that your strategy of asking an assumptive question is subtle. Assumptive questions indicate that you believe your employee is ready to make a decision and only the details need to be worked out. Your timing and sensitivity in reading the state of mind of your employee are very important if the assumptive question is to be used appropriately and effectively. Otherwise, it may be seen as a "trap" to force a decision and thus would reduce your credibility and trustworthiness in the eyes of the employee.

Some examples of assumptive questions are as follows:

"When shall we schedule our next counseling session?"

"Did you want to do your performance appraisal this week or next?"

"How soon did you want to take action on the new suggestion?"

"When is a good time for you to meet with Harry?"

Third-Party Questions. Third-party questions combine a statement and a question. They probe indirectly by relating to the employee how others feel or react to a particular situation. They then ask the employee to give his opinions and/or reactions concerning that same subject. Research indicates that there will be greater acceptance of a statement by an individual if a respected person or group of people endorse that statement. You should be aware of this phenomenon and use it to your advantage when appropriate. Third-party questions can be either specific or general. Specific third-party questions take the following form:

> "Mary Personnel believes that our MBO program is working quite well. How do you feel about this?"
>
> "John Vice-President feels that we could lower our costs and at the same time increase our revenues by dropping our losing product lines. What's your opinion?"

On the other hand, general third-party questions take this format:

> "Most of the people I talk to in this company tell me this is the case. Do you find this to be true?"
>
> "Many of my employees tell me that this is the most rewarding aspect of the job. What's your opinion?"
>
> "A lot of people feel that mutual goal setting is important. How do you feel about it?"

Testing Questions. These questions act as gauges or barometers of an employee's state of mind or present position on a specific topic or issue. They are good to use when you need to determine your employee's level of agreement or disagreement on the specific factors or points that have been brought up in the conversation. They are most appropriately used during the solution process of interactive management. Testing questions take the following form:

> "How does that strike you?"
>
> "How important is that to you?"
>
> "Does that sound sensible to you?"
>
> "How agreeable are you to that issue?"
>
> "Do you think you can live with that?"

Closure Questions. These questions are good devices to encourage agreement and promote successful implementation of any suggested plan or solution. Closure questions are typically open-ended questions with direction. For instance, "Where do we go from here?" is a classic closure question. It is an open question; yet it directs the employee to commit to a position on a particular topic—that is, that she will or will not go in the proposed direction. Either way, the employee is asked to make a commitment. Other closure questions include the following:

"How would you like to proceed with this?"
"What action would you like to take?"
"What do you see as the next step in the decision process?"
"How should we come to closure on this situation?"
"What's the next move?"

Once you are fully aware of why you should be asking questions, for what purposes they can be used, and the various structures and types of questions, you can move to the final step—the strategies and techniques of putting it all together. That is the last section of this chapter—the "how to" skills of asking questions.

QUESTIONING STRATEGIES AND TECHNIQUES

By skillful questioning, you initiate and maintain conversation that will eventually lead to a successful manager–employee relationship. Regardless of whether your employee is the quiet type or likes to take control of the conversation, your questioning skills and techniques will help you obtain valid and useful information as well as develop a trust bond between you and your employee. The manner in which a question is asked can be as important as the content of the question. Since you want truthful, complete answers to your queries about employee needs and motivations, structure your questions to maximize your chances of getting accurate information while maintaining your employee's good will and respect. Without honest and conscientious input by the employee, the questioning process will accomplish nothing. Keep in mind the following general strategies as you select questions.

Use Correct Timing.   If your employee is not in the proper frame of mind to receive questions, you will not get accurate and effective answers. Questions must be properly timed. Asking questions too soon or too late will dull their impact, as they are more than likely falling on deaf ears. Utilize sensitivity and insight in judging your employee's frame of mind to determine if it is an appropriate time to ask questions.

Correct timing can be viewed from another perspective. Questions should not be asked too quickly or too slowly. Timing is important in getting answers. After asking questions, allow enough time for your employee to think and come up with an answer. Asking questions too quickly gives the impression of impatience and comes across more as an interrogation than an interview. Asking questions too slowly can lead to a quick case of boredom.

Have a Questioning Plan.   Although it is not generally advisable to have specifically worded questions to ask in a particular sequence to each and every one of your employees, it is advisable to have a questioning plan. This simply means that you should have a general idea of what you would like to ask to get the particular information you require. A questioning plan gives you a starting point but also allows you the flexibility to explore additional fruitful areas as they arise in conversation. When you leave your planned questions to explore these other areas, you can use directive questions to bring yourself back on track. Remember that you only need a hazy idea of the type of information you desire and the types of questions you must ask to get that information. You do not need specifically worded questions prior to your interviews with employees.

You should take care to avoid being maneuvered into a corner by employee answers. When questioning, try to imagine the worst possible answer you could receive. In what position would that dreaded answer leave you? If the answer could leave you without recourse, perhaps the question should be avoided. Instead of asking such a potentially troublesome question, you could investigate the worker's position by asking other questions that skirt the dangerous subject yet help provide information on the employee's problems. If subsequent queries show that the employee is not likely to answer the question, you can return to the original line of inquiry. The important point is that the employee's answers aren't necessarily those most favorable to your position. To do this properly requires foresight and planning prior to the questioning process.

Know Your Audience. It is important to know something about the person you are questioning. Having information about a person's personal background, political beliefs, religious beliefs, attitudes, interests, and opinions, as well as his behavioral style, transactional style, decision style, and learning style can be an incredible aid in framing and delivering questions for that person. You will not always enjoy the luxury of having all this information about each and every one of your employees, especially the new ones. However, in every interview, you will get to learn more and more about each particular person, thus allowing your subsequent questions to be more relevant for each individual employee. With a little practice, you will be able to adjust the timing and delivery of your questions as well as their framing and structure according to each individual.

Ask Permission to Ask Questions. Although this is not always required, it is a good rule of thumb. Even though you might feel that in your role as a manager, you have the right to ask employees questions, you will find that utilizing the simple courtesy of asking permission will put your employees more at ease. This simple show of respect for another person will set a positive tone for the interview session; it is a good first step toward building trust and will allow a more honest, straightforward, free-flowing exchange of information.

Move from Broad Questions to Narrow Questions. "Tell me a little about your concerns" is an excellent example. This broad, open-ended question allows your employee total autonomy to answer whichever way she wishes. From her answer, specific areas of concern may come to light that you may want to focus on with more specific directive questions.

This broad response opportunity also allows your employees to reveal their "styles" more readily than is possible under a more specific narrow probe. When your employees are free to talk about their goals, problems, and concerns in their own way, they will tend to reveal how they typically interact with others, process information, and make decisions. Your ability to listen to their "open" responses will also guide you to your next question choice, which will tend to narrow your inquiry based on the previous response. For instance, your second response might be: "You mentioned that overtime has caused some problems for you personally. Would you mind elaborating on that?" Subsequent probes may narrow even further to explore in more detail the problems this employee has encountered with overtime. The bottom-line benefit of asking broad questions first is that many specific questions may be answered by the employee before they are ever asked by you; that is, some narrow questions may be answered in the course of responding to the broad questions.

Build on Previous Responses.   Simply stated, listen before questioning. Rather than becoming preoccupied with what you want to ask next and missing most if not all of what your employee is communicating to you, concentrate and attend to what your employee is saying. With this information, you can easily frame your subsequent questions based on your employee's responses. This technique has many advantages. First, you concentrate on listening to your employee rather than letting your mind wander. Second, the questioning process is orderly, logical, and focused. Third, by building on the employee's previous responses, you show through actions that you are, in fact, listening to what the employee is telling you. Fourth, you get the opportunity to explore areas of interest to the employee that you might not have chosen on your own had you not truly listened and built your questions on your employee's previous responses.

Focus Your Questions.   Questions should also allow the employee to think logically about a particular subject. Rather than asking numerous questions on various subjects, pursue one line of thought so that the employee can easily follow that line of thought. By guiding your respondent through these questioning steps, you can maximize your chances for a successful interview and problem solution.

Have One Main Thought.   The employee must understand the questions being asked him. If the question is poorly phrased and the employee doesn't understand it, his answer may provide you with inaccurate information; at best, the answer will be incomplete. Without the successful transfer of accurate information, there has been no communication, and misunderstandings and confusion abound. Rather than risking this, you should carefully structure your questions so that they contain only one main idea. This will reduce the likelihood of confusion. The employee can then concentrate on that one specific thought. Questions that have more than one basic idea can cause a breakdown of understanding, which in turn may decrease the trust bond. An example of a question containing too many thoughts is: "Would you mind telling me a little bit about your personal and professional objectives, as well as some of the things you find that have been helping or hindering you in accomplishing those goals, as well as some suggestions that you might have to overcome some of the hindrances, as well as. . . ." As you can easily see, by the time the manager gets to the end of the question, the employee will have forgotten the whole first half of it. Phrase your questions so they contain only one major thought at a time.

Avoid Ambiguous Questions. An ambiguous question is one that, because of its phrasing, is misleading and open to various interpretations. An example would be, "Would you mind looking over my figures and then giving me your okay?" In the case of this ambiguous question, whether you receive a no or a yes, you are still not quite sure where the employee stands. A no might mean that the person would not mind looking over your figures, whereas the yes might indicate that the employee will sign off on your figures. This type of vague, ambiguous question often confuses the employee and very often fails to elicit the desired response. Remember that if your employee does not understand the question, she cannot give you an accurate or complete answer; so to avoid breakdowns in communication, carefully structure your questions to avoid confusion and promote understanding.

Use Common Language. Keep your questions free of buzzwords, slang, or technical jargon that may or may not be understood by your employee. In addition, avoid flowery, formal, haughty, or legal language. In phrasing your questions, keep in mind the famous K.I.S.S. formula—"Keep it simple, stupid." Also try to avoid complex, "hundred-dollar" words that you believe might impress your employee. More than likely, they will depress the employee because he may not understand them. In such a case, he will tune you out, and a total breakdown of communication will result. By using simple, common language devoid of all superfluous terminology, you can ask questions that will be easy to understand and more likely to get you accurate, straightforward, meaningful information.

Balance the Number of Questions.   When you are with an employee in a counseling session, performance appraisal, problem-solving interview, coaching session, or any other interview, it is important to balance the number of questions you ask. Asking too few questions can be seen as shallow from the employee's perspective. For instance, you might ask your employee, "How are you?" or "How's the job treating you?" and, after receiving answers to these questions, move right into your own verbal dissertation about a particular topic. It will not be too long before your employees see you for what you really are—a shallow, ritualistic questioner only using questions as springboards for your own conversation. On the other hand, asking too many questions without sharing some of yourself can be seen as an interrogation. Asking too many questions can create an information imbalance whereby the employee has provided you with too much information and you have not provided her with enough. This can easily serve to increase interpersonal tension and decrease trust, the net result being a breakdown in communication. Always try to balance the number of questions you are asking against the information you need and the "style" of the employee. For instance, you can get away with asking more questions of an Amiable behavioral style than you can of a Driver behavioral style.

Mix Them Up.   During an interview with your employee, try to use as many different types of questions as possible. Although we stress that you should use more open questions than closed ones, there should be a sprinkling of closed questions throughout your conversation wherever appropriate. Generously use fact-finding and feeling-finding questions as well as clarifying, continuing, directive, echo, testing, and, finally, closure questions. Using too many of one type of question quickly becomes boring to the interviewee. For instance, if you ask questions that consistently provoke one-word or very short answers, you won't get adequate information about your employee's needs or current situation. Unless questions can be framed to encourage employee input and participation, you will be unable to get a complete picture. By encouraging employee participation through using a mix of different types of questions, you may even receive helpful voluntary information that you had not previously thought to request.

Do Not Use Slanted or Manipulative Questions. Questions should not be slanted or manipulative, thus limiting your employee's personal autonomy. Your questions should not force him into an answer or put him on the spot. It is much better to say, "How do your mornings look for a meeting this week?" than "Would you prefer to see me at 10:00 A.M. on Tuesday or at 8:30 A.M. on Thursday?" Good interactive managers realize the importance of protecting their employees' dignity and know that if they insult their employees' intelligence with blatant manipulation, they will be poorly received and less respected.

Do Not Use Threatening Questions. Take care to stay away from questions that might threaten or offend your employees. Such questions will probably raise their tension levels and cause decreased trust. In addition, questions that embarrass a subordinate may encourage her to provide inaccurate or incomplete information. In most cases, the employee has no reason to lie. But when questions touch sensitive areas, you must be wary of inaccuracies. If it becomes obvious that your subordinate is uncomfortable with a question, move on to a different subject immediately. Unfortunately, at times you must ask questions that are in this category. The ability to handle family problems so that they don't interfere with job performance is one area that may cause embarrassment for the employee, but it must be pursued by you to resolve the problem. In such cases, your questions should be straightforward and businesslike but also must project sensitivity and empathy for the employee's position. Although indirect questions could be used to preserve the employee's dignity, you cannot rely on these ambiguous references. You need straightforward, accurate information. Employees usually respect this need to know and usually are willing to provide the necessary information. If an employee hesitates at disclosing the minimal information necessary, you may be wasting your time. Aside from personal questions about family problems, queries about medical problems and ability to meet financial obligations may make an employee anxious and uneasy. If you are reasonably sure that these potentially embarrassing subjects are in fact interfering with job performance, you should take the time to phrase these questions properly so as not to offend your employees. For instance, when a worker is consistently coming to work late, you might say, "Do you know what time it is?" when he has come in late one day too many. The employee will perceive this question (and rightfully so) as a threatening one that is not necessarily meant to gather information but to discipline and embarrass him. Another way to handle the same situation in a more open, consultative manner would be: "Do you have a problem that is causing you to come in late that I can help you with?" This latter question brings up the same, potentially sensitive subject but without the sarcasm of the earlier version.

Provide Rationale for Sensitive Questions.   When questions must touch on sensitive areas, be sure to explain why you are asking them. By explaining why the information is necessary, you are more likely to get a complete, truthful, and accurate response. If the employee can determine why you want the information, she may see a benefit to her situation in providing pertinent and complete data to you. If a foundation is laid for the question before it is asked, the employee may anticipate the question and be prepared to answer it. This helps eliminate suspicion and may even reduce anxiety over provocative questions. Instead of "Where did you get that pen?" you might be able to say: "I would like to buy a pen like yours. Where did you get it?" With this method, the employee already knows or at least suspects what you are trying to achieve before you ask any further questions. If she seems anxious over a question, it may be productive to back off a bit, explain your purpose, and ask the question a second time. However, if you don't really need the information that is causing her anxiety or if it impinges on her security or privacy, it is wise to change to a less threatening subject.

Use End versus Means Questions.   If you want your questions to produce the most useful and complete information, do not assume that your employee is already aware of his needs. The questions you ask should not put your employee on the spot. Instead of making him feel uneasy, structure your questions to ask about the results he is trying to achieve rather than the specific means he must use to get to his ultimate goal. To focus your discussion around general needs, end results, and ultimate objectives allows your employee to speak more knowledgeably and freely; at the same time, it provides you with more latitude in coming up with more meaningful solutions (means) to obtain those ends. Specific means may not be as easy to provide as the more general ends. Structure your questions around the results your employee is trying to achieve, not the specific "How am I going to get there?" methods and solutions.

Maintain a Consultative Atmosphere. Remember that your ultimate role in the interview process is that of a helper. When asking questions of an employee, remember that role. Don't ask questions in an interrogative, rapid-fire meanner. You are not an attorney with your employee on the witness stand. Pressuring usually is counterproductive. Use a relaxed and quiet tone of voice. There is nothing to be gained by shouting. Give your employee time to contemplate the question, even if it means a period of silence. By pausing and allowing her time to think about it, you will likely get a more accurate and complete reply. Allow her to answer one of your questions completely without being interrupted. Once she has fully answered, you are in a better position to proceed with the questioning process. Above all, show empathy, sensitivity, and understanding during the whole process, not only in the words you use but in how you say them and in the nonverbal signals you make.

The problem-solving, interactive management approach relies on skillful questioning. In order to help someone solve his problems, you have to uncover what they are. The interactive manager conducts the interview so that the employee's problems are fully determined. In addition, she leaves a subordinate feeling somewhat uplifted because she shows sensitivity and concern for that employee. By effectively mastering the art of questioning, the interactive manager becomes highly flexible in her role as problem solver, counselor, and consultant to her employees.

7

"It is better to remain quiet and be thought a fool than to speak and remove all doubt."
    Anonymous

The Power of Listening

A while ago, a team of professors at Loyola University in Chicago participated in a study to determine what is the most important single attribute of an effective manager. For a year and a half, they queried hundreds of businesses across the country and finally decided that, of all the sources of information to help a manager know and evaluate the personalities of the people in his department, listening to the individual employee is the most important.

Unfortunately, however, listening skills are very often ignored or just forgotten in business. Since listening is taken for granted, many communications problems develop. These problems might easily be avoided if people were aware of the listening fundamentals and knew how to avoid the pitfalls caused by inadequate and incomplete listening. Many businesses, in an effort to improve interpersonal communications, have developed courses that teach reading, writing, and speaking. However, although businesses may be willing to finance sending executives to such courses, they rarely direct personnel to courses to improve listening habits. The reason for this may be the misconception, held by many, that listening is related to hearing. Although people usually hear the entire message, its

120

meaning may be lost or distorted and the communication incomplete. A person may have perfect hearing, but because his listening skills are inadequate, what he understands is not necessarily what has been said. Listening is more than the physical process of hearing. It is an intellectual and emotional process in which one integrates physical, emotional, and intellectual inputs in search of meaning.

In order to be a good listener, you must attempt to be objective. Although complete objectivity is rarely possible, listening requires a conscious attempt to understand the speaker without letting personal opinions influence the intent of the speaker's words. This means that you must try to understand what the speaker wants to communicate—not what you want to understand. Empathy allows the listener to see and feel what the speaker sees and feels. It helps her penetrate the symbols of communication and come closer to reality.

Effective listening does not come easily. It is hard work. It not only involves considerable concentration, sensitivity, and a "sixth" sense but is also characterized by various physical changes. During concentrated listening, heart action increases, body temperature rises slightly, and blood circulation becomes faster.

Unfortunately, not enough people know how to be effective listeners. The normal, untrained listener is likely to understand and retain only about 50 percent of a conversation, and this relatively poor percentage drops to an even less impressive 25 percent retention rate forty-eight hours later. This means that recall of a particular conversation that took place more than a couple of days ago will always be incomplete and usually inaccurate. No wonder people can seldom agree about what has been discussed!

Managers who are poor listeners miss numerous opportunities in their employees' words. They miss current or emerging problems. They miss the importance of messages to the employees. The solutions that these managers propose are usually faulty and inappropriate, and they sometimes address the wrong problems. Lack of listening by the manager creates tension and distrust in the employee; and when it comes time for the manager to speak, the employee will reciprocate appropriately by not listening. On the other hand, managers who are good listeners quickly build and enhance rapport and trust with their employees. Listening to your workers is one of the most valuable and effective tools for having them feel understood by you. You can accurately determine your employees' problems and goals and how they really feel about them. The solutions you propose will be meaningful and relevant and at least tried by the employees. In addition, your employees will really listen to you when you speak.

The focus of this chapter is on skills you can use to listen to your employees effectively. It also presents ways to avoid misunderstanding your employees through poor listening habits. In addition to a number of powerful listening skills, exercises are presented to help you improve your listening ability. The net result of this chapter, if you implement its ideas and suggestions, will be that your employees will feel good about you because you have made a concerted effort to listen to them and understand them from *their* point of view. This will lead to more effective management and greater productivity by your employees. Isn't that a powerful payoff for exercising your ears more than your lips?

GRIPES ABOUT MANAGERS

Employees talk a lot about their managers. Some good, a lot bad. Let's examine some of the more common statements employees make about their managers when it comes to listening. While reading these, try to determine objectively if you are guilty of any of them. If so, you will know where to begin your listening improvement program.

"He Does All the Talking; I Go in with a Problem and Never Get a Chance to Open My Mouth."   The classic managerial problem—verbal diarrhea. Many managers are of the old school that believes that speech is power. These managers monopolize the conversation by doing all the talking. They tell their employees what their problems are. They tell their employees how to solve these apparent problems. They remain oblivious to what is really happening around them when it comes to their employees. If they only allowed their employees to speak their piece, they'd learn something very important— how to be an effective manager.

"She Interrupts Me When I Talk."   This is as bad as or worse than the previous statement. How do you feel when

somebody finishes your statement or tells you, "I know what you mean," before you've even finished your message? Don't step on your employees' sentences—pay them the courtesy of allowing them to finish their train of thought.

"My Manager Never Looks at Me When I Talk. I'm Not Sure He's Listening." Isn't it ironic that although you listen with your ears, people judge whether you are listening by looking at your eyes? This is easily one of the most common complaints. Maintaining a gentle, intermittent eye contact is a skill that is integral to being an effective listener. If you don't believe it, think about how you feel when somebody doesn't look at you when you are speaking.

"My Manager Makes Me Feel I'm Wasting Her Time." This is primarily an attitudinal problem. However, it is communicated to your employees through the way you say and do things. For instance, you can communicate boredom through toying with a pencil, paper, or some other item while your employee is talking. Other managers communicate disinterest through doodling, shuffling through papers, wiping glasses, or playing with a pipe or cigarettes. Another classic way of communicating that the employee is wasting your time is by frequently looking at your watch or the clock while the employee is speaking, or by not stopping what you are doing and giving your full attention to the employee who enters. Always acting rushed and making comments about your busy day will also tell your employees that they are wasting your time when they come in to speak with you. It seems contradictory that a manager should feel that her employees are wasting her time when they come in to seek managerial guidance. Unfortunately, too many managers have this attitude; whether they realize it or not, they communicate it nonverbally to their employees.

"My Manager Seems Too Preoccupied with the Telephone." Managers frequently ignore an employee by taking incoming phone calls or making outgoing calls while the employee is in the office for a serious conversation. When a manager interrupts his employee to make a phone call, that employee has to believe that the manager's attention throughout the conversation was focused more on the upcoming call than on the conversation. Obviously, this makes the employee feel unimportant, to say the least. Why not hold all incoming

calls while employees are in your office to talk to you, or even take the phone off the hook?

"My Manager's Facial Expressions and Body Language Keep Me Guessing as to Whether She Is Listening to Me or Not." A number of managers must believe that they are in a negotiation session when talking to their employees, because they show a total lack of emotion in facial expression. This effectively keeps the employee wondering whether her manager is following her message or not. It is also an ideal way for the manager to show a total lack of empathy for the employee. Of course, some managers overcompensate with facial expressions and body language while listening to their employees. For instance, some managers try to "stare down" their employees with eye contact. Sometimes the eye contact is so intense that the employees begin to wonder if something is wrong with their appearance. Although they are careful not to verbalize it, some managers nonverbally show that they disagree with what the employee is saying before the employee is finished. This is extremely frustrating for the employee and counterproductive for the relationship between the two. Many managers also project impatience, acting as though they are just waiting for the employee to finish so they can interject something of their own.

"My Manager Sits Too Close to Me." This is the proverbial territorial violation. The manager violates the employee's personal space, often without even realizing it. We talk more about personal space and territory in a later chapter; but just to drive the point home, how would you feel if you were in an elevator all by yourself and one other person entered and stood right next to you? Most people would feel extremely uncomfortable, tense, and distrustful of the "intruder." Although we allow those we know to get closer to us than those we do not know, when someone gets inappropriately close—regardless of the relationship—we get the same feelings we experienced with that person in the elevator.

"I Think My Manager Just Came Back from a Seminar on Listening. He's Overdoing It." Sometimes managers get carried away with their newly found active listening skills. They were taught to have eye contact during listening, and they

overdo it by staring down the speaker. They were taught to nod their heads to show that they are following the speaker, and they use all too many head nods. They were taught to project appropriate facial expressions while listening, and they put their faces through all types of contortions. The bottom line is superficial listening. The employee very easily sees through this ruse. They know their manager is trying to listen the way he was told a manager should appear to be listening, but it is obviously artificial. All good things, including listening, require moderation and appropriate application. Too much exaggerated listening is just as bad as, if not worse than, not listening at all.

"My Manager Stays on the Surface of the Conversation or Problem." There seems to be great reluctance by managers to go below the surface of a conversation to get to the root issues. At times it may be a lack of questioning expertise by the manager that prevents her from appropriately going below the surface. Some managers are reluctant because of a fear of opening a "can of worms." And some managers don't go below the surface of conversations with their employees because they just don't give a damn. They are too caught up in their own problems, their own lives, and their own tasks. They see their employees as interruptions in the accomplishment of their jobs. This latter point was shockingly driven home in a listening seminar that one of the authors conducted for a group of sales managers. During the seminar, one of the participants raised the question of what could be done about employees who frequently entered her office to tell her their problems. The participant felt that this wasted a lot of her time and was curious to know whether there was any solution to her dilemma. Before the seminar leader could answer, another participant blurted out, "I have the answer!" This person related his method for dealing with those "bothersome" employees. He had a desk-size model of a parking meter on his desk. Every time an employee came in to talk with this manager, he immediately explained that the parking meter was his retirement fund and that he would put in the first dime for the first ten minutes of conversation, but if the employee wanted to speak beyond that, the employee had to put the money in—ten cents for every ten minutes of conversation. The story initially struck me as a little tongue-in-cheek humor. Immediately after this gentleman's story, however, at least a dozen people in the audience wanted

to know where to get one of those parking meters. Where is this kind of manager coming from?

"My Manager Is Too Easily Distracted From Listening to Me and My Problems."   Employees resent managers who are too easily distracted by external noise, passersby, and employee statements that remind them of prior experiences they've had or heard of. They resent managers who are always trying to get ahead of their story . . . and guess what their point is. They resent managers who consistently interrupt the conversation by saying, "That reminds me of. . . ." They resent managers who always look out the window to see if anything more interesting is happening outside their office than inside it. They resent managers who continue to read or write while employees are trying to converse with them. They resent managers who give the impression that they couldn't care less about employees and their problems.

Here are some other highly irritating listening habits that employees complain about when it comes to their managers.

"He paces back and forth while I'm talking."

"She never smiles—I'm afraid to talk to her."

"He asks questions as if doubting everything I say."

"Her questions and comments get me off the subject."

"Whenever I make a suggestion, he pooh-poohs it."

"My manager puts me on the defensive when I ask a question or make a suggestion about improving things."

"My manager changes what I say by putting words into my mouth that I didn't mean."

"My manager rephrases what I say as if I hadn't said it right: 'Oh, do you mean . . . ?' "

"My manager frequently answers my questions with other questions."

"My manager smiles or wisecracks all the time, even when I am telling her about a serious problem of mine."

"My manager postpones the problems."

"My manager walks away from me while I am talking."

"My manager acts as if he knows it all and doesn't give me the benefit of the doubt to have the least bit of intelligence for meaningful input into the job situation."

If any of these poor listening habits apply to your style of listening, we suggest that you make haste and read on. We present some important barriers that might be standing in the way of your becoming an effective listener, as well as some ways to overcome those barriers so that you can improve your listening. The end result of improvement in your listening skills will be your employees saying: "I like my manager—he listens to me. I can talk to him." And, "She really understands me and my problems. I like working with her."

CATEGORIES OF LISTENERS

We have identified four general categories of listeners. Whenever people listen, they are typically at one of these four basic levels of attentiveness. Each category requires a particular depth of concentration and sensitivity on the part of the listener. These levels are not distinct lines of difference but general categories into which people fall. Depending on the situation or circumstance in which listeners find themselves, these categories may even overlap or interchange. As you move from the first, to the second, to the third, to the fourth level, your potential for understanding, trust, and effective communication increases.

The Nonlistener. At this first level, you do not hear your employees at all. In fact, you do not even make an effort to hear what the other person is saying. The nonlistener manifests blank stares as well as nervous mannerisms and gestures. He fakes attention while thinking about unrelated matters. He is too busy with preparing what he wants to say next to listen to what is being said to him now. The nonlistener is primarily concerned with doing most of the speaking. He is constantly interrupting the speaker's sentences, rarely interested in what anyone else has to say, and must always have the last word. He is usually perceived as a social bore and a know-it-all, as insensitive and nonunderstanding; he is typically disliked or "tolerated" by most people.

The Marginal Listener. At this second level, you are hearing the sounds and words but not really listening. The message is toyed with, not really heard. The marginal listener is a superficial listener. She stays on the surface of the argument or problem, never risking going deeper. She postpones problems into the future rather than dealing with them in the present. This behavior only tends to make the problems get bigger, which in turn scares the marginal listener into putting them off even more. Eventually, these problems explode. The marginal listener is easily distracted by her own thinking and by outside occurrences. In fact, many marginal listeners selectively look for outside distractions, so that they have an excuse to draw themselves away from the conversation. They prefer to evade difficult or technical presentations or discussions, and when they do listen, they tend to listen only for the facts—the bottom line—rather than the main ideas. Marginal listening is extremely dangerous because there is enormous room for misunderstanding when a manager is only superficially concentrating on what is being said to her. At least at level one—nonlistening— the speaker receives many noticeable clues that the nonlistener is indeed not listening. However, at the marginal listening level, the speaker may be lulled into a false sense of security that he or she is in fact being listened to and understood; this is not the case. Marginal listening may be funny in situation comedies where family members continually respond to each other with, "Yes, dear." However, it is not funny in real life. It is downright devastating.

Evaluative Listening.   This third level takes somewhat more concentration and attention by the listener than the first two levels. At this level the listener is actively trying to hear what the speaker is saying but isn't making an effort to understand the speaker's intent. He tends to be a more logical listener, who is more concerned about content than feelings. The evaluative listener tends to remain emotionally detached from the conversation. He does well in "parroting back" the words his employee has just delivered but totally ignores that part of the message that is carried in the speaker's vocal intonation, body language, and facial expressions. He is great in semantics, facts, and statistics but poor in sensitivity, empathy, and true understanding. The evaluative listener believes that he understands his employees, but the employees do not feel understood by this type of manager. Evaluative listening greatly speeds up conversation because the manager anticipates the employee's words and is ready with a retort almost as soon as the employee finishes speaking, whether in agreement or rebuttal. The concentration of the evaluative listener, however, is misplaced, and the results are potentially dangerous to the relationship. The evaluative listener forms opinions about his employee's words even before the message is complete and thus risks not understanding the true meaning of the message. This promotes the opportunity for highly provocative words to arouse emotion or distraction in the evaluative listener, who may then concentrate entirely on an examination and possible rebuttal of the employee's remarks. This obviously leads to tense behavior and deterioration of the trust bond.

The Active Listener. This is by far the highest and most effective level of listening. If you can refrain from evaluating your employee's words and place yourself in his position—attempting to see things from his point of view—you are using the fourth and most effective level of listening—active listening. This is the level where real communication takes place. You are not only attentive to the words being spoken; you are also trying to project your mind into that of the worker so that you can align your own thoughts and feelings more closely with those of your employee. In doing so, you must actively try to suspend your own thoughts and feelings and give your attention solely to listening to your employee. It figuratively means "putting yourself in the other person's shoes." Active listening requires that you listen not only for the content of your employee's message but, more importantly, for the intent and feeling of the message as well. It also requires you to show your employee, both verbally and nonverbally, that you are truly listening. The active listening manager does not interrupt her employee. In fact, active listeners are extremely perceptive. They are always looking for verbal and/or visual cues that might signify that the other person would like to say something. When one appears, the active listener promptly gives the floor to the other person. The active listener continually tries to get a deeper understanding of the other person. She listens for feelings and emotions, as well as words, from the speaker. She listens not only to what is said and how it is said but also is perceptive to what is *not* being said. The active listener is a skillful questioner. She uses questions to encourage the employee to extend the conversation and clarify the message; then she probes into areas that need to be developed further in order to get a better total picture of what the employee is trying to communicate.

The active listener also has three very important skills that none of the other three levels of listeners have. The active listener is good at sensing, attending, and responding. *Sensing* is the ability of the active listener to recognize and appreciate the silent messages that the speaker is sending—that is, vocal intonation, body language, facial expressions, and so forth. *Attending* refers to the verbal, vocal, and visual messages that the active listener sends to the speaker indicating attentiveness, receptiveness, and acknowledgment of the speaker and the message. This includes eye contact; open body language; affirmative head nods; appropriate facial expressions; avoidance of nervous, bored, or angry gestures; and verbal expressions such as "uh-huh," "yes," "go on," "I see," and "keep going." Attending also includes the establishment of a receptive listening setting, such as an atmosphere of privacy that is away from phone calls, people talking, or people within earshot. It includes not violating the speaker's "personal space," as well as eliminating such communication barriers as a large desk between manager and employee. The active listener is *responding* when she tries to get feedback on the accuracy of the employee's content and feeling, tries to keep the speaker talking, tries to gather more information, tries to make the speaker feel understood, and tries to get the employee to understand herself and/ or her problems or concerns better.

It can be very tiring to listen in this manner, as it takes great concentration. But if you really want to develop the skill of active listening, you must attain this power of attention.

Unless a manager understands the definition of active listening and practices it in her managerial relationships, she doesn't know what it means to be a "good listener."

Many people assume they are good listeners; few actually are. The average employee spends about three-quarters of each working day in verbal communications. Nearly half of that is spent on listening. Incredibly, on the average, these employees are only about 25 percent effective as listeners. This means that if you receive a salary of $15,000 per year as a manager, over $3,500 of it is paid for time you spend being *ineffective* as a listener. These depressing facts emerged from intensive research by Dr. Ralph C. Nichols. In his book *Are You Listening?* he emphasizes that most people are more concerned with developing their speaking skills than their listening skills. Today, more and more companies are discovering that one bad listener within the managerial ranks can cause much more damage than a number of good listeners can correct. Nonlistening, marginal listening, and evaluative listening can be the reason that performance appraisal and counseling sessions between manager and employee fail to produce desired outcomes. These first three levels of ineffective listening are often the cause of errors in work, failures in internal communications, interpersonal inefficiency, employee dissatisfaction, and lower overall organizational productivity. It would not be wrong to suggest that ineffective listening contributes to the majority of the business problems you encounter.

Do not despair. The case is not hopeless. With the proper motivation and skills, you can in fact become a much better listener—an active listener. In order to do this effectively, you must first understand the barriers to effective listening. Having a deeper understanding of these physical, mental, and emotional roadblocks is the first step toward the elimination of poor listening habits. Later in this chapter, we present a number of rules for better listening. These are the steps for good listening—those good listening habits you must adopt to be perceived by other people as an active listener. Finally, we present some exercises that you can use to improve your listening ability. By practicing these exercises, you will become an active listener more quickly, and you will feel much more comfortable in acting the part of an active listener. Let's start by looking at the barriers to effective listening.

BARRIERS TO EFFECTIVE LISTENING

In today's society, there are numerous deterrents to listening. Some are obvious, some more subtle. If you are not aware that these barriers exist, you do not have much chance of dealing with and overcoming them in your quest to become a better listener. We hope this section will make you more consciously aware of the physical, psychological, behavioral, and educational barriers to effective listening. Armed with this new insight, you will be much better prepared to take them on and win.

Motivation and Attitude. This is probably the biggest deterrent to effective listening. We hear what we want to hear, and we don't hear what we don't want to hear. When you enter a listening environment without the proper attitude or motivation, there is no way that you are going to hear, comprehend, or understand what the other person is communicating. You might as well have stayed home. If you are not going to listen to the other person, go somewhere else rather than ignore and insult the speaker.

Lack of Concentration and Attention. Many people are ineffective listeners because of a lack of concentration and attention. There are a number of people who simply have a short attention span and find it difficult to concentrate on an outside activity for any period of time. However, there are other people who have poor powers of concentration because they allow outside influences to distract them. For instance, one of the biggest deterrents to concentration and attention is the mistaken assumption that you can do two things at the same time. The classic example is a person who believes that he can read and listen to another person at the same time. Nothing could be further from the truth. In order to concentrate fully on what you are reading, you cannot listen to someone speak. In order to listen to the person fully, you must concentrate and attend to her, not the reading material. The best you can possibly hope for when doing two things at the same time is equally dividing your interest between both of them. Neither act—listening or reading—is accomplished fully, appropriately, or effectively. Another major culprit that contributes to lack of concentration and attention is outside distractions. Things such as outside noises, movements of people, nearby conversations, and phone calls can easily distract the listener from a conversation. It is not easy to ignore these outside distractions, but it is possible with practice. If you are motivated to listen to another person, you can bear down, concentrate more, and ignore those distractions.

Negative Attitudes toward Listening. Many people identify listening as a passive, compliant act. This attitude is considered by many people to be the most obstinate barrier to effective listening. Our schools generally produce good talkers who are very poor listeners. From early childhood onward in our society, we are encouraged to put our emphasis on speaking and talking as opposed to listening. As we become adults, we mistakenly perceive listening as a passive act—something others must do, but not ourselves. We believe that talk is power—that when we have the floor, we are in control. Ironically, this couldn't be further from the truth. When two people are vying for attention, control, and "the podium," they not only aren't listening to each other; they are also building up hostilities toward each other. The net result is increased tension, decreased trust, and decreased productivity. On the other hand, there is true "power" in listening. When you listen to others—truly listen—they tell you how best to approach them in meeting their needs. They start feeling good about you because you gave them the floor. When it comes your turn to speak, they will be much more attentive to you and your message. Both sides win.

Experience and Background. Prior learning and experience have a great bearing on how good a listener you are right now. For instance, those people who have poor vocabularies find it much more difficult to listen to people who have more developed vocabularies. Think of how you feel when you listen to someone who uses words you cannot understand. You are probably a little ashamed to ask the speaker for the definitions of those words for fear of appearing ignorant. After a while, if the speaker is using a lot of words that you can't comprehend, you are very likely to become mildly depressed with the situation and totally tune out the speaker, with some rationalization that what he or she is saying isn't worthwhile anyway. Similar problems are encountered when there are language, dialect, and slang problems. When you have difficulty understanding what the other person is communicating, you have two choices. You can ask the person to explain what he just said in clearer language, or you can tune the person out. Unfortunately, many of us take the latter course. The difficulty level of the material being spoken also creates barriers to effective listening. If the listener's experience and background do not include exposure to the speaker's material, it is very likely, again, that the listener will tune out the speaker.

Poor Listening Setting. Where you choose to do your communicating and listening can have a great bearing on how effectively you are able to listen. If you are trying to listen to another person near sources of external distractions, such as outside noises and people passing by, you will find that your attention and concentration will be severely challenged. Why put yourself in this "tempting" situation when you can choose an environment that is without these distractions? One of the authors had lunch on a couple of occasions with a business acquaintance at a restaurant that was frequented by many other people. During the conversation, the business acquaintance was constantly distracted by the other patrons passing by. The net result on both occasions was that not much was accomplished, and what was communicated was misperceived. Is it any wonder that all their meetings now take place in a room that has no windows, no telephone, no distractions? They now get twice as much done in one-fourth the time.

It is also difficult for people to listen when they are sitting too close to, or too far from, the speaker. Being too close to the speaker may violate the listener's "personal space." This may cause the listener to think about the physical closeness of the two rather than the message being communicated. By sitting too far from the speaker, the listener may miss important parts of the message, both verbally and vocally. When the setting is too hot, too cold, too comfortable, or too uncomfortable, a poor listening environment is created. The listener becomes much more aware of and concerned with the surroundings than she is with the message.

Emotions.   Many ineffective listeners classify and/or prejudge the speaker. This tends to distort the message positively or negatively. For instance, many listeners prejudge the quality and believability of a speaker's message solely on the speaker's image. If the speaker projects a particular image, the listener might classify the speaker as "one of us" and positively distort the message, purposely viewing it in a very positive light. On the other hand, if the speaker's image is not in line with that of the listener, the listener will judge the speaker as "one of them" and negatively distort the message. Hence, when we like a speaker, we view his message in favorable and/or sympathetic ways; when we dislike a speaker, we do just the opposite.

The net result is that any classification of the speaker will distort the speaker's information to fit that classification, whether it is right or wrong. This is pure and unadulterated selective perception. If we label the speaker a bore, what we will hear will be perceived as boring. If we label the speaker as brilliant, we are dazzled by her speech.

Our prior and current beliefs and values also determine how well and how objectively we listen to the message content. If the actual message is in line with what we currently believe, we tend to listen to it much more attentively and in a much more favorable light. However, if the message contradicts our current values and beliefs, we tend to argue and criticize the message mentally. This internal mental distraction effectively cuts off the listening process. It is very important to realize that when you become too emotionally involved with the content of the message or with the speaker, you will systematically distort the message. The net result must be a breakdown in communication.

Daydreaming and Fantasizing. Daydreaming and fantasizing are perceived by many psychologists and psychiatrists to be a healthy aspect of life. However, if we cannot control how often and when we do it, it can be extremely detrimental both to our emotional health and our listening effectiveness. One of the factors contributing to daydreaming and fantasizing during the listening process is the simple fact that people can think nearly four times as fast as they can speak. In normal interpersonal conversation, people usually speak at the rate of 125 to 150 words per minute. However, the human mind can comprehend approximately 500 words per minute. This leaves the listener with three- to fourfold the mental time he actually needs to comprehend the message. This "dead space" is used to his advantage by the skilled listener and as an opportunity to let his mind wander by the ineffective listener.

Delivery. Certain speakers are much easier to listen to than others. Speakers who take the time to organize their message are easier to listen to than speakers who talk in a stream of consciousness. Some speakers talk quickly, others more slowly. Some listeners prefer faster speech delivery, whereas other listeners prefer slower delivery. In other words, different listeners feel more comfortable with different rates of input, depending on the speaking norm of their environment. For instance, people from the Southeast are used to listening to a slower rate of input than are people from the Northeast. Any deviations from the geographic or cultural norm will create listening problems. However, these problems can be overcome if the listener realizes what is happening and consciously concentrates on rates of input and delivery styles different from the norm of her area.

People of different learning, decision, and behavioral styles have difficulty listening to one another. For instance, some people tend to be much more auditory, whereas others are more visual or conceptual. This means that some people are more prone to take in information better from a listening mode than others, who may be better at taking in information from a visual mode. Some styles like to communicate and listen to more formalized and factual information, whereas other styles prefer more personal and generalized information. As you can see, there are potentials for obvious listening problems among people with different delivery styles and listening preferences. The typical response of a listener confronted with a speaker who has a difficult delivery style is simply to tune out that speaker or distort the message. If the listener is aware of those delivery styles that are difficult for him to listen to, he can train himself to increase his attention and concentration to an even greater degree when confronted with these styles in the future.

Lack of Listening Skills.   One of the simplest barriers to overcome, but one of the most commonly ignored, is the lack of learned listening skills. Steps toward the elimination of this barrier are an awareness and knowledge of the previously discussed barriers as well as a motivation to overcome them. Another step to overcome this particular barrier is the application of the listening skills that are discussed in the next section of this chapter. Above all, however, the best way to overcome the lack of listening skills is to increase your motivation to become a better listener. Reading this book, and this chapter specifically, is an important first step. It is our hope that you continually try to upgrade your listening skills, as well as your other communication skills, and put into practice what you learn. That in itself will help you overcome many of the barriers to effective listening and contribute to making you a better communicator and manager.

THE NINETEEN COMMANDMENTS OF POWER LISTENING

Rules for being a good listener involve courtesy and common sense. Some of the rules may seem obvious or trivial, but it is amazing how many people forget them and insult the speaker unintentionally. Often, you don't mean to be rude, but your enthusiasm for a subject and your own desire to hear yourself talk make you forget courtesy. Other times you are so intent with your own point of view that you forget to listen to what your employee is saying; you just plain stop listening! When conversing with another person, you must therefore be aware of and practice the following rules.

1. **Remember that it is impossible to listen and talk at the same time.**—*This most basic rule of effective listening is broken most often. People, anxious to add their own views to the conversation, try to interject comments while another person is still speaking. They wait for a pause in the conversation and "rapid fire" their comments at the other person. This injection of random comments is irritating to the speaker and actually slows the conversation, because the initial speaker must dodge the comments and still keep his train of thought to continue with what he was saying. Rather than interrupting a speaker, you should wait until his point is made. Then you will have your chance—hopefully, uninterrupted—to make your own views known. A good listener relaxes and does not give the impression of wanting to jump right in and talk. The only interruption a person likes is applause. The speaker will accept this form of assent and approval with a smile. But even so, he may lose his stream of thought and have to digress in order to continue. Other accepted gestures to a speaker's words are nods and smiles of encouragement. Be careful, however, to refrain from disturbing the speaker's train of thought.*

2. **Listen for the speaker's main ideas.**—*Specific facts are only important as they pertain to the main theme. And they can cause misinterpretation if taken out of context. Relate stated facts to the arguments of the speaker, and weigh the verbal evidence used. Take advantage of the superior speed of thought over words, and periodically review a portion of the discussion that has already been completed. Take care, however, to review carefully, and don't assume something that hasn't been stated. A good listener should try to guess the points the speaker will make. Ask yourself: "What is the speaker getting at?"*

Or "What is her point?" If you guess correctly, your understanding is enhanced, and your attention is increased. If your guess is incorrect, you learn from your mistake. However, unless you are very experienced in active listening, don't get too far ahead of the speaker. Otherwise, critical points may be missed.

3. **Be sensitive to your emotional deaf spots.**—*Deaf spots are words that make your mind wander or go off on a mental tangent. They set off a chain reaction that produces a mental barrier in your mind, which in turn inhibits the continued flow of the speaker's message. Everyone is affected by certain words, so it is important to discover your own individual stumbling blocks and analyze why these words have such a profound effect on you. When one of the authors was doing a training session with savings and loan personnel, he inadvertently used the work* **bank.** *It just so happens that savings and loan association employees do not like to have their institutions called "banks." A number of people in the audience had the word* **bank** *as one of their own emotional deaf spots. Sensitive to what had happened, the author stopped his presentation and backtracked to determine what had caused the inhibition. The audience was kind to him in relating the negative effect that the word* **bank** *had on them. Sadly, you may not be so fortunate in your relationships. Most important is a conscious attempt to continue to listen whenever these emotion-arousing words are mentioned by the speaker.*

4. **Fight off distractions.**—*Train yourself to listen carefully to your employee's words, despite such external distractions as a ringing telephone, passersby, or other office noise. Other distractions, such as the idiosyncrasies of the speaker, may also be irritating, but you should make a conscious attempt to judge the content of the message—not the delivery. Particular speech patterns can be distracting, but resist the tendency to listen for quirks in delivery. Focus attention solely on the words, ideas, feelings, and underlying intent of your employee. Through practice, you can improve your power of concentration, so that you can block out all the external and internal distractions and attend totally to the speaker.*

5. **Try not to get angry.**—*Emotions of any kind hinder the listening process, but anger in particular is detrimental to message reception. A good listener will put aside her emotions as best she can, so that she is open to the message being conveyed. She will try hard to understand the speaker without making value judgments.*

6. **Do not trust to memory certain data that may be important.**—*Take notes. However, keep the notes brief, as listening ability is impaired while you are writing. Remember—you cannot do two things at the same time effectively. Write notes in words and phrases rather than putting down complete thoughts. All you need is something*

to jog your memory; later you can recall the complete content of the message. Read your notes to make sure you understand what you put down on paper, and always review them again before subsequent contacts with your employees.

7. **Let your employees tell their own stories first.**—*When employees explain their situations, they may reveal interesting facts and valuable clues that will aid you in helping them solve their problems or satisfy their needs. By letting them speak first, you will also save time, because when their interests are revealed, you can tailor your discussion to their particular needs, goals, and objectives. You can thus dispense with those aspects of the conversation that may have been inappropriate to a specific employee.*

8. **Empathize with your employees.**—*Make a determined effort to see their point of view.*

9. **Withold judgment.**—*Judge the value of the message, not the speaker's delivery ability. In addition, wait to see in what context the speaker uses words and phrases before evaluating her intent and meaning. Don't make hasty judgments.*

10. **React to the message, not the person.**—*Don't allow your mental impression of the speaker to influence your interpretation of his message. Good thoughts, ideas, and arguments can come from people whose image or personality you don't like.*

11. **Try to appreciate the emotion behind the speaker's words (vocal and visual messages) more than the literal meaning of the words.**—*Try always to ask yourself the following four questions when another person is speaking:*

    a. What are the other person's feelings?
    b. What does she mean by what she is saying?
    c. Why is she saying this?
    d. What is implied by what she says?

12. **Use feedback.**—*Constantly try to check your understanding of what you hear. Do not only hear what you want to hear. In addition, consistently check to see if the other person wants to comment or respond to what you have previously said.*

13. **Listen selectively.**—*Very often in conversation, your employee will tell you specific things that will help you identify his problems, needs, goals, or objectives. These critical messages may be hidden within the much broader context of the conversation. You must listen in such a way that you can separate the wheat from the chaff. Always ask yourself: "What is my employee telling me that can specifically*

help me to help him satisfy his needs, solve his problems, and accomplish his goals?"

14. **Relax.**—*When another person is speaking to you, try to put her at ease by creating a relaxed, accepting environment. Try not to give the speaker the impression you want to jump right in and speak. Be attentive, lean slightly forward, assume an interested facial expression—act like a good listener.*

15. **Try not be critical, either mentally or verbally, of someone else's point of view, even if it is different from your own.**—*Hold your temper and your emotional feelings, and try to listen to truly understand. Be patient. Allow your employee plenty of time to fully finish his train of thought. You might find that what you were initially going to disagree with wasn't such a bad idea after all. If you give the other person half a chance to tell you his views and allow your mind to be open, you might find that you have learned something from what he has said—and like it, too.*

16. **Listen attentively.**—*Face your employee straight on with uncrossed arms and legs; lean slightly forward. Establish good, gentle, intermittent eye contact. Use affirmative head nods and appropriate facial expressions when called for, but do not overdo it. Intermittently respond to your employee with "uh huh," "go on," "yes," and the like.*

17. **To the degree that it is in your power, try to create a positive listening environment.**—*Try to ensure an atmosphere of privacy away from sources of distraction. Do not violate the speaker's "personal space." Take great efforts to make sure that the environment is conducive to effective listening.*

18. **Ask questions.**—*Ask open-ended, feeling-finding questions to allow your employee to express her feelings and thoughts. Use continuing questions, echo, and clarifying questions to keep your employee talking and to clarify any potential ambiguities. The effective use of questions shows the other person that you are interested, that you are listening; and it allows you to contribute to the conversation.*

19. **Be motivated to listen.**—*Without the proper attitude, all the foregoing suggestions for effective listening are for naught. Try to keep in mind that there is no such thing as a disinteresting speaker; there are only disinterested listeners. Answering the following questions after each discussion with an employee may help you to sharpen your listening skills:*

1. *Did I comprehend each point he was trying to make?*
2. *Did I make judgments of the words before she was through speaking?*
3. *Did I make decisions in my mind while she was still speaking?*

4. *Did I assess his information at the conclusion of his remarks?*
5. *Did I try to hunt for evidence that would prove her wrong while she was speaking?*
6. *Did I hunt for evidence that would prove her right?*
7. *Did I hunt for evidence that would prove my own point of view wrong?*
8. *Did I hunt for evidence that would prove my own point of view right?*
9. *Did I become upset while listening to him?*
10. *Did I feel that his ideas were wrong when he was discussing them with me?*
11. *Did I generally jump to conclusions while listening to her?*
12. *Did I let him speak at least 50 percent of the time?*
13. *Did I understand her words in terms of their intended meanings?*
14. *Did I restate her ideas and feelings accurately?*
15. *Did I pinpoint her assumptions and compare them with my own?*
16. *Did I study his voice, posture, actions, and facial expressions as he talked?*
17. *Did I listen between the lines for unspoken meanings behind the words?*
18. *Did I weigh the verbal evidence used by the speaker to support her points?*
19. *Did I really try to listen to him?*
20. *Did I really want to listen to him?*
21. *Did I really show him that I was, in fact, motivated and interested in listening to him?*

Through positive listener reaction, your employees should be prompted to talk more freely about their needs, wants, goals, objectives, and problems. On the other hand, poor listening habits and negative listener reaction can make your employees uncomfortable, defensive, and even hostile. Which reaction do you want?

EXERCISES TO IMPROVE YOUR LISTENING SKILLS

The following exercises are a few examples of those the authors use in their listening and communications seminars. As with any behavior that you are trying to improve, practice makes perfect. Through constant practice, these exercises will help take the listening concepts from these pages and make them an actual part of your everyday behavior.

In addition, completion of the "Listening Action Plan" that follows can specifically aid you toward your goal of being a true active listener.

Exercise 1. Try to listen to a number of speeches that might have quite a few words that are not familiar to you. As you are listening, try to guess the meaning of the unknown words based on the context in which they are used. You should practice a number of these exercises, because they will improve your vocabulary and help your listening effectiveness. The objective of this exercise is to improve your listening vocabulary, so that you will not become so frustrated by complex or unidentifiable words that might otherwise prompt you to tune out the speaker.

Exercise 2. Go out of your way to converse with others who have speaking styles that cause difficulty for you in your role as listener. By exposing yourself constantly to a number of difficult delivery styles and having the opportunity to practice your listening skills during the conversation, you will become much more comfortable and effective in listening to these diverse styles.

Exercise 3. Imagine that you have an appointment in a few minutes with someone who wants to talk with you. This person who is coming to your office really wants to see you, but you have very ambivalent feelings about the meeting. The person is someone you prefer not to see or hear at this time. As you are waiting for the individual to enter your office, try to picture both the person and the encounter that you will be having for the next thirty to sixty minutes. The person has just entered your office. How would you describe this individual? Young or old? Male or female? Liberal or conservative? What is the person's physical image? How does he or she dress? What is the intended topic of conversation? What makes this person someone you really do not want to see or talk to at this time? Do exactly the same exercise with an individual you really would like to be seeing at this moment. Ask and answer the same types of questions. At the end of your imagining exercise, compare your notes on each individual. You may make some startling discoveries. This exercise is intended to point out those types of people you feel most comfortable with and those with whom you have a difficult time relating. With this increased

Figure 7-1

LISTENING ACTION PLAN

1. I can listen effectively when _____

_____

_____

2. I do not listen effectively when _____

_____

_____

3. Three listening areas where I feel strongest: _____

_____

_____

4. Three listening areas that I feel represent areas of potential improvement: _____

_____

_____

_____

5. For each of the above areas of potential improvement, I plan to take the following long-term and short-term action steps to improve my listening:

    Short-Term Action Steps   Long-Term Action Steps

a. _____

_____

_____

b. _____

_____

_____

c. _____

_____

_____

awareness and knowledge, you can make an extra effort to be more open, less emotional, and more understanding with those people you previously had difficulty communicating with.

Exercise 4.   Videotape or tape-record a fifteen- to twenty-minute interview between you and another person in which you are playing the role of an effective listener. Play back the tape, and try to tally the number of times you found yourself: (a) distracted by external stimulations; (b) distracted by internal personal thoughts; (c) mentally racing ahead of the person speaking; (d) making value judgments as the person spoke; (e) cutting off the person because of something he or she said; (f) filling the voids or silences with your own words.

LISTENING AND INTERACTIVE MANAGEMENT

If you are really willing to learn how to listen, it will take a lot of hard work to learn the skills, and constant practice to keep them in shape. The most important step is realizing that listening is a necessary skill, as important as other communication skills such as reading, writing, and speaking. Especially necessary is the understanding that listening should not take a secondary position to speaking, its verbal counterpart. Speaking has traditionally been a favorite child, but you should realize that when no one listens, it is pointless to speak. Employees feel relieved when they find managers who understand what they have to say about their problems. Once you truly try to understand your employees by actively listening to them, they will most likely reciprocate by listening to you and trying to understand your point of view. Isn't this what management—interactive management—is all about?

Projecting
the Appropriate
Image

Have you ever seen yourself on TV or videotape? Have you ever heard your voice on a tape recorder? Have you ever examined photographs of yourself? How did you look and sound—to yourself? Were you projecting the type of image you would like others to see? These self-images are very important because they give you an idea of how you may be coming across to other people, either positively or negatively. Projecting this "proper" image to other people significantly hastens the development of trust and rapport with other people. They will feel much more comfortable and much more at ease around you when your image is appropriate, thus making it easier for you to communicate with them. On the other hand, if your image is inappropriate to the other person or the situation, it will create a roadblock that will severely hamper effective communication. The critical importance of the image you project is underscored by the well-accepted fact that the famous debate between Kennedy and Nixon was won by Kennedy primarily because of his physical image, not through the verbal content of his speech. That turned out to be a turning point in that election.

As irrational as it may seem, people do indeed judge a

book by its cover. It is the unusual person who can overcome bad initial impressions in order to allow the other person to discover some genuine assets and skills hidden underneath. People also react in a generally predictable manner to certain qualities of the "cover," the image. People are more comfortable in dealing with an element of predictability. This may be equally irrational, but managers who attend guidelines of image tend to be more successful than those who do not. Those managers who look and act like executives have a decided edge over those managers who do not convey the executive image.

Not long ago, a friend of ours was on a long business trip when he developed a severe rash all over his body. Being away from home and his family doctor, he decided to go to a large medical center in the city in which he was staying. It was late at night, and he had to wait more than an hour for someone to examine him. Finally, after what seemed to be an eternity, in walked a young woman. She didn't appear to be much more than twenty-five years old. She had long straight hair, tight-fitting fashion jeans, and a loose overblouse. She said she was the doctor. She stared at our friend's rash for a few minutes but never touched him. She diagnosed his condition, wrote a prescription, and left. Our friend was not very impressed. In fact, because of the image this doctor projected and her apparent lack of professionalism, he was rather skeptical of both the diagnosis and the prescription. As a result, the very next morning he went to another doctor in the same town. He was examined thoroughly for nearly three hours. He felt he was finally in good hands. When the second doctor gave him a prescription, it turned out to be the same exact medication the first doctor had given him the night before. However, this time he was much more motivated and confident to take it. The moral of the story centers on the image of the doctors. The demeanor, the clothing, and the grooming of the first doctor projected an image in the mind of our friend that created skepticism, tension, and distrust. The opposite was true of the second doctor. Our friend's opinion of the first doctor had nothing to do with her competence. In fact, she must have been quite good to come up in only three minutes with the same diagnosis and prescription that took the second doctor nearly three hours. The image made the difference—just like the Kennedy and Nixon debates. It might help those of you who suspect our friend is biased against women doctors to know that his personal doctor at home is a woman.

COMPONENTS OF IMAGE

The total image you project to others consists of many things. Among these are the first impressions you project, the depth of your knowledge, the breadth of your knowledge, your flexibility, your enthusiasm, and your sincerity. These six areas are the critical components of image. Let's examine them in detail.

First Impressions. "First impressions are lasting impressions." You probably heard that saying before, but have you ever given it serious thought? Have you ever contemplated the ramifications of your first impressions on other people? Your first impression is the initial impact you make on another person. In this regard, it covers the areas of dress, voice, grooming, handshake, eye contact, and body posture. The way you choose to manipulate each of these various factors has a profound effect on how other people will perceive you initially. Positive first impressions make initial and subsequent communications with other people much easier and more comfortable. Negative initial impressions can cut off a relationship before it ever gets started. Some people can overcome poor initial first impressions, but it is not easy. Many people give up rather than trying to reverse another person's negative first impression.

Have you ever judged another person's personality and/or competence solely on the first impression they made on you? What is the first thing that comes to mind when you think about a person with a heavy Brooklyn accent? A New England accent? What about a weak handshake? How about sloppy grooming, poor hygiene, bad vocabulary, poor posture, or ill-fitting clothing? At this point, you may think that none of these potential weak spots apply to you. Don't kid yourself! We have met very few people who could not do with some improvement in the initial impressions they project to others. Read on.

One of our friends from graduate school initially had a very difficult time landing a job. He was interviewed at a number of universities for a faculty position, but something elusive stood in the way of his getting a solid job offer from any of them. It had nothing to do with his competency. He was truly a brilliant individual. Nobody questioned that aspect of his credentials. At one of the universities, a particular department head took a personal liking to him. Although our friend did not get the job offer there either, the department head did him an extremely big favor that no one else had done. He took

147

our friend to the side and told him that his image had caused some problems in his interviews. Other faculty members in the university wondered if he really would "fit." You see, our friend did not create the most favorable first impression. Once you got to know him, he was the most friendly, warm, and helpful individual you could possibly know. However, his initial impression left something to be desired. First of all, his clothing selection was atrocious. He wore obviously inexpensive clothing and indiscriminately combined stripes with plaids and colors that clashed. That was only the beginning. His shoes were seldom polished. His hair always looked overly greasy. He had an extremely limp handshake. When he spoke, it was in a low, monotone voice. He also maintained very little eye contact while speaking to other people. In other words, his overall image was rather poor.

We do not tell this story to be cruel to our friend. We truly respect him professionally and cherish him personally. But our friendship has gone beyond the initial impression stage. We know how he thinks and acts and feels and treats other people. Unfortunately, because of his initial first impression and his image, a number of other people will never allow a meaningful relationship to develop with him. Thus, they will never get to know and appreciate him the way we do. We feel that this story vividly relates the cruelty of first impressions. Most people always have judged a book by its cover and unfortunately always will. The only thing you can do to get around that fact is to take utmost care in projecting the most flattering facets of your image.

Research has shown that you can change reactions to yourself simply by changing some aspects of your image that relate specifically to your first impressions on other people. For instance, one thing you can easily work on is your handshake. This should be firm, yet not too hard. People who try to crush the bones in your hand evoke as negative a response as those who are limp as a dishrag. In addition, make sure you do not hold the other person's hand too long. Strange ideas may enter the other person's mind as to your intentions. Establish good eye contact with the other person while you are shaking hands. This helps get the relationship started.

Before you get the opportunity to shake somebody's hand, they have an opportunity to see the way you sit or walk. They also get to see the way you dress and how you are groomed.

When it comes to sitting and standing body postures, the only thing we recommend is that you avoid any extremes. People who walk with a strut, a shuffle, a bounce, or even with hunched shoulders project an image that may or may not be positive. Likewise, when you sit slouched in a chair or with one of your legs over the arm of the chair or in any other unusual posture, you again may be projecting an unflattering image. Avoid extremes. Sit and walk straight and relaxed.

Not enough can be said about personal hygiene and grooming. Good grooming and hygiene are so obviously important; yet they are so often neglected. How many people do you see in your organization, regardless of where they are in the hierarchy, with dirt under their fingernails? How about dandruff on their collar or jacket? Have you ever seen any of your male co-workers with too much hair coming out of their ears or nostrils? How about any female co-workers with too much hairspray or makeup or perfume? After lunch, have you ever spoken with people who had a strong odor of tuna fish, onion, garlic, or alcohol on their breath? Have you ever noticed an odor coming from a suit, shirt, blouse, dress, or shoes that a co-worker wore once too often? Are you completely innocent of all these grooming violations? Be very concerned and aware of the impressions you project to people through personal hygiene and grooming. You can and should improve them immediately if necessary.

The manner in which you dress has a profound effect on your acceptance by others. Clothes may not make the person, but they make a lasting statement about who the person is. Therefore, it becomes very important for you to understand what you are saying to other people about yourself simply through your mode of dress.

Clothing is a powerful image maker. Through skillful dressing, you can evoke positive responses to your personality. This enhances your chances of success in interactions with other people. However, as a manager, you must walk a clothing tightrope. In order to move up the organizational hierarchy, you must project an aura of authority and success through your clothing. At the same time, you don't want to come off as overpowering with your employees. Although this sounds like a tough order, it can be accomplished.

To project authority and success, dress in a conservative manner where appropriate. Try to buy clothing made of natural fibers. Although this will cost you a little more at first, it will last longer and look much better. This includes wool or cotton suits; cotton shirts; silk blouses, ties, and scarfs; and leather shoes, belts, and briefcases. The colors, patterns, and styles of your clothing should also be conservative. Whites, blues, and soft pastels are recommended for shirts and blouses, as are conservative plaids and pinstripes. Effective colors for suits are all shades of gray, blue (except very light blue for males), and beige. Proper styling and fit are imperative in all your clothing.

We must admit that we have seen people who, even though they followed all the foregoing rules, still projected a poor first impression because they didn't know how to put it all together. You, too, have probably seen a person wearing a pinstripe suit with a plaid shirt and a patterned tie. In order to complete the image you are trying to project to other people, you must know how to combine your clothing properly. Make sure the colors you wear are complementary to each other. Your tie or scarf should pick up some of the color in your suit and/or in your shirt or blouse. Men's socks should blend with shoes and/or suit. A long-sleeve shirt or blouse is recommended with a suit to put the finishing touches on that successful, authoritative image. Jewelry and accessories should be simple and functional.

If your height, weight, or age is creating an emotional problem or an image problem for you, you can use clothing to help alleviate those problems. For instance, a very tall person can wear soft colors and textures and avoid dark, heavy, overpowering clothing. Short people can do just the opposite. They can wear more authoritative clothing, such as dark pinstripe suits, vests, solid white shirts, and wing-tip shoes for men; for women, dark-colored, tailored suits and plain, high-quality blouses. Heavy people can wear dark suits and outer clothing to de-emphasize their weight, whereas thin people can wear lighter clothing to make them look a bit heavier. Young people, who may need to project more power and authority, can follow the same guidelines as those recommended for shorter people. Older people, whose age already carries power and authority, can follow the same advice as that recommended for taller people. This conservative, authoritative, and success-ful mode of dress projects the type of image you would like to those people within the organization who make decisions about your upward mobility. There is no doubt that this image will prompt your employees to take you more seriously. Recommendations and instructions are much more likely to be carried out promptly and accurately when you project an authoritative and successful image. When you need to relate to your employees on *their* level, simply alter your image with minor adjustments. You can loosen your tie or scarf, unbutton the top button of your shirt or blouse, and take off your vest and/or jacket. This projects a much more relaxed image and will make it easier for your employees to communicate openly with you. When meeting with a superior and an employee at the same time, you must make a value judgment on what image you need to project with those people in that situation. Knowing what you now know about image and clothing, you are much more likely to make the right decision in future situations than you were in the past.

Your clothes, voice, grooming, handshake, and body postures make a significant difference in the reception you receive from other people. First impressions do count—and if you do not present an appropriate image to create a positive impression on other people, those impressions will count against you. Do the best you can to make it count for you.

Depth of Knowledge. This refers to how well you know your subject—your particular area of expertise. How well do you know your company? How well do you know your industry? Are you up-to-date on your company's strengths and weaknesses relative to your competitors? Are you familiar with the skills and techniques of being a good manager within your company? Do other people come to you with questions about your company and your industry because they respect your expertise? Or do your employees, peers, and superiors avoid you because of the shallowness of your knowledge? Does the depth of your knowledge project credibility and command respect from your employees and fellow workers, or can you hear them saying: "I could do his job as well as he can"?

If you don't think the depth of your knowledge has an effect on your image, you are sadly mistaken. Make every effort to learn as much as possible about your company and your industry. Be thoroughly familiar with your firm's policies and procedures. Get to know your products and personnel as well as possible. Study the current situation and trends within your industry, and find out how you rate within the industry compared to your competitors. Take advantage of any training programs your company may offer. By increasing the depth of your knowledge, you will command respect from your employees, fellow workers, and superiors by projecting an image of intelligence and credibility.

Breadth of Knowledge. This area deals with your ability to converse with others in fields outside your particular area of expertise. For instance, who won the football game on Saturday? What are the latest developments in the world events? Are you familiar with the latest popular books and movies? Can you converse with people about things that are of interest to them?

By increasing the breadth of your knowledge, you will be able to develop rapport more easily with others. By not restricting the topic of conversation to something you alone desire, you will allow people to be more comfortable in conversing with you. When you are willing and able to talk with people about topics that are of interest and importance to them, they will feel much more confortable in your presence. In fact, people will go out of their way to talk with you. They will feel that you share something in common. Research has shown that the more people feel they have in common, the better they like each other. So by increasing the breadth of your knowledge, you will increase your circle of influence with various types of people.

The responsibility for increasing the breadth of your knowledge falls totally on your shoulders. There are a number of things you can do *today*—regardless of your age or background—to increase the breadth of your knowledge. We recommend that you read a local newspaper every day, front to back. Don't just read the sports section or the funnies or the fashion section or the classifieds. Read everything! In addition to reading the daily paper, you should try to read one of the major news magazines weekly. This will give you a good background in national and international events, as well as some additional knowledge in education, the arts, sports, books, movies, etc. Make an effort to read at least two books a year outside your normal area of interest, and try to mix fiction and nonfiction.

Make optimum use of typical nonproductive time, such as when bathing, shaving, putting on makeup, driving to and from work, cooking, cleaning and other time you can think of. You can make use of this nonproductive time by watching a morning or evening television news show, listening to radio news anytime, or listening to books and/or educational materials on audio cassettes. Finally, even if you are not up-to-date or knowledgeable about another person's topic of conversation, show interest in it by asking questions. That is one of the best ways to learn. Remember that increasing the breadth of your knowledge comes most easily from reading, listening, and interacting with other people.

Flexibility. Flexibility is your willingness and skill to adapt your behavior to relate best to other people. It is where you step out of your own "comfort zone" in order to communicate and interact effectively with other people on their level. Flexibility is something you do to yourself, not to others. You practice flexibility every time you slow down to interact with another person who does not feel comfortable moving as fast as you do. You are practicing flexibility when you take time to listen to a personal story rather than getting right down to the task at hand. You are practicing flexibility when you make an effort to speak on the same level as the other person. You are practicing flexibility when you cover things in much more detail than is typical of your style. You are practicing flexibility when you are simply making an effort to meet the personal and professional needs of others.

Flexibility is required because of the fact that people are different and need to be treated differently. When you treat all people the same or treat them inappropriately, they will feel uncomfortable with you, and tension will rise. This will have an adverse effect on the trust relationship you are trying to establish. Interactive management requires open, honest, and tension-free relationships with others. You do this by negotiating relationships and sharing, so that everybody wins. You do this by being tactful, reasonable, and understanding. You do this by exhibiting flexible behavior.

Enthusiasm. Who's your favorite entertainer? Let us make believe that you are going to a benefit concert tonight to see your favorite entertainer. Because it's a benefit concert, the tickets cost $25 per person. By the time you and your date get to the concert and are seated, you are out $50 without ever seeing a thing. The entertainer comes out, and the house thunders with applause. An entertainer typically sings twelve to fifteen songs during the course of a concert. When the singer comes onstage, he walks up to the microphone and starts singing. He sings fifteen songs as well as you have ever heard him sing them. But he sings them in succession, with no "rapping" or rapport building with the audience. At the end of the fifteenth song, the entertainer thanks the audience for coming to see him and walks off the stage. How much do you think you and your date would have enjoyed that concert? If you are like most people, you would feel cheated because he did not talk with his audience, did not build rapport, and did not show any enthusiasm at all. Even though the entertainer sang those fifteen songs as well as you have ever heard them sung by anybody, including himself, you feel cheated. Would it improve your opinion of his performance if you knew that he didn't feel very well because he stayed out late the night before and had a hangover? Would it improve your attitude any if you knew that just prior to coming out onstage, he had an argument with his business manager about an advertising contract? Again, if you are like most people, these revelations would not in any way change your feeling of being cheated. If the entertainer had just shown a bit more enthusiasm and warmth toward the audience, you'd probably feel much differently. *You* might even feel enthused.

When you show a lack of enthusiasm for your job, your company, or your personnel, do you think your fellow employees really know or even care why you are not enthused? Shouldn't they have the same feelings toward you as you had toward the nightclub singer? Wouldn't they feel cheated by a manager who lacked enthusiasm, just as you felt cheated by the entertainer who lacked enthusiasm?

Most managers like to see enthusiasm in their employees. Enthusiastic employees seem to work harder, longer, and more accurately than those who are not enthused. If you want your employees to have enthusiasm, you must project that quality yourself. It doesn't just happen. Enthusiasm is like a disease—it's catching—positive or negative. When you outwardly show enthusiasm about yourself, your fellow workers, and your company, the same attitude will rub off on your employees. They will be enthused. If you show a lack of enthusiasm, it, too, will eventually be projected to your employees; and they, in turn, will show a lack of enthusiasm about themselves, their fellow workers, their jobs, and their company. The choice is yours—bitterness or enthusiasm. Which do you choose?

Sincerity. This is our final aspect of image. This simply means that you cannot and should not fake it. You should make a concentrated and sincere effort to improve your first impressions, the depth and breadth of your knowledge, your flexibility, and your enthusiasm. As with any change of behavior, when you first do it, it will feel a little uncomfortable. But if you do it long enough and are sincere about it, it will become part of you. This sincerity, or the lack thereof, will be projected to other people and will become part of your total image. If you come across as insincere to other people, it will have a more damaging effect on your relationships with them than if you fall short in all the foregoing components of image. So above all else, be sincere in your interactions with other people, and project that sincerity to them.

IMAGE AND INTERACTIVE MANAGEMENT

The response you receive from the world around you is a measure of your success in interpersonal relations. The image you project will help to maximize or minimize your interpersonal success. From the beginning to the end of every transaction with another person, you are onstage. Every word, gesture, expression, and impression will be seen and evaluated, consciously or subconsciously, by that other person. Therefore, go through great pains to make sure the image you project—in each and every transaction—is one that helps facilitate and foster open, honest, trusting communications.

9

Communicating Through Voice Tones

What do you think a person who is speaking loud and fast is feeling? You probably said that the person was excited or enthused or angry or even frustrated. However, just to know that somebody is currently speaking loud and fast doesn't mean anything on its own. The person may be from the Northeast and just naturally speaks loud and fast. The person may come from a large family and has always had to speak loud and fast to be heard. So what does it mean when a person is speaking loud and fast? Nothing! However, if that person typically speaks slower and lower and, at a particular point during your conversation, starts speaking louder and faster, that probably does mean something. Generally, this is a positive sign, but it might also be negative. In this chapter, we take a closer look at the many different emotions people can project simply through the tone of their voice.

Voice intonation, or vocal behavior, is a form of nonverbal communication. This is important to remember not only in management but in personal relationships as well. Nonverbal communications, in the case of voice intonations, means dividing the vocal information from the verbal information. There is certainly a difference between these two types of information.

Vocal information is that part of the meaning of a message that is lost when speech is written rather than spoken. The verbal and vocal parts of messages do not always communicate the same meaning or feeling.

Added meaning can be derived from the words others speak, and additional meaning can be added to the words you speak simply by changing your voice intonations. Simple changes in voice qualities can change the meaning or emotion of the same group of words from one thing to another. A good example is an acting teacher who can verbalize the word *oh* eight different ways. By simple changes in vocal qualities, the actor can convey eight totally separate and unique feelings and emotions to the audience. Just a simple two-letter word—*oh*—can be used to demonstrate the critical importance of vocal intonation in communications. A lack of emotional sensitivity to voice tones can damage the trust bond with your employees. Spending too much time on superfluous topics and not enough time on pertinent ones can increase the tension between you and your employees. The most important thing to remember when paying attention to voice intonations is to concentrate primarily on changes in your employees' voice qualities.

Voice Qualities. Some people naturally speak slow, loud, or clear. When these people *change* their normal voice qualities, they are communicating something extra to you. It is up to you to know what these vocal qualities are, when they are changing, and what to do about these changes. The seven major vocal qualities are as follows:

1. **Resonance**—*The ability of one's voice to fill space; an intensification and enrichment of the voice tone.*
2. **Rhythm**—*The flow, pace, and movement of the voice.*
3. **Speed**—*How fast the voice is used.*
4. **Pitch**—*The tightening or relaxing of the vocal cords (e.g., the nervous laugh); the highness or lowness of sound.*
5. **Volume**—*The degree of loudness or intensity of the voice.*
6. **Inflection**—*The changes in pitch or volume of the voice.*
7. **Clarity**—*The crisp articulation and enunciation of the words.*

You should realize that the way someone says something can have a great effect on what meaning is being communicated. An example of this is sarcasm, where the information being transmitted vocally has quite a different meaning from what is being transmitted verbally. This is why it is very important for managers to learn what different voice intonations mean, how to identify them, and how to use them effectively to get their message across. There is a very good example of how differing vocal intonations can totally change the meaning of the message being communicated in a film distributed by CRM/McGraw-Hill Films called *Communication: The Nonverbal Agenda.* In the film, a manager must relate the same message verbatim to three of his employees. He has ambivalent feelings toward one of the employees, dislike for another, and friendship for another. The three scenarios clearly show that although the manager's words were exactly the same with all three employees, his feelings, likes, dislikes, and biases were clearly projected in his vocal intonation as well as other observable behavior. Although the manager did not consciously realize what he was doing, the subconscious vocal message was clearly communicated to and identified by each of the three employees.

By learning more about vocal behavior and voice intonations, you will have a much better idea of your employee's true feelings. In addition, you will have a better understanding of how others perceive you through your voice intonations.

Projecting Emotions Vocally.   The way in which a person varies any or all of the seven vocal qualities in conversations can significantly change the feeling or emotion of the message. By having the knowledge and awareness of the combinations of these vocal qualities and the respective emotions and feelings they project, you will be able to respond appropriately to these "silent" messages communicated to you through your employee's vocal behavior. Listed next are twelve feelings and emotions that can be communicated simply through changes in voice qualities.

1. **Affection**—*Upward inflection, resonant, low volume, slow speed.*

2. **Anger**—*Loud volume, terse speech, irregular inflection.*

3. **Boredom**—*Moderate to low volume, resonant, somewhat slow speed, descending inflection, little clarity.*

4. **Cheerfulness**—*Somewhat high volume, fast speed, irregular inflection.*

5. **Impatience**—*Normal to high pitch, fast speed.*

6. **Joyfulness**—*Loud volume, fast speed, ascending inflection.*

7. **Astonishment**—*Ascending inflection.*

8. **Defensiveness**—*Terse speech.*

9. **Enthusiasm**—*Loud volume, emphatic pitch.*

10. **Sadness**—*Low volume, resonant, slow speed, descending inflection, little clarity.*

11. **Disbelief**—*High pitch, drawn-out words.*

12. **Satisfaction**—*Ascending inflection, little clarity.*

You must remember to keep two very important things in mind when paying attention to the vocal qualities of other people. First, identify the other person's personal and *habitual* vocal qualities. Second, note any *changes* from that characteristic vocal quality, both in kind and direction of change. When it comes to vocal qualities, what is characteristic for one person is not characteristic for another. This should have been recognized just in reading about behavioral styles. The Amiables and the Analyticals characteristically speak more slowly and in a lower volume than do the Expressives and the Drivers. Try to recognize how the other person typically speaks in relationship to the seven vocal qualities, and during your conversation, note any changes from that characteristic style. When changes do occur, the person more likely is communicating something extra that isn't carried in the words alone. It may indicate a point of emphasis, something of importance, something of concern, or simply a shift in the way that person is feeling. If you are aware and sensitive to these clues as they are happening, you can take appropriate action if necessary. This skill refines your interpersonal communications ability. It helps in building and improving good, solid, long-lasting working relationships with your employees.

Generally speaking, upward changes in a person's volume and speed indicate a positive change in attitude. But if the rhythm is clipped, it could project anger. Downward changes in volume and speed, greater resonance, and lessened clarity usually project a change in a negative direction. But they could also indicate affection or satisfaction on the part of your employee. Any changes in rhythm usually mean a change in mood, which also can be positive or negative. The important thing to keep in mind with any of the foregoing changes is that when they are happening, be aware of their occurrence. Then use your clarification skills to determine specifically what those changes are indicating on the part of your employee. Your responsibility is to fall back on your listening, probing, and feedback skills to get at the root of the change. Once you have determined the exact nature of the change, you can do something about it. If it's positive, you can capitalize on it. If it's negative, you can try to turn the negative situation around before it is too late. When using your feedback skills for confirmation, make sure that you speak to your employee in terms of how the message is coming across to you, not in terms of the specific vocal qualities you are hearing. Remember that you are trying to show your *sensitivity* skills, not your analytical skills.

Using Vocal Qualities.   Not very many people enjoy being shouted at or belittled by the tone of voice another person uses. Harshness, irritability, and patronization are just some of the attitudes that are very easily communicated through tones of voice. Your tone of voice should be pleasant, cheerful, friendly, and straightforward without attempting to overpower or convince your employees. Your tone of voice often has more impact than your actual words. A good example is in dealing with animals. An animal will accept a derogatory remark when given in a friendly voice but react negatively when even positive remarks are expressed in an angry tone. Surprisingly enough, people are not much different.

Your tone of voice communicates an important part of you and your personality to others, especially over the telephone. You might find it a worthwhile exercise to tape-record only your half of several phone calls. After each call, replay the tape. How are you coming across—to yourself? How does it sound? Are the volume and speed appropriate? What about the rhythm, inflection, resonance, and clarity? Do you feel that you were accurately communicating to the other person the emotions that you meant to communicate to him? By analyzing and constructively critiquing several of these phone calls, you can determine if any of your vocal qualities need improvement. As soon as you can identify these, think about how to improve them so you can start projecting the type of voice you would like to have.

Language can communicate almost anything, but through

the use of vocal qualities you can learn to communicate your feelings, likes, and dislikes. By varying tone, you can always reinforce what you are saying verbally. It can be very helpful to you as a manager to convey competence and trust through the tone of your voice. Five aids to an assured voice that can help you project competence and trust to your employees are as follows:

1. Project a strong, full, but not overwhelming resonance.
2. Fully using your mouth and lips, speak clearly and distinctly.
3. Show enthusiasm by using the appropriate pitch, volume, and inflection.
4. Be interesting by varying your vocal qualities—do not speak in a monotone voice.
5. Speak naturally and at ease, not phony or put-on.

Your part of the conversation should never be monotonous, or you will bore your employees. On the other hand, do not vary your intonations in the same manner every time and risk coming across like a machine. A mechanical voice will bore your employee and give the impression that your message is canned. Both the uninteresting voice and the voice that follows a mechanical pattern are monotonous. You can avoid this monotony by simply varying your vocal qualities as the situation requires.

Speak rapidly when the subject matter permits; then emphasize an important point by speaking more slowly. By watching the employee's facial expressions and other nonverbal communications, you can determine the degree of involvement. You should emphasize points that apparently interest the employee and then pause to let the idea sink in. As you can see, timing in speech can be highly informative and effective to both you and your employees.

A study at Yale University showed that the more errors a person made while speaking (errors meaning poor tone, volume, monotony, etc.), the more that speaker's discomfort and anxiety increased. Through practice and awareness, you can reduce these errors. By doing this, you will become much more comfortable with your speaking voice. This in turn will make your employees more comfortable and subsequently will increase the trust bond.

Your carelessness in enunciation is likely to be taken by

your employees as an indication of carelessness in other areas. Poor enunciation is also likely to result in the employee misunderstanding what you are saying. It can easily lead to a breakdown in the communication process. Good enunciation strengthens your trust bond, and that makes each subsequent communications step a little bit easier.

The foregoing vocal suggestions can be very effective if they are used appropriately. Overuse or overemphasis of these methods may annoy your employees and take their attention away from the conversation. Your use of these vocal skills must seem natural and spontaneous, or they will appear insincere. By using the proper vocal intonation, you can draw attention to those areas of your message that are of utmost importance and benefit to your employees.

The interactive manager knows the importance of using effective vocal behavior when speaking with employees. An awareness of the subtle nuances, feelings, meanings, and emotions of vocal behavior is critical. It allows you to be aware of what you are (nonverbally) communicating to your employees and what they are (nonverbally) communicating to you. The effective or ineffective use of vocal intonations can play a crucial role in the development of the manager–employee trust bond. It can make or break the relationship. It may even determine whether you get higher or lower productivity from your employees. If you can become more aware of and sensitive to your vocal intonations and those of your employees, you can increase the trust bond, your credibility, and the productivity of the relationship and the employees. That payoff seems well worth the effort.

10

Using Body Language Effectively

Suppose that you have just called one of your employees into your office. He is not aware that you intend to talk to him about a recent discipline problem that you just discovered. You are determined to get to the bottom of this problem here and now. The employee enters your office, and you cordially ask him to have a seat. As you open the conversation on a social note, your employee is looking at you with his head slightly tilted, legs and arms uncrossed, and suit jacket unbuttoned; he is leaning slightly forward in his chair with his hands open and relaxed. As you broach the sensitive topic, the employee's body becomes more rigid. His arms and legs become tightly crossed, his lips pursed, and his fists clenched. He now is also maintaining little eye contact with you. As he begins telling you his side of the story, he still fails to maintain eye contact and even resists your glances. All during his end of the conversation, he seems to be squinting, rubbing his nose, and casually covering his mouth with his hands. As you are listening, you are peering at him over the rims of your glasses, occasionally giving him sideways glances, and intermittently raising an eyebrow. Toward the end of the conversation, you tell your employee that you intend to keep an open mind about this situation and will look into the matter further in a very objective way.

As the employee is leaving your office, you lean back in your chair with your fingers laced behind your head and your feet on the desk. You have a funny feeling that something else went on during the conversation in addition to the words that were spoken, but you can't put your finger on it. You didn't believe a word he said because of the way he was acting, but you didn't want to let on to him that you were suspicious. That's why you told him that you would keep an open mind and be objective in this matter. Little do you realize that both you and the employee were openly communicating with each other, not through words, but through body language. Your body movements, facial expressions, and gestures revealed much more about your attitudes and emotional state than your words. If you, the manager, only knew how to read body language, your interview with the employee might have gone in an entirely different direction, and the problem could have been resolved right then and there.

Body language is certainly not a new phenomenon. People have known about it and used it since the beginning of time. Before people developed language as a communications tool, they used body language to make their needs and desires known to other people. Also known as *kinesics*, body language describes human interaction excluding the use of written and spoken words. This broad definition encompasses everything from the most subtle raising of an eyebrow to the precise movements of the sophisticated sign language used by the deaf.

There are some nonverbal gestures that have universal symbolism. The position at the head of the table has long been reserved for the leader of the group. In recent times, this position of honor has also been extended to the host of the table. It is a custom that was honored as far back as the time of King Arthur, when the round table was developed as an attempt to administer democracy by eliminating the appearance of having one leader. Another universal gesture is raising the hands above the head, which has long symbolized surrender and submission.

Some gestures are even more expressive than words. Conjure up the image of a person slapping his forehead. This may be accompanied by an audible groan. Don't you already know that he has just remembered something he should have done?

Implicit in this gesture is an apology to the audience for his oversight.

Other well-known gestures are saluting, tipping one's hat, shaking hands, shrugging shoulders, waving good-bye, forming an o with thumb and forefinger, and blowing a kiss.

Nonverbal communication in the form of body language is rather quick. Research has substantiated that even when exposure to a situation is reduced to 1/24 of a second (the time it takes to show a single frame of film), people often grasp what it means. At 3/24 of a second, comprehension goes up dramatically, and there is increased understanding up to slightly more than one second of exposure.

Ability to understand body language is apparently not related to IQ, the ability to take tests, or the grades one makes in school. Practice tends to improve how well people understand body language. People tested for body language comprehension generally score higher on second and subsequent tests than on their first tries.

Researchers in the area of nonverbal communications claim that as much as 90 percent of the meaning that is transmitted between two people in face-to-face communications can come via nonverbal channels. This means that as little as 10 percent of the meaning we derive from others comes through words alone. If these figures even come close to reality (and research supports that they do), then the importance of nonverbal communications is obvious.

With a plethora of courses and seminars offered in speaking, and so relatively few available in the study of nonverbal communications and body language, it seems that an uninformed public should be guided to a more thorough understanding of the importance of this subject.

Sigmund Freud, an early believer in the importance of body language, distrusted the spoken word and based much of his work on the assumption that words hide much more than they reveal. Freud believed, as do many researchers, that although we cannot rely on the truth of words, nonverbal behavior often does project the truth.

Through kinesic behavior, people express their conscious and subconscious emotions, desires, and attitudes. Body language, which is stimulated by a subconscious need to express inner feelings, is more reliable than verbal communication and may even contradict verbal expressions. Body language is an outlet for your feelings and can function as a lie detector to aid a watchful listener in interpreting your words. Your body language communicates your sincerity and commitment to those who are observant.

In the field of management, the communication of ideas is of primary importance. The benefits derived from a study of body language are therefore numerous for you as a manager. By increasing your awareness of kinesic behavior, you can read the emotions and attitudes of your employees. As a result, you will have a greater feeling for and awareness of all your employee transactions. This increased rapport with and understanding of your employees will probably result in increased trust and productivity.

In addition to increasing your understanding of your employees, the study of body language can also help improve your employees' understanding of you. Body language is an important part of having your employees perceive your messages the way they were intended to be received and perceived. The better able you are to transmit messages so that they are received by your employees as they were intended, the more effective you will be as a manager. Therefore, be acutely aware of your own body projections as well as those of your employees. You can increase tension and decrease trust simply by projecting negative body language or by lacking sensitivity in observing your employees' nonverbal communication. The "bad vibes" that result can be disastrous to present and future relationships with employees.

INTERPRETING BODY LANGUAGE GESTURES

Body language involves interpretation of many kinds of gestures. Some of the major areas involved in this form of nonverbal communication are the eyes, face, hands, arms, legs, and posture (sitting and walking). You can tell a great deal about others and they about you simply by noting body gestures. However, each individual, isolated gesture is like a word in a sentence; it is very difficult and dangerous to interpret in and of itself. Unless it is a one-word sentence, it takes more than one to provide full meaning. Therefore, you should consider the gesture in light of everything else that is going on around you. Just as individual words have definitions, individual gestures have some meaning. When words are put together in a full sentence, they communicate a fuller meaning. When individual gestures are put together in clusters, they give a more complete and exact meaning of what the other person is feeling and thinking. Before looking at the attitudes and meanings projected by clusters of gestures, let us look at some of the more common interpretations of individual isolated gestures.

Eyes. The eyes, known as the windows of the soul, are excellent indicators of a person's feelings. The expressions *shifty eyes*, *beady eyes*, and *look of steel* demonstrate the awareness people have for this area of the body. It is a long-held belief that the honest person has a tendency to look you straight in the eye when speaking. Recent work in this area has shown that there is some scientific basis for this belief. It has been discovered that speakers who were rated as "sincere" looked at their audience an average of three times longer than those speakers who were rated as "insincere."

People avoid eye contact with another person when an uncomfortable question is asked. You should be aware of this and steer clear of topics that result in the avoidance of eye contact. Try to reduce tension and build trust rather than increase the tension.

Eye gestures are often easily interpreted. The raising of one eyebrow shows disbelief, whereas two eyebrows raised shows surprise. Winking can be flirtatious or sometimes indicative of agreement, especially when accompanied by a nod or smile. You should be sensitive to the body language of an employee who looks upward with a fixed expression while blinking rapidly. Chances are that what you are talking about is being seriously considered by the employee. In fact, a favorable decision may have already been made on the big issue, and the employee may simply be meditating on the details. Patience on your part is needed here. You should refrain from further intense discussion until the employee's thought process is complete.

Some very interesting work has been done with eye direction. It has been found that people look either to the right or to the left, depending on what thoughts dominate their mental activity. Most people are generally classified as right lookers or left lookers. Left lookers are found to be more emotional, subjective, and suggestible; whereas right lookers are more influenced by logic and precision.

The Face.   The face is one of the most reliable indicators of a person's attitudes, emotions, and feelings. Facial expressions sometimes betray emotions and states of mind. By analyzing facial expressions, interpersonal attitudes can be discerned and feedback obtained. "You can read her face like an open book" is a common statement used to describe a person whose facial expressions are very demonstrative. Sometimes facial expressions are very guarded because one does not want to betray one's position prematurely by expressing a nonverbal opinion. The term *poker face* describes an attempt to keep others from knowing your true emotions.

The Hands.   Tightly clenched hands or wringing hands usually indicate that the person is experiencing undue pressure. This person will usually be difficult to relate to, as he is highly tense and in strong disagreement with you. Steepling, joining the fingertips together and forming what might be described as a church steeple, indicates a smugness and great self-confidence. Superiority and authority are usually indicated when you are standing and joining your hands together behind your back.

A number of attitudes and emotions can be conveyed by what a person does with her hands around the face or head. For instance, rubbing gently behind or beside the ear with the index finger usually shows signs of doubt. Casually rubbing the eye with one finger also usually means the other person doesn't know about what you are saying. Of course, it may also indicate that the other person has an itch or a "sleeper" in the eye. Rubbing the back of the head or palming the nape of the neck typically indicates frustration with the other person or the situation. Leaning back with both hands supporting the head usually indicates a feeling of confidence or superiority. Cupping one or both hands over the mouth, especially when talking, may well indicate that the person is trying to hide something. Boredom is often communicated by placing your head in your open palm and dropping your chin in a nodding manner while allowing your eyelids to droop. Putting your hand to your cheek or stroking your chin generally portrays thinking, interest, or consideration. On the other hand, pinching the bridge of your nose with your eyes closed, or placing your forefinger near your nose with your chin resting in the palm of your hand and your fingers bent across the chin or below the mouth most often shows that critical evaluation is taking place.

The Arms and Legs. Crossed arms tend to signal defensiveness. They seemingly act as a protective guard against an anticipated attack or a fixed position from which the other person would rather not move. Conversely, arms open and extended toward you generally indicate openness and acceptance.

Crossed legs tend to signal disagreement. People who tightly cross their legs seem to be saying that they disagree with what you are saying or doing. If people have tightly crossed legs and tightly crossed arms, their inner attitude is usually one of extreme negativeness toward what is going on around them. As long as they are in this position, it is unlikely you will get their full agreement to what you are saying or doing.

Posture—Sitting and Walking. Sitting with a leg over the arm of a chair usually signals an uncooperative attitude. Sitting with a chair back facing forward and straddling the seat with your arms on the chair back tends to express a dominant, superior attitude. Sitting with your legs crossed and the elevated foot moving in a slight circular motion indicates boredom or impatience. Interest and involvement are usually projected by sitting on the edge of the chair and leaning slightly forward.

Generally, people who walk fast and swing their arms freely tend to know what they want and to go after it. People who walk with their shoulders hunched and hands in their pockets tend to be secretive and critical. They don't seem to like much of what is going on around them. Dejected people usually scuffle along with their hands in their pockets, heads down, and shoulders hunched over. People who are preoccupied or thinking usually walk with their heads down, hands clasped behind their backs, and pace very slow.

INTERPRETING GESTURE CLUSTERS

Certain combinations of gestures are especially reliable indicators of a person's true feelings. These combinations are called gesture *clusters*. Each body language gesture is dependent on others, so analysis of a person's body language should be based on a series of signals to ensure that the body language is clearly and accurately understood. Interpreting gesture clusters ensures a more meaningful analysis of the person's state of mind if the individual gestures that make up the cluster are congruent. In other words, all the individual gestures must fit together to project a common, unified message. When they do not, you are faced with a case of incongruity. A good example of incongruity is the nervous laugh. A laugh should signal amusement and relaxation. Yet when it sounds strained or nervous, when other body signals are nervous arm and leg movements, and when the entire body shifts as though it were trying to escape an unpleasant situation, you know that laugh does not mean amusement or relaxation. The laughter is probably there to try to cover up discomfort and possibly fear. So, in reading body language, make sure that you focus on gesture clusters and congruency. Remember that body language may augment, emphasize, contradict, or be totally unrelated to the words that someone is speaking. Therefore, reading body language is a continuous process of analysis. Let's look at some of the more common gesture clusters and their associated meanings.

Openness. Several gestures indicate openness and sincerity, such as open hands, unbuttoned coat or collar, removing coat or jacket, moving closer together, leaning slightly forward in the chair, and uncrossed arms and legs. When people are proud of what they've done, they usually show their hands quite openly. When they are not, they often put their hands in their pockets or behind their backs. Carefully watch the hands of a child the next time one is trying to hide something. When people take their coats off, unbutton their collars, or extend their arms toward you, they are generally beginning to feel comfortable in your presence. These are all very positive signs.

Defensiveness. People who are defensive usually have a rigid body, arms or legs tightly crossed, eyes glancing sideways or darting occasionally, minimal eye contact, lips pursed, fists clenched, and a downcast head. What's the first thing that comes to mind when you think of a person with arms tightly crossed over his chest? A baseball umpire, right? Picture the manager rushing out of the dugout, arms swinging or stuck in his back pockets. As the manager approaches, the umpire crosses his arms. He has already signaled nonverbally his intention to defend his decision. As part of this cluster, the umpire may curtly turn his back on the manager, saying nonverbally, "You've talked enough." Arm gripping and tightly clenched fists are more extreme forms of the crossed-arm gesture. Especially watch for tightly clenched fists. They show that the other person is really turned off.

When someone puts his leg over the arm of a chair, it might seem to suggest relaxation and openness. It does not. Research has shown that when this happens, that person is dropping out of the conversation. You can't expect much more participation from this person unless you can reverse his or her position. Straddling a chair again might look informal and open, but it is not. It is domineering. The person has raised his defenses. Quite often, in work situations the boss will do this to an employee. It is defensive, and you won't get anywhere dealing with a person in this posture.

Evaluation. Evaluation gestures say that the other person is being thoughtful or is considering what you are saying—sometimes in a friendly way, sometimes unfriendly. Typical evaluation gestures include the tilted head, hand to cheek, leaning forward, and chin stroking. Have you ever seen Auguste Rodin's famous statue *The Thinker?* Isn't this the model of a person deep in thought? In addition to the hand-to-cheek gesture, a person who tilts her head and leans slightly forward is usually considering what you are saying. A gesture indicating serious contemplation of what is being said is the chin-stroking gesture. It has been said that this gesture signifies a wise person making a judgment.

Sometimes evaluation gestures take on a critical aspect. In this posture, the body is usually more drawn back. The hand is to the face, but the chin is in the palm of the hand with one finger going up the cheek and the other fingers positioned below the mouth. This is generally an unfavorable gesture. The typical delaying gesture to give a person more time to evaluate the situation is removing one's glasses and putting the earpiece of the frame in the mouth. People who smoke cigarettes sometimes light one to gain time. However, the classic stall gesture is pipe smoking. With little effort, this can be turned into a ritual of delay. The pipe must be filled, cleaned, tapped, and lighted. Pipe smokers generally give the impression that they are more patient and moderate than cigarette smokers, who sometimes look like sprinters as they fish for a cigarette. If you are dealing with someone who is going through these stalling evaluation rituals, it is usually a good idea to let the person have the time needed to think things through.

A person who pinches the bridge of her nose, closes her eyes, and slumps her head down slightly is expressing self-conflict. She is probably trying to decide if she is in a bad situation or not. Don't try to reason her out of it. Give her time. A final negative evaluation gesture is a person's dropping his eyeglasses to the lower bridge of the nose and peering over them. This gesture usually causes a negative emotional reaction in other people. Those on the receiving end feel that they are being closely scrutinized and looked down upon. Sometimes this gesture is made unintentionally by people who have ill-fitting glasses or granny glasses for reading.

Suspicion, Secrecy, Rejection, and Doubt. These rather negative emotions are communicated typically by sideways glances, minimal or no eye contact, shifting the body away from the speaker, and touching or rubbing the nose. When a person won't look at you, it sometimes means that she is being secretive, has secret feelings in opposition to what you are saying, or is hiding something. A sideways glance sometimes registers as suspicion and doubt. It is sometimes called "the cold shoulder." Have you ever tried to help someone across the street who really preferred to proceed alone? You quickly discovered what the cold shoulder means. The individual may cross the street with you but turn away from you at a forty-five degree angle. It is a gesture of rejection toward your "helping" hand. Shifting your body away from a person who is speaking or sitting so that your feet are pointing toward the door usually means that you wish to end the meeting, conversation, or whatever is going on. Touching or slightly rubbing the nose, as opposed to scratching the nose, may indicate puzzlement, doubt, or concealment.

Readiness. Readiness is related to the goal-oriented high achiever with a concern for getting things done. It communicates dedication to a goal and is usually communicated by placing your hands on your hips or sitting forward at the edge of a chair. The most common of these gestures is hands on hips. Athletes standing on the sidelines waiting to enter a sporting event often take this position. At a business meeting, it is usually assumed by someone who wants and expects other people to follow. A young child takes this position when challenging a parent's authority.

If you are about to sign an agreement you are pleased with, you would sit at the edge of your chair. If you did not like the agreement, you would sit back. Salespeople are usually taught that a person sitting on the edge of the seat is usually ready to make a purchase decision. These are positive gestures and should not be feared. The individual is merely saying nonverbally that she is ready and able to take action. However, be careful when you project these gestures to others. You may give the appearance of being overly anxious.

Reassurance. This is usually conveyed by someone pinching the fleshy part of the hand; picking at fingernails; gently rubbing or caressing some personal object such as a watch, ring, or necklace; or chewing on some object such as a pencil, pen, or paper clip. We usually see these gestures quite vividly when people from the audience participate on a TV program. Many people are afraid of the television camera for numerous reasons. They think it will make them look heavier or older or will reveal some strange idiosyncrasies in their behavior. During the actual videotaping and the subsequent playback of the tape, people make all kinds of gestures to reassure themselves.

Frustration. The next time you watch a football game, pay close attention to what happens after a quarterback fades back and throws a pass that goes in and out of the hands of his teammate. You will probably see the teammate kick the ground, slap the side of his helmet, or even do a double karate chop in the air. These are all frustration gestures of an extreme kind. More common frustration gestures are tightly clenched hands, rubbing the nape of the neck, hand wringing, and running one's hands through the hair. These are all negative gestures. If your employees are doing this in your presence, you should immediately back away from whatever you are doing, and give them some more breathing room. If you don't, the frustration level will just keep increasing until it eventually explodes.

Confidence, Superiority, and Authority. These emotions are usually conveyed through relaxation and expansiveness gestures, such as steepling, feet up or on the desk, leaning back with fingers laced behind the head, and hands together at the back with chin thrust upward.

Nervousness.   Clearing one's throat is a typical nervous gesture. Speakers often do this before they talk in front of an audience. Chain smoking is another gesture of nervousness. Yet when a smoker is extremely nervous, the first thing the person does is put out the cigarette. Covering the mouth while speaking is one nervousness gesture that police officers often see during interrogations. They say that this gesture means anything from self-doubt to lying. Other nervousness gestures include twitching lips or face, fidgeting, shifting weight from one foot to another, tapping fingers, pacing, jingling money in one's pocket, and whistling.

Self-Control.   Gestures such as tightly locking ankles and gripping your wrists behind your back usually mean that you are holding back. Do you do this in a dentist's waiting room? The Army has an old phrase—"keeping your heels locked." It means holding back and not disclosing anything—self-control.

Boredom or Impatience.   These unproductive feelings are usually conveyed by the drumming of fingers, cupping the head in the palm of the hand, foot swinging, brushing or picking at lint, doodling, pointing the body toward an exit, or looking at your watch or the exit.

Enthusiasm.   This is an emotion that you love to see in other people and they in you. Enthusiasm is conveyed by a small upper or inward smile, an erect body stance, hands open and arms extended outward, eyes wide and alert, a lively and bouncy walk, and a lively and well-modulated voice. This attitude should be projected by you to others and should be cultivated and reinforced in your employees.

USING BODY LANGUAGE

When the relationship between two people is that of manager and employee, the ability to project favorable body postures and to read the body language of others is undoubtedly a special asset.

The body language of your employees is very important to you. It tells you how your words are being accepted by expressing their emotions and attitudes nonverbally. You may show agreement with their words by nodding your head slowly or perhaps bobbing your head enthusiastically. Disagreement may be evident when your employee shakes her head or raises her eyebrows to indicate amazement or doubt. Regardless of the attitude expressed, you should know the effect of your words before you finish speaking simply by keying in on the body language projected by your employee.

In interactive management, always be aware of your employees' body language. Their body projections should guide your conversation, and each interaction should be geared toward the individual employee's emotions and attitudes as interpreted through individual body language. Constantly monitor your employee's body language, and be alert to any changes in postures and gestures that might indicate a change in mental attitude. You can then adjust your presentation accordingly.

The changes in body projections that an employee manifests may mean that he is ready to make a commitment to a new action plan. The most obvious things to observe are signs of relaxation—unlocking of ankles, palms and arms extending outward toward you, and movements toward the front of the chair—all of which indicate that your employee is listening to you and tuning in to your message. If, on the other hand, your employee crosses his legs, folds his arms tightly across his chest, and continues to lean back in his chair, you are probably not being very effective. He is not being receptive to what you are trying to say, and a change in approach is necessary to win him back.

If your employee starts to nod her head with you and copies your gestures, especially to the degree of leaning forward in the chair and balancing on the balls of her feet, you have someone who is really on the same wavelength as you. It is important to recognize these signals early and get a commitment on a new action plan if appropriate. Otherwise, you may keep talking beyond the point of appropriateness and eventually bore the employee. By carefully reading the body language of your employees, you will know when to continue along the same line of conversation and when to change the subject, ask for a commitment, or totally end the conversation.

In addition to your employees' body language, you should

be aware of your own body language. You must realize that you are sending out signals of your own. Even if your employees are not trained in kinesics, they will still be affected by your body projections. They may not consciously interpret these signals, but they will react to them nonetheless. What makes it worse is if your body language and your words are not saying the same thing, which often happens. This can create an enormous credibility problem for you in the eyes of your employees. It may condition them to look for double messages in their conversations with you.

Defensiveness, anger, or frustration on the part of your employees may be a direct result of your aggressiveness, dominance, or manipulative body language. Manager–employee games and a deterioration of the trust bond result from these postures. You can create either beneficial or dangerous emotional environments through body movements. Research has found that people who sit in open, relaxed positions are seen as more persuasive and active and are better liked than those who sit in a tight, closed manner. Managers who sit in an open, relaxed way are able to effect greater opinion change in their employees than those who do not. These tips can help you maintain or increase employee cooperation.

The relevance of reading body language should be obvious to you as a manager. Studies have demonstrated that people who exhibit "expressionless stimuli"—blank face, aloof, uninterested—produce low levels of self-expression in others. A simple head nod in agreement seems to offer more feeling of expression, and a combination of head nods and warm smiles allows your employees to express their own feelings fully. Your actions and role are equally important to that of observing the employee.

As already demonstrated, body language is an essential part of interpersonal communications. For you, knowledge and mastery of reading body language is an integral part of your interactive management success. The mastery of this skill allows you to perceive the needs and desires of your employees and is also an aid in your own self-expression. However, it should be remembered that body language is an inexact science. Gesture clusters are clues to the attitudes and emotions of another person, but they do not provide conclusive evidence. You should test and validate your understanding of an employee's body language rather than jeopardizing your position with that employee by making snap decisions. Body language provides the basis for making assumptions that ought to be tested and validated, not for concluding facts.

If all else fails, you can always revert to the use of words.

11

Spatial Arrangements Say Things

Have you ever had someone stand so close to you that you were prompted to ask, "Did you enjoy your tuna sandwich at lunch?" How do you feel when you return to your office and find a colleague sorting through your filing cabinet? What is your reaction when you return to a meeting after a break and find that someone else is sitting in your place? The uncomfortable feelings most of us experience in such situations result from violations of personal space. Answers to these types of questions can give you a clue to how you use *proxemics*—that is, space and the movement of people within it—to communicate with others. There are at least six aspects of proxemics that we can study to help understand how we use space for communicating with others: territory, environment, things, proxemic zones, dyad arrangements, and group arrangements.

TERRITORY

Your reactions to the foregoing questions probably confirm the conclusion of anthropologists that human beings are territorial animals with inherent compulsions to possess and defend space as exclusive property. Your office is a *fixed feature territory* with unmovable boundaries such as walls and doors. When you enter a meeting, you establish a *semifixed feature territory*, which is bounded by movable objects such as your notebook, coffee cup, and jacket hanging on your chair. Although you have no legal rights to certain geographic areas because you arrived there first and staked out your claim with your jacket, notebook, and coffee cup, your immediate reaction in returning to the meeting and finding someone else in your seat is probably a feeling of loss, followed by anger and a desire to regain your space.

People like to protect and control their territory. This is much easier to do with fixed feature territories, where it is possible to shut your door or even lock it. In semifixed feature territories, the best protection is your physical presence. If you are absent for a while, your only protection is other people's respect for honoring your territory. If it is a very desirable territory, you may return and find that someone else has claimed it.

There are times when others invade even our fixed feature territory or cause us to lose control over it. This is a more severe social violation than ignoring semifixed boundaries, and your angry feelings are apt to be even greater. If you have your door closed and someone walks into your office without knocking and without being invited, the tension between you will skyrocket, and your trust of the perpetrator will plummet. Similar reactions would probably occur if a visitor sits in your chair, uses your pen, or grabs your personal appointment book to check a date for a future meeting.

In attempting to establish a trust bond with subordinates, be careful not to violate their territory, even though you're the boss. When dealing with territory, mutual respect is the norm, and trust is based on honoring it. People value their privacy and need to protect and control their personal territory. Studies have even demonstrated that if you are talking to subordinates and inadvertently violate some aspect of their personal space, they may not say anything to you directly, but internally they may be so upset that they don't hear a word you say.

ENVIRONMENT

Architects have long been aware that the design, color, and placement of objects such as furniture, plants, and pictures in an environment can facilitate or hinder the quality of communications and productivity of other interactions among co-workers. Several commonly accepted feelings about the use of space in work environments have been identified by Dr. Anthony Athos. Attention to these environmental clues can help you understand what others are trying to say or why they react as they do to this important form of nonverbal communication. Awareness of these variables can also facilitate the breadth and clarity of your own communications.

More Is Better than Less. One way to communicate to others their importance is by the amount of space assigned to them in the total organizational environment. Presidents of companies usually have larger offices than middle managers, and so forth. Space is a limited resource, so the more space people are assigned for their personal territory, the more valuable and important they can be assumed to be.

People not only desire large offices but offices with a view. Although there may be practical reasons for windows such as ventilation or lighting, views also provide the illusion of greater space. In any event, if you check out office assignments in most organizations, you will surely find that newer and lower-status employees occupy the inside offices without windows or desirable views. Higher-status persons with more power and assumed importance will usually occupy larger offices with nicer views. When you notice an incongruence in this pattern, it may be worth your time to check out what is being communicated.

Private Is Better than Public. Another way of communicating status is by assigning someone personal territory (not public) that can be closed off for privacy out of the sight and sound of others. In most organizations, to go from open, public space—characterized as a semifixed feature territory—to a private office—which is an enclosed fixed feature territory—is a signal of increased importance and status. Think of most administrative offices you have visited. The typists are usually situated in a common "pool" area and sometimes do not even have the same table or typewriter to use every day. The executive secretaries often have assigned fixed feature territories characterized by partitions giving them some privacy. The manager of the typists and secretaries probably has a private office with a door and other fixed feature characteristics.

If we have private space, how we use it communicates

things to other people. If some people are invited into our office for a closed-door meeting, they are assumed to be privileged and to have access to important information denied those not included. It is better to be with the "insiders" than with the "outsiders." Those without the privilege of private space are not considered important enough to need a door or the option of privacy. Important assumptions are attributed to this nonverbal communication concerning factors such as trust and importance of function.

Taking privacy away is often perceived as a territorial violation. If inadvertent, the trespasser may not understand why such tension has been created. Such a case occurred when a group of filing clerks were moved to a new work space shared by another group of workers. They were used to their own private environment and thus suffered decreased morale and productivity and increased errors and turnover. Intentional territory violations are sometimes used by "aware" supervisors as a form of punishment. While collective bargaining was in process, a group of workers engaged in a work slowdown procedure including much longer breaks than formally allowed. When supervisors started policing the break area to enforce the standard time allowable, the workers began to spend much longer periods of time in the rest rooms with reading material. Management's reaction to this ploy was to remove the doors from the toilet stalls. Although effective in shortening rest room breaks, this action brought a much greater response than anticipated from the workers. When a space is designed for activities close to our bodies, we value its privacy all the more. A related example that supports the common acceptance of this aspect of privacy as associated with status is the usual assignment of rest room space. Top executives often have rest rooms within their own offices. Managers have shared, but private, rest rooms in the hallways, which may be locked and made private. Workers usually share a common rest room area designed to be public and serve many at one time.

Higher Is Better than Lower. Remember the childhood game "King of the Mountain"? We have all probably played a version of this game at one time or another, with the objective of being higher up in space than others. As adults, we play the same game but of a much more serious nature. The wealthy people are called the "upper class," and the poor are the "lower class." As we advance, we "climb *up* the organizational ladder." The executive offices are usually on the top floor, and the work area is on the bottom floor. If you're higher than others, you "look down" on them. Although there are specific exceptions, in general it is a sign of higher status to occupy higher territorial space than others.

Knowledge of this form of nonverbal space communication can be helpful in assigning space to organization members in a fashion congruent with their expectations. It can also be helpful in interpersonal situations when you might appear to be talking down to someone if you remain standing over them when they are seated. You can probably think of several more applications.

Near Is Better than Far.   It is usually a sign of higher status to be assigned space close to the top executive rather than space far away. Being near the boss allows for more exposure and the chance of being noticed. It also allows for increased interaction potential and more opportunities for being in on important information and decisions. The territory assignment itself, being formally situated close to the boss, is a sign of importance.

This principle sometimes works in reverse. If, for example, you don't like the boss, or if you're trying to catch up on some work before you are noticed, being located far away may be more desirable than being near. Even if you like the increased status of being assigned space near the boss, it is a mixed blessing. It is an opportunity for recognition and advancement but also a responsibility always to appear on top of everything and to cope with the associated pressures.

One common procedure for using space to communicate rank is through the assignment of parking spaces. The lowest-ranked employees may not even have a parking area available but have to use public streets or pay for parking outside. Those with a little more status usually have access to the company parking lot, and their cars are designated by a "hunter's permit" that allows them to find a space on a first come, first served basis. Upper-level managers and executives have their own private area and usually specially designed spaces with their names on them.

At a large, urban, state-supported university where one of the authors was once employed, lip service was paid to the importance of the students in the educational community, but the nonverbal communications told another story. Although administrators and faculty had access to either faculty/staff parking lots or private spaces according to status differentials, students had no formally designated parking area on campus. They had to compete for metered lots and public street parking or ride the university bus from their formally assigned parking lot, which was located five miles from campus. The author is now associated with a private university that also expounds on the importance of the student in its educational community. In this case, for philosophical and financial reasons, the importance of and respect for students is real, and space assignments communicate a congruent message. Only one type of parking permit is issued, and faculty and students share the parking facilities equally.

In Is Better than Out. This principle is closely related to the concept of near being better than far. The difference is one of a fixed boundary versus a matter of degree. Higher status people are usually located within the main office building; but within that building, additional differences in rank are indicated by nearness to the boss, which floor you're on, and how much space your office has.

People are usually more satisfied and productive if they are working within their own office or work area than when they are required to work in an unfamiliar area. This phenomenon is similar to sports teams that usually prefer to perform on their own turf than to have to adjust to an area "owned" by their opponents.

THINGS

The kinds of things that are in your assigned territory also communicate meaning about your status in the organization. Just as the various aspects of space interact to present combined status communications (e.g., a small but private office near the boss), so do the type and use of things within our space. Several commonly accepted generalities about the value of different aspects of things are mentioned next.

Bigger Is Better than Smaller. Higher-level executives usually have larger desks and larger pieces of furniture in their larger offices than lower-ranking managers. The president of a company often drives a Cadillac or Continental, whereas the vice-presidents drive Buicks or Oldsmobiles, and managers are allowed the use of Chevrolets and Fords from the car pool when needed for business engagements.

More Is Better than Few.   Top executives often have two offices, two secretaries, two telephones, and more furniture and decorations in their offices than their lower-ranking associates. Higher-ranking organization members also usually have access to more privileges, such as club memberships, expense accounts, and dining facilities. Not only do they have more things assigned for their own private use, but they also usually have access to the facilities made available for their underlings.

Clean Is Better than Dirty.   Maintenance people have the responsibility for daily cleanings of executive offices, whereas shop workers usually have to keep their areas clean themselves. On the other hand, administrators are expected to maintain a clean and neat appearance, but the workers in the plant may be able to wear their work clothes several days before changing.

Neat Is Better than Messy.   Most high-ranking officials have neat and orderly desks, at least in their public offices where they meet with others. A clean desk communicates efficiency, whereas a messy one indicates disorganization and confusion. Clean and neat reception areas communicate that the organization cares enough about its visitors to keep their environment pleasant. The same message is communicated by the condition of visitors' rest rooms and dining areas.

Expensive Is Better than Cheap.   This is a truism, or expensive things wouldn't be that way in the first place. It is evidenced every day in the kind of clothes people wear, the furniture in offices, the cars we drive, and the food we eat. Although in some subcultures, "economical" may be of value, "expensive" is usually the signal of status in organizations.

Very Old or Very New Are Better than Recent.   Offices furnished with antiques or modern types of furniture are usually more impressive than those with contemporary furniture. The same is true of antique automobiles and brand new ones versus those three to five years old.

Personal Is Better than Public. Your own personal desk or chair is a sign of status when others have to compete for public facilities. The same is true of your own versus company-provided trophies, pens, photographs, and other decorations. Finally, expense accounts and other special funds assigned exclusively to you are of higher status than those that must be shared with others.

USING TERRITORY AND ENVIRONMENT TO FACILITATE COMMUNICATION

Based on the preceding discussion, there are several ways to utilize feelings about territory and environment to facilitate communication and relationships. It is always best, for example, to arrange for meetings in an attractive location so that participants will feel comfortable and important. If they enjoy their surroundings, they will probably have more desire to continue their activities and do a good job worthy of the setting. The meeting place should, of course, be a neutral location so that territorial problems won't intimidate those meeting on another's turf. Finally, flexible seating should be encouraged to allow participants to establish their own *semifixed* territories and appropriate spatial arrangements.

If a supervisor wants to establish more intimacy in relationships with subordinates, it sometimes helps to have one-to-one meetings in subordinates' offices or in a neutral place. The supervisor should also apply appropriate body language during the conversation. Standing or leaning over someone who is seated conveys power and can be intimidating and uncomfortable for the person sitting. On the other hand, leaning back and appearing too casual can also convey a feeling of superiority and create a negative reaction in the subordinate.

The way you arrange your office furniture communicates the degree of formality you wish to maintain in your interactions with visitors. If your chair is behind your desk, which creates a barrier between you and your visitors, the outcome will probably be relatively short and formal interactions. A chair closer to the visitor, without the barrier of a desk, creates a much more informal and relaxed atmosphere, which encourages longer and more open interactions.

PERSONAL SPACE

Another aspect of space that we use to communicate to others is air space around us personally. We assume that this is our personal territory, much like a private air bubble. We feel a proprietary right to this space and resent others entering it unless they are invited. The exact dimensions of these private bubbles vary from culture to culture and with different personality styles, but some generalities can be useful in helping us receive and send messages more clearly through the use of this medium. How many times have you sat next to a stranger on an airplane or in a movie theater and jockeyed for the single armrest between you? Since touching is definitely a personal space violation in our culture, the more aggressive person who is not afraid of touching someone usually wins the territory.

INTERPERSONAL SPACE

Research in proxemics has revealed that adult American business people have four basic distances of interaction. These are defined next and are illustrated in Figure 11-1.

  1. **Intimate Zone**—*ranges from actual physical contact to about two feet.*
  2. **Personal Zone**—*ranges from approximately two feet to four feet in distance.*
  3. **Social Zone**—*extends from nearly four feet to roughly twelve feet.*
  4. **Public Zone**—*stretches from twelve feet away to the limits of hearing and sight.*

People are not necessarily conscious of the importance of

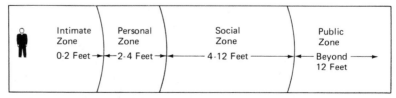

Figure 11-1 Proxemic Zones

186

maintaining these distances until violations occur. This can easily lead to increased tension and distrust.

How you feel about people entering these different zones depends upon who they are. You might feel quite uncomfortable and resentful if a business associate entered your Intimate or Personal Zone during a conversation. If the person were your spouse, however, you would probably feel quite good, even if he or she were so close as to touch you. Manager–subordinate relationships usually begin in the Social Zone of four to twelve feet, although they often move to the Personal Zone over time after a trust bond has been built.

People can generally be classified into two major proxemic categories—*contact* and *noncontact*. According to Edward Hall, Americans and Northern Europeans typify the noncontact group due to the small amount of touching that takes place during their transactions. On the other hand, Arabs and Latins normally use much contact in their conversations. In addition, although Americans are considered a noncontact group in general, there are obviously significant numbers of Americans who are "contact" people.

When these two major patterns of proxemic behavior meet, their interaction normally ends in a clash. The contact people unknowingly get too close or touch the noncontact people. This leads to discomfort, tension, distrust, and misunderstanding between the two. A commonly used example is that of the South American and North American businessmen interacting at a cocktail party. For the South American, the appropriate zone for interaction was Personal to Intimate and included frequent touching to make a point. This was about half the distance minus touch that the North American needed to be in his comfortable Social Zone. The South American would step closer, and the North American backward, in a strange proxemic dance until both gave up the relationship as a lost cause because of the other's "cold" or "pushy" behavior.

Contact and noncontact people have conflicting perceptions of each other based solely on their proxemic behavior. The noncontact people are seen as shy, cold, and impolite by the contact people. On the other hand, noncontact people perceive contact people as pushy, aggressive, and impolite. Often people are bewildered by interactions with other persons displaying different proxemic behaviors. When a proxemic violation occurs, a person generally has a feeling that something is not right but may not be able to focus directly on the cause. Attention usually focuses on the other person and why the other person is not behaving in the "proper" manner. Attention may even be focused on yourself, causing you to become self-conscious. In either case, attention shifts to the behavior of the two transactions and away from the conversation at hand and interferes with effective communication.

Most business relationships are impersonal and begin at a social distance. After the supervisory relationship has been established and trust is developed, the distance will usually decrease, and interactions will take place in the Personal Zone without any discomfort for either party. Even within the North American business culture, however, proxemic violations occur because of the different personality styles of the participants. A warm Amiable or Expressive executive who feels comfortable touching the arm or shoulder of an Analytical or Driver subordinate, for example, may create considerable discomfort for the latter. Again, the keys are being able to read the styles of others and behavioral flexibility.

INTERPERSONAL SPACE STRATEGIES

Because we become uncomfortable when someone violates our personal space, we develop specific behaviors to reduce tension and protect ourselves from further invasion. Charles and Marie Dalton have summarized several interpersonal space strategies. Perhaps the most commonly used strategy is simply to move away and create a greater distance until the intruder is in a more comfortable zone. Other strategies include avoiding eye contact or placing an object between yourself and the other person, such as a footstool, your leg, or an elbow. The most comfortable position for any given conversation will depend upon the nature of the other person and the situation.

Dyad Arrangements. When two people, or a *dyad*, are interacting in a *casual* conversation in which both feel at ease with the topic and each other, a *corner-to-corner* arrangement is often preferred. As illustrated in Figure 11-2, this position allows for unlimited eye contact and maximum use of other

Figure 11-2 Corner-to-Corner Seating Position

nonverbal signals such as facial expressions and gestures. *Side-by-side* seating arrangements are often preferred for cooperative task interactions where both parties intend to concentrate mainly on the work they are doing. As illustrated in Figure 11-3, the reading of nonverbal expressions is difficult in this position, and the physical proximity is closer than usually tolerated. Because the participants are concentrating on the task and intend to cooperate with each other, the associated

Figure 11-3 Side-by-Side Seating Position

Figure 11-4 Competitive Seating Position

assumed trust makes these disadvantages tolerable for the task at hand.

Figure 11-4 illustrates the across-the-table arrangement, which is sometimes used for casual conversations but is almost always used for *competitive* situations. It permits close monitoring of nonverbal clues and provides the safety of a barrier between the participants.

When participants are in the same location but are working independently, the *co-action* position illustrated in Figure 11-5

Figure 11-5 Co-Action Seating Position

is preferable. It provides a kind of privacy within semifixed boundaries for shutting the other person out so that one can be alone with the work.

Group Arrangements.   We have just seen how the nature of the interaction affects the positions of participants. Although more complex, the same type of phenomenon operates within groups and affects things like the communication pattern, leadership, and quality of the decisions.

Leaders usually sit at the end of a table, which is a position conducive to active participation no matter who occupies it. As can be determined in Figure 11-6, the individual at the end of the table probably has high status in the group and will tend to be the most active participant. Since more communication will be sent in his or her direction, this individual will be more influential in any decision that is made and will probably enjoy the discussion more than those seated at the sides of the table. A formal leader usually will assume a position at the head of the table. In a group of "equals," the person occupying that position has the best chance of becoming the most influential person because of the advantages in giving and receiving both verbal and nonverbal communications.

To balance the influence of a dominant leader, other group

Figure 11-6 Group with Dominant Leader Seating Arrangement

members sometimes bunch together, as illustrated in Figure 11-7. Although this grouping is most often an unconscious reaction, it does allow for easier reading of nonverbal clues between the leader and other group members. It explains the usual void of bodies in the chairs immediately adjacent to formal leaders when formal meetings are held.

Research has also provided several other interesting points about individual location in group situations. Conflict is more likely, for example, between people sitting opposite each other. Also, when a person stops talking, someone across the table is more likely to pick up the conversation than someone sitting on the side. Side-by-side conversations are often attempted to pool power or gain support before making a verbal commitment.

SPECIAL ARRANGEMENT DETERMINANTS

Many factors are involved in determining the special arrangements between people in dyads or groups. Among them are angle of approach, personality, previous relationship, race, and sex.

Figure 11-7 Seating Arrangement Balancing Dominant Leader

Angle of Approach. Women tend to permit closer approaches at the sides than at the front. This is in contrast to men, who permit others to approach closer frontally than from the sides before becoming uncomfortable. Women also use the side-by-side seating arrangement when talking to others more than men, and they are more prone to talk to others seated next to them during group discussions. Also, as a passing note, women seem to be more comfortable with the closer physical presence of others, in general, than men.

Personality. As mentioned earlier, Amiables and Expressives prefer closer interpersonal spaces than do Drivers and Analyticals. Similar findings apply to extroverts, who prefer closer interpersonal distances than do introverts. Also, individuals who feel that they have control over their lives like closer distances to others than do people who feel that their lives are controlled externally. With respect to learning style, Accommodators and Divergers prefer working closely with others, whereas Convergers and Assimilators prefer distance and minimal contact. Finally, with respect to decision-making situations, Flexibles and Integratives are better at working closely with others, as opposed to Decisives and Hierarchics, who would prefer to keep their distance and not interact at all (except maybe over the phone) if possible.

Previous Relationships. People who have interacted successfully with each other in the past prefer closer distances than individuals who do not feel comfortable with each other. The same is true for people who are attracted to each other or desire to communicate positive feelings to one another, as opposed to those who are indifferent or hostile to each other.

Race. In general, people prefer greater distances between themselves and others of different races than others of the same race. When people of the same race are interacting, black females prefer more intimate distances, followed by black males, then white females, and finally white males, who like the most distant positions from each other.

Sex. It should come as no surprise that men and women like to be closer to others of the opposite sex than to others of the same sex. When interacting with members of the same sex, however, females are capable of tolerating less space between each other than males are comfortable with when interacting with other males. Research has demonstrated that male employees permit female supervisors to get closer to them than male supervisors. For female employees, on the other hand, there was no difference in the space they permitted between themselves and their supervisors, whether female or male.

IMPLICATIONS FOR
INTERACTIVE MANAGEMENT

By watching your own behavior and checking your feelings to see how you use your own space and react to others who behave differently, you can learn a lot about what the use of personal space means to you. You can become more skillful at communicating what you mean to others and at understanding what they mean in return.

If the *manager* violates a subordinate's proxemic zones without verbal or nonverbal invitation, it most likely will lead to an increased tension level and a decreased trust level. The supervisory relationship is then likely to become nonproductive, with little or no cooperation. In attempting to establish a trust bond, you must be careful not to offend your subordinates by intruding on their proxemic zones or territory. They value their privacy and do not appreciate clumsy attempts to invade it. There are dire consequences for managers who are insensitive to the proxemic rules of behavior: an increase in tension, a decrease in trust, a decrease in the manager's credibility, and a lesser chance of gaining commitment.

You can use the concepts of proxemics to further the trust bond with your subordinates. The supervisory process can be viewed as initially meeting your subordinate face to face at a social distance and slowly moving 180 degrees to a side-by-side personal distance. Care should be exercised in not moving too fast (increasing tension) or too slow (refusing your subordinate's invitation). The interactive manager respects, understands, and effectively utilizes the concepts of proxemics. The net result is more attention, more trust, better communication, and a better chance for a productive supervisory relationship.

REFERENCES

ALESSANDRA, A. J., "Body Language," Chapter 8 in *Non-Manipulative Selling* (San Diego, Calif.: Courseware, 1979), pp. 95–118.

ATHOS, A. G., and GABARRO, J. J., "Communication: The Use of Time, Space, and Things," Chapter 1 in *Interpersonal Behavior: Communication and Understanding in Relationships* (Englewood Cliffs, N.J.: Prentice-Hall, 1978), pp. 7–22.

DALTON, C., and DALTON, M., "Personal Communications: The Space Factor," *Machine Design* (September 23, 1976), pp. 94–98.

HALL, E. J., *The Silent Dimension* (New York: Doubleday, 1959).

HALL, E. J., *The Hidden Dimension* (New York: Doubleday, 1966).

12

How Your Use of Time Talks

How do you feel when you are kept waiting for an appointment to discuss something with your boss? When a colleague or subordinate is chronically late to meetings? When someone arrives early for a meeting with you? When you are asked to work overtime during the weekend? When your boss stops talking with you as much as usual and begins spending more time with a colleague?

The foregoing examples are meant to demonstrate that how we use time communicates things to people about how we feel about them—especially feelings of liking, importance, and status. Time is a continuous and irreversible scarce resource. Consequently, who you give it to, how much you give, and when you give it are important variables in communicating your feelings to others.

Professor Anthony Athos has identified *accuracy*, *scarcity*, and *repetition* as three major variables that we use to assign meaning to time. Although the rules about how time is used, with respect to these three variables, vary from one situation to another, our use of time to communicate would make a lot of noise if "talking" with time were audible.

ACCURACY

Our concern for time accuracy is enormous. Watches are advertised as not being more than a few seconds off a year, and we literally strap them to our bodies so that we can know *exactly* what time it is and be sure to keep on schedule. Because of our concern for accuracy, the way we use time communicates things to other people.

Think back to your first date. Many men probably arrived quite a bit early and drove around the block for a while so as not to communicate their eagerness. It would not be unusual for a woman, on the other hand, to wait in her room for a few minutes after her date arrived in order to mask her anxiety. If either party had been very late, however, an explanation would have been in order to erase the assumption of indifference. Similarly, it is not uncommon for a manager to assume that a subordinate who is frequently late to department meetings doesn't care, and that manager may well get angry as a result. Subordinates also tend to assume that managers who are late to meetings don't care very much. Consequently, how accurate we are with time often "tells" about caring, whether accurately or not.

Time can also be used to tell how we feel about others in terms of their relative status and power. If the president of the company calls a junior manager to her office for a meeting, the manager will probably arrive well before the appointed time. Because of the difference in status, most managers would probably feel that any inconvenience in waiting ought to be theirs. The president's time is assumed to be worth more and, therefore, is not to be wasted, as opposed to the less expensive time of others.

Time use is also a mechanism for defining relationships. If two managers of equal status are very competitive, one might try to structure the other's time in order to demonstrate greater status and power. Assume that one manager calls the other and asks him to come to his office for a meeting later that morning. First, the initiation indicates a higher status. Second, specifying the place and time diminishes the other's influence. Third, the immediacy of the intended meeting implies that the other has nothing more important to do. If he agrees, the chances are high that the second manager will not arrive for the meeting exactly at the agreed-upon time. He will probably be slightly late and offer no apology. This is enough to irritate his colleague but not enough to comprise an open insult. The silent message is: "Now we've each got one put-down. My time is equal to yours, and I am at least equal to you."

Using time to manipulate or control others is common, although we are not usually aware of it, whether we are on the initiating or the receiving end. When we allow others to structure our time, it is usually in deference to their relative greater status or power. This is especially true when we would rather be doing something else. Private time is becoming more and more valued, as evidenced in the growing reluctance to work overtime in the evening or on weekends.

The longer we keep people waiting, the worse they are likely to feel. Imagine a middle manager who has been summoned to a meeting with the president at 1:00 P.M. and arrives at a "respectful" 12:50. He remains comfortable until 1:10, when he asks the secretary to remind the president that he is there. If the secretary checks and conveys that the president will be right with him, the manager will probably remain comfortable until around 1:25. By 1:45, however, he is likely to be quite angry and assume that the president doesn't really care about seeing him. If the president then has the manager sent in and proceeds directly to the business at hand without offering an explanation, the manager may appear—and act—cranky and irritable. This may negatively affect the meeting and the relationship. If the president apologizes for being late and shares some inside information with her explanation, the manager is more apt to forgive the boss because, after all, her time is more important.

In general, the longer a person is kept waiting, the more "stroking" is required to neutralize the collection of brown stamps. Awareness of this process can help you understand your feelings better when you are the person who is waiting and can increase your skill at helping others not feel put down when they have to wait for you because of some legitimate commitment. Speaking our intentions and checking our assumptions about the use of time can contribute to more productive and satisfactory relationships.

SCARCITY

Time and money are both limited resources for most of us. Just as what we spend our money on tells others what we value, who we spend our time with tells people things about how we feel toward them. Because we forego some option when we choose to spend our time with someone, it is a signal of our sentiments and what we think is important.

Sociologists have discovered that liking increases with increases in frequency of interaction, although you can probably think of several exceptions. On the other hand, people may read withdrawal or decreases in frequency as an indication of decreased liking; again, however, there may be a more relevant alternative explanation, such as your necessary involvement in another very important activity that has no bearing on the other person whatsoever. These reactions may be especially true of your own subordinates, who probably read your use of time more carefully than you know. Problems arise when their interpretations are incorrect or differ with respect to who, or what, is important.

You may, for example, find that you need to spend a larger amount of time than usual with a particular subordinate because of a new procedure or special problem in the area in which he is working. If this causes your time with other subordinates to be temporarily reduced, this may cause them to feel that you care more about what the first subordinate is doing and may come to care more about him than them.

The "cost" of your time varies from moment to moment, depending on how much you have to do and how much time you have to do it in. Communications may be strained, for example, when you are in a big hurry to complete a report and a subordinate drops in to chat for a while. If, on the other hand, the time being spent has approximately the same value for both participants (e.g., neither has anything else better to do), the chat will probably lack this stress. This type of tension can contribute to a deterioration in your relationship if read as noncaring, or: "You're not OK, and I don't want to waste my time with you." The tension can sometimes be avoided by explaining your situation and why you're in a hurry. It also helps to make a date in the future to make up the time if necessary.

In general, since time is viewed as a scarce resource, who we spend it with is often taken as a signal of who we care about. Being aware of this can help you build more productive relationships by simply stating out loud what the meaning is for you of spending your time as you do. It can help others from jumping to the wrong conclusions and prevent you from having your own feelings hurt because you have responded to conditioned reactions without checking out your automatic assumptions.

REPETITION

Time also has meaning for us in its repetition of activities. Most of us become irritated when someone interrupts a pattern to which we have become accustomed. Examples are having to miss a customary 10:00 A.M. coffee break or having to work late and miss dinner with your family.

How we use and feel about the seasons of the year—another pattern of time—also varies. People become accustomed to certain activities and feelings associated with different seasons and holidays. Christmas, for example, is usually thought of as a time set aside for ritual, being with friends and family, and expressing warmth and affection. Usually there is less work done during the Christmas holidays, and trying to get subordinates to work overtime during this season can be deeply resented.

Any disruption of established patterns of activities will be experienced as a deprivation, and if you are perceived as the source of the disruption, hostile feelings will be directed your way. Consequently, care should be used when planning changes in work load, especially during holiday seasons. You should also use your questioning skills to determine unique individual patterns and expectations.

Because our use of time is such an expressive language, being aware of its meanings can facilitate our communications and relationships with others. This is especially true for managers because of the tendencies of subordinates to watch them intensely for nonverbal feedback. Being accurate and openly stating the reasons for our use of time can go a long way in avoiding misunderstandings and building more trusting and productive relationships.

REFERENCES

ATHOS, A. G., and GABARRO, J. J., "Communication: The Use of Time, Space, and Things," Chapter 1 in *Interpersonal Behavior: Communication and Understanding in Relationships* (Englewood Cliffs, N.J.: Prentice-Hall, 1978), pp. 7–22.

13

Making Sure
with Feedback

Quickly jot down what you feel would be meant if someone said the following to you:

"In a little while."
"I'll be there in a minute."
"It isn't very far."
"We've got to get together socially sometime."
"I need it quickly."
"I want you to do a good job."
"We'll provide you with a small number of these at no cost."
"We need to communicate better."
"I wish every man had long hair."
"That will cost a lot of money."
"Call me later and we'll discuss it."

You have probably already come to realize that most, if not all, of these statements are highly ambiguous. When used in normal conversation, there is a very high probability that these statements will be misinterpreted unless they are fully clarified. For instance, when a person says: "Call me later and we'll discuss it," do they mean fifteen minutes from now, one hour from now, tomorrow, or next week? Additionally, when a person says: "I wish every man had long hair," does she mean covering the ears, to the collar, past the collar, or even to the waist? All of these statements, in addition to millions of others not mentioned here, can have unlimited meaning. They create a high probability of misunderstanding in communication. Unfortunately, we use these statements in everyday conversation and expect the other person to understand clearly what we say. The same is true when other people are communicating with us. Unless statements such as these are clarified and confirmed between the two communicating parties, there is great likelihood that the statement will be miscommunicated, that the directions and instructions will not be followed according to the supposed agreement, and that the relationship between the parties will be further strained. Through the simple use of feedback skills, these highly ambiguous statements can be transformed into very specific, effective communications.

The use of feedback in communication is very often taken for granted. In the management process, no other communication activity is so widely used yet so misunderstood. Feedback may be the most important aspect of interpersonal communications if conversation is to continue for any length of time and still have meaning for the parties involved. If there wasn't feedback, how would each person "really" know what the other person was talking about and communicating? In conversations with your employees, your fellow managers, and your superiors, how often have you felt like saying: "I know you think you understand what I said, but I'm not so sure that what you heard is what I meant"? The effective use of feedback skills helps reduce the probability of this type of misinterpretation and misunderstanding.

One of the authors recently went to the post office to mail a package COD. When he arrived at the post office window and explained to the postal clerk what he wanted to mail and how he wanted to mail it, the postal clerk began filling out the COD form. This required the clerk to ask a number of specific questions, the answers of which were put down on the COD form. The beginning was easy. The name and address of the sender and the name and address of the receiver posed no difficulty for either party. The problem arose when the postal clerk said, "How much is this item worth?" The immediate answer was $79.50. So the clerk went about filling in the rest of the spaces on the COD form and about two minutes later was in the process of explaining how the COD process worked and when and how much he would be receiving from the person to whom the package was being sent. When the postal clerk mentioned that the author would receive $79.50, the author promptly replied, "I'm only charging the recipient of this package $59.50." With that, the postal clerk became irate. He stated: "You told me it was $79.50, and that's what I filled in on all the blanks. Now you tell me it's $59.50. Which one is it? Can't you make up your mind?" Rather than being pulled further into the argument, the author realized what was happening and why and tried to clarify the misinterpretation. He explained to the clerk that when he asked how much it was worth, that was a very ambiguous question. The item was in fact worth $79.50. That was its typical retail price. However, in this specific case, the recipient was being charged $59.50. In a situation like this one, both participants should take responsibility for the misunderstanding. The postal clerk asked a question that was rather ambiguous and could be answered correctly in more than one way. The author should also accept part of the blame; he should have used the feedback we are talking about now and asked the postal clerk specifically what he meant when he asked, "What is this worth?" When trying to clarify this type of misunderstanding, it is important to avoid any judgment, criticism, or preaching in vocal intonation or body language. The net result can be a mini-lesson in communication for both parties. Effective two-way communication is never a destination; it is always a journey. It must constantly be worked on by everyone—novices and experts alike.

Whenever you verbally, vocally, or visibly react to what another person says or does, or seek a reaction from another person to what you say or do, you are using feedback. Effective two-way communication depends on it. This chapter explores the feedback skills you can use to communicate effectively and clearly with your employees.

TYPES OF FEEDBACK

Feedback comes in a number of forms. There is verbal feedback, nonverbal feedback, fact feedback, and feeling feedback. Each serves a specific purpose in the communications process.

Verbal Feedback. Verbal feedback is the type we are most frequently aware of and most often use. From verbal feedback, you—as an interactive manager—can accomplish a number of very favorable objectives. First, you can use verbal feedback to ask for clarification of your employee's message. Second, you can use verbal feedback to give positive and/or negative strokes to your employees. Third, you can use verbal feedback to determine how you should structure a presentation to your employees.

By asking simple questions of your employee, you can determine whether you should keep proceeding in the same direction or modify your approach. For instance, if you think you are going a bit too fast for your employee to comprehend your message, you might simply ask: "I sometimes get carried away with my enthusiasm and move along a bit too quickly on this topic. Would it be more helpful to you if I covered these issues a bit slower?" The same can be done if you are getting the impression that you should speed up your presentation. Questions such as "Shall we explore that issue some more?" allow you to determine your employee's interest and understanding of the conversation. Answers can help you avoid capriciously cutting the topic too short or dragging it on too long. You are simply asking your employee for direction. "Would you like me to get right into the details of this job, or do you have some other questions that you'd like to ask me first?" allows you to determine your employee's present state of mind and level of receptivity. Without this information, you may get into the details of the job when, in fact, your employee does have a number of questions he would have liked to ask first. In this situation, the employee is dwelling on his questions and not paying too much attention to what you are explaining. Through questions such as the preceding, you can determine how to tailor your delivery style and presentation to fit the needs of each individual employee. Although this takes a bit more time in the short run, it saves much time in the long run, because it prevents communication problems and improves the employee's receptivity, understanding, and productivity.

Verbal feedback should also be used by managers to give positive and negative strokes to their employees. When an employee is doing something that is positive, that behavior should be positively reinforced. Simple statements are in order, such as: "You did a really good job"; "I haven't seen anybody do as thorough a job as you have on this project"; "I really trust you"; and "Keep up the good work." Specifically show the employee that you recognize and appreciate what she is doing. Given effectively and consistently, this type of feedback prompts the employee to continue performing in a positive manner. On the other hand, when an employee's behavior requires some negative feedback, it too should be given. One of the worst things you can do is ignore ineffective personal or work behavior on the part of an employee. Silence may be construed as tacit approval. Phrases such as: "Phil told me he is afraid to have you in his office because you always come on too strong with him"; "You did a sloppy job folding these"; and "You didn't complete the job when you said you would" provide the employee with the type of verbal feedback he needs to correct the ineffective behavior. To improve the accuracy and clarity of a message during a conversation, you should make an effort to describe to your employee the relevant aspects of the image in your mind, just to make sure that you understand what your employee is communicating to you. Encourage your employees to do the same with you. If your employee does not feed back your message, it is wise to ask her to do so. Make sure that each person feeds back her interpretation of the other person's message rather than the specific words the other person used.

Clarifying feedback statements typically begin as follows:

1. "Let me be sure I understand what you have said."
2. "Let me see if I can summarize the key points we've discussed."
3. "I hear you saying . . ."
4. "I think I hear you saying that your central concern is . . ."
5. "As I understand it, your major objectives are . . ."

They usually end as follows:

1. "Did I understand you properly?"
2. "Did I hear you correctly?"
3. "Was I on target with what you meant?"
4. "Were those your major concerns?"
5. "Can you add anything to my summary?"

Nonverbal Feedback. Many of us can remember when the word *vibes* was in vogue. Both good and bad vibes are a direct form of nonverbal feedback. Through the use of their bodies, eyes, faces, postures, and senses, people can communicate a variety of positive or negative attitudes, feelings, and opinions. You do this consciously or unconsciously with your employees, and they do the same with you. These are the forms of nonverbal feedback that people communicate to each other. The sensitive, perceptive communicator utilizes nonverbal feedback from the other person to structure the content and direction of a message. The subsequent outcome is a positive continuance of their interaction and increased trust and credibility in their relationship.

The *amount* of nonverbal feedback you receive and send is not as important as how you *interpret* it and react to it. It is critically important for you to realize when you are losing your employee's interest. With this sensitivity to and perception of your employee's nonverbal feedback, you can react by changing your pace, topic, or anything else that is needed to recapture your employee's attention, interest, or trust. Also be sensitive to the nonverbal feedback you are projecting to the employee. Many ineffective managers send "mixed messages" to their employees. This simply means that while they are saying one thing, they are communicating something totally different through vocal intonation and body language. These mixed messages force the employee to choose between the verbal aspect of the message and the observable aspect. Most often, they choose the nonverbal aspect of the message. When your employee receives mixed messages from you, it immediately creates tension and distrust on the part of the employee. Right or wrong, the employee feels that you are purposely hiding something or that you are being less than candid. The unfortunate thing is that many managers do not realize they are sending mixed messages. Be aware of the terrible toll that mixed messages take on your relationship with employees. Keep your nonverbal feedback and your verbal feedback in sync with each other.

In an earlier chapter on listening skills, we mentioned the process of attending. This is nothing other than projecting nonverbal feedback to the employee. It lets the employee know that his message is getting through to you, and it also lets him know how you feel about that message. People do not like to speak to others who are emotionless, who do not respond. They want feedback, and they seek feedback. You must make a concerted effort to give them that feedback, especially nonverbal forms.

Fact Feedback.   In an earlier chapter on questioning skills, we mentioned that one type was the fact-finding question. This type of question is meant to elicit specific data and information from your employees. If the facts are worth asking for *from* your employee, they are certainly worth being heard accurately. This is where fact feedback comes into play. There are also times when you are relating specific information *to* your employees. These data are important for your employees to receive as accurately as possible, and again, fact feedback can help.

When you are depending on other people's facts and they are depending on yours, it is critically important to get and give the information exactly. When you want clarification, agreement, or correction, fact feedback should be used. Fact feedback is also used in translating messages and interpreting words or phrases. The following messages contain words or phrases that are unclear. They are perfect candidates for fact feedback statements.

"Due to recent layoffs, all employees are expected to work harder from now on."
"There will be a short wait for a table."
"Don't spend too much time on that job."
"In this company, we are very liberal and democratic."
"*Major* credit cards are accepted."
"We will be visiting Philadelphia and New York City. We expect to open our first unit there."

When there is a chance for something to be misunderstood, it will be misunderstood. Use fact feedback to keep your messages clear.

Feeling Feedback.   A firm understanding and clarification of the words, phrases, and facts of your employee's message are obviously important. Without them, you two would not be speaking the same language. However, this increased accuracy in communications still only stays on the surface of the discussion. Why is your employee saying the things she is saying? What are the underlying causes and motivations behind her message and her facts? How much personal feeling does her message carry for her? How does she really feel about what she is saying to you? Does she know whether her message is really getting through to you—at the feeling level? Is she aware that you really care about what she is saying to you? All these questions underscore the importance of feeling feedback in two-way communications. Feeling feedback should be two-directional. You, as the interactive manager, should make a concerted effort to understand the feelings, emotions, and attitudes that underlie your employee's message. In addition, you should project feeling feedback to your employee to let her know that her message has gotten through to you—at the gut level. Fact feedback is simply a meeting of the minds, whereas feeling feedback is a meeting of the hearts. Feeling feedback is nothing more than the effective use of empathy. That is, putting yourself into your employee's shoes so that you can see things from her point of view. When you can really experience your employee's true feelings and understand where she's coming from and at the same time project this emotional awareness to your employee, it serves to reinforce rapport, lower interpersonal tension, and significantly increase trust. Probing questions, supportive and understanding responses, and an awareness and projection of appropriate nonverbal signals are the key tools used in sending and receiving feeling feedback. Until you and your employee really know how each other truly feels, the "facts" don't matter at all. Improve the accuracy of communications through fact feedback—and improve the rapport of your relationships by practicing empathy through feeling feedback.

USING FEEDBACK EFFECTIVELY

If you took a few moments and really thought about it, you could probably recall numerous times you could have smoothed over some problems in communications simply by using some of the forms of feedback that we have discussed. Effective communication between two people is not easy. You really have to practice to make it work. The proper use of questioning skills helps. Utilizing active listening helps. Sensitivity to nonverbal behavior helps. But without feedback, all of these skills are for naught. Through effective use of feedback skills, you can create a good communications climate. The following guidelines will help you use your feedback skills effectively.

Give and Get Definitions. Tony grew up in the Northeast. When he went away to college in the Midwest, he got his first taste of communication difficulties. Shortly after arriving in Indiana, he went into a coffee shop to get something to eat and drink. He ordered a sandwich and a cherry soda. When his order arrived, he received the sandwich as expected, but his beverage had a scoop of ice cream in it. Tony told the waitress that he didn't order an ice cream soda and asked her to take it back and bring him a cherry soda. The waitress insisted that was, in fact, a cherry soda. Tony disagreed. The waitress was insistent on her definition. So was Tony. Tensions rose and tempers flared. Tony learned a good lesson in communications. Even in the United States, across regions the same word may have different meanings. In the New York City area, when someone orders a cherry soda, he receives carbonated water with cherry syrup. However, in the Midwest, when somebody orders a soda, he gets it with a scoop of ice cream. Both Tony and the waitress were right and wrong at the same time. They could have circumvented the entire problem by simply giving and getting definitions.

Interpretation of words or phrases may vary from person to person, group to group, region to region, or society to society. When people believe or assume that words are used for one and only one meaning, they create situations in which they pretend to understand others but really do not. The words you use in everyday conversations almost inevitably have multiple meanings. In fact, the 500 most commonly used words in our language have more than 14,000 dictionary definitions. For instance, "a person is considered 'fast' when he can run rather quickly. However, when one is tied down and cannot move at all, he is also considered 'fast.' 'Fast' also relates to periods of noneating, a ship's mooring line, a race track in good running condition, and a person who hangs around with the 'wrong' crowd of people. In addition, photographic film is 'fast' when it is sensitive to light. On the other hand, bacteria are 'fast' when they are insensitive to antiseptics."*

* William V. Haney, *Communication and Organizational Behavior, Text and Cases,* rev. ed. (Homewood, Ill.: Richard D. Irwin, Inc., 1967), p. 223.

The abundance of meanings of even "simple" words prompts managers to assume (or pretend) that they understand the true meaning of the employee's communication when, in fact, they do not. This eventually leads to subsequent misunderstandings, breakdowns in the communications process, and decreased trust. Therefore, during the process of questioning and listening, use feedback. Give and get definitions.

Don't Assume. Making assumptions invariably gets you into trouble. During interpersonal communications, it is highly dangerous to make the assumption that the other person either thinks or feels as you do at that moment. The other person may have a frame of reference that is totally different from your own. She reacts and perceives according to what she knows and believes to be true, and that may be very different from your reactions, perceptions, and beliefs. Do not assume anything in communications. If you do, you stand a very good chance of being incorrect. Don't assume that you and the other person are talking about the same thing. Don't assume that the words and phrases you are both using are automatically being understood. The classic phrase of people who make assumptions is: "I know exactly what you mean." People usually use that statement without ever using feedback skills to determine exactly what the other person means.

Use more feedback and fewer assumptions, and you'll be happier and more accurate in your interpersonal communications.

Ask Questions. Questions have many uses. We've discussed a number of these in Chapter 6. Remember to use questions to test for feedback. A good rule of thumb is: "When in doubt, check it out." One of the best ways to check it out is through the effective use of questioning skills. Clarifying questions, echo questions, continuing questions, fact-finding questions, feeling-finding questions, and open questions should be used freely during conversation to test for feedback.

Speak the Same Language. Abstain from using words that can easily be misinterpreted or mistranslated, especially technical terms and company jargon. These terms, which are so familiar to you, may be totally foreign to the people with whom you talk. Simplify your language and your technical terms so that every one of your employees can understand you, even though you might think they do or should know what the terms mean.

Keep Tuned In. Constantly be on the lookout for and recognize those nonverbal signals that indicate that your line of approach is causing your employees to become uncomfortable and lose interest. When this happens, change your approach and your message accordingly. This fact was stated earlier, but it is so important that it cannot be repeated too often. Observe the other person. Be sensitive to the feelings they are experiencing during your interaction; above all else, respond to those feelings appropriately.

Give Feedback on the Behavior, Not the Person. This relates to the appropriate use of positive and negative strokes with your employees. When they do something especially well, give them positive feedback, and relate it specifically to the action or behavior that was performed. When they do something especially bad, give them negative feedback specifically directed toward the action or behavior that you would like corrected. Do not under any circumstances criticize your employee personally because of an inappropriate action or behavior. This is not only degrading but also counterproductive. Many ineffective managers, upon learning that one of their employees has done something wrong, criticize that employee personally: "You're an idiot"; "That was really stupid"; "You can't do anything right, can you?" These statements constitute inappropriate feedback. After a while, the employee starts believing these statements, and they become a self-fulfilling prophecy. How can an employee improve performance on a particular task or behavior unless he knows specifically what behaviors or actions he must improve? Therefore, direct your praise and punishment specifically toward your employee's behavior and actions, not toward the employee personally.

Withholding Feedback. There are times when it's best not to give feedback. You should bite your tongue and restrain your body language and facial expressions in these situations. A few months ago, one of the authors was visiting a married couple. While waiting for the husband to finish getting dressed for an appointment, the author was chatting with the wife in the dining room. All of a sudden, the husband came into the dining room in what appeared to be a huff. In a loud and harsh vocal intonation, he asked his wife, "Where did you get this shirt cleaned?!" While "asking" this assertion, he was shaking the collar of the shirt and seemed to be peering at his wife. My initial interpretation of this occurrence was that the husband was rather upset about the condition of his shirt. Most spouses would tend to act rather defensively, and some would even counterattack. His spouse was rather expert in withholding inappropriate feedback while at the same time asking for feedback. In a gentle voice with no disturbing body language, she simply told her husband: "I got it done at XYZ Cleaners. Why do you ask?" His reply almost floored me. He said it was the first time that any cleaners had done his shirt properly. He told his wife she should always take his shirts to that specific cleaners from now on. As you can see, there are times when it is best to withhold inappropriate feedback until you utilize effective feedback to clarify the intent of another person's message.

Feedback can reduce interpersonal tension and create a sense of trust and credibility between you and your employee if used properly. Use feedback to let yourself know when you uncover a very important need or problem of an employee. Use feedback to clarify your employee's needs so that there is no misunderstanding. Use feedback to improve your relationship with your employee by letting each other know what is going on in the relationship. Most of all, use feedback to improve your part of the conversation. Through feedback, you can determine which areas to spend more time on and which ones need less time. Do not abuse feedback, either, because a misinterpreted nonverbal cue can cause a lot of problems. It is important to confirm all uncertain verbal, vocal, and observable cues through feedback. The proper and effective use of feedback skills should lead to improved communication with your employees. This increased sense of mutual understanding will lead to less interpersonal tension, increased trust and credibility, and higher employee productivity. Both sides win in this type of relationship—the interactive management relationship.

INTERACTIVE PROBLEM-SOLVING

Back in Chapter 1, we used a bicycle to illustrate the importance of a manager having both people knowledge and technical knowledge. Parts I and II of this book—"Understanding People" and "Interactive Communication Skills"—provided you with the "front-wheel" knowledge, the people knowledge. They provided you with the direction and sensitivity for effectively and appropriately applying the technical knowledge of interactive management. The final part of this book provides the "back-wheel" technical knowledge for implementing the interactive management problem-solving process.

The following five chapters present a step-by-step approach to the interactive management problem-solving process. In detail, we take you through the steps of defining problems, developing action plans, implementing those action plans, and tracking results. This knowledge will provide the power to drive the interactive management process. Combined with the first two parts, this final one provides you with the detailed technical information to implement the interactive management philosophy successfully. It provides the last crucial part of the "bicycle." It is now up to you to get on it and ride—effectively and successfully.

14

Problem-Solving Together

When managers are asked how they make decisions and solve problems, the typical response is usually something like: "I don't know. I just do what has to be done." Although they may not be able to specify what steps they take or what rules they apply, all would probably agree that making "good" decisions and effectively solving problems are the essence of good management. Even though they may not be aware of it, most managers proceed through fairly common processes when making decisions and solving problems. This process includes at least the following sequential steps:

1. Problem awareness
2. Problem definition
3. Finding a solution
4. Implementing the solution

How rapidly and thoroughly managers move through this process will vary depending upon their decision styles, the effectiveness of their communication skills, and the quality of their relationships with their employees. Decisives make quick decisions but often give too little thought to analyzing all the facts, considering other people's feelings, and determining the impact of specific decisions on other areas of concern. Flexibles quickly jump from one alternative to another and never seem to make a solid, lasting decision. At the other extreme are the Hierarchics, who seem to take weeks to decide. They want to look into every facet of the problem and want all the facts before making a decision. Once it's made, however, it's permanent regardless of any shortcomings that may exist. Integratives take at least as long as Hierarchics to analyze the data; worse yet, they may never make a decision because "all the facts aren't in yet," and the opportunity to take action to solve a problem passes.

The problem-solving process recommended for interactive management is an elaboration of the natural steps most managers go through—in one way or another—to make decisions anyway, albeit unconsciously. It has been improved considerably, however, by adding updated methods of problem solving and decision making currently found in most "management by objectives" (MBO) programs. It also highlights the differences between the technical and interactive approaches to managing others. The interactive management approach to problem solving is outlined in Table 14.1. Being aware of, and consistently applying, this approach can overcome most decision-style shortcomings and provide a vast improvement over the technical approach.

What goes on within the problem-solving processes spells a dramatic difference between the technical and interactive management approaches. Interactive management differs from technical management in that it stresses trust building and *centering on the employee's* real needs and problems, rather than focusing solely on organizational goals or considering employee needs only to get compliance. The rest of the chapter provides an overview of the essential differences between interactive and technical management in helping employees accomplish objectives. The following chapters detail each phase of the interactive management problem-solving process.

PROBLEM DEFINITION

At the problem definition stage, the manager and employee gather information and diagnose the current problem situation to determine if there is something the employee needs or wants

Table 14-1 Interactive Problem-Solving Process*

1. DEFINE THE PROBLEM
   a. Establish Trust Bond
   b. Clarify Objectives
   c. Assess Current Situation
   d. Identify Problems
   e. Define and Analyze Problems
   f. Agree on Problems to Be Solved
2. DEVELOP ACTION PLAN
   a. Check Trust Bond
   b. Establish Decision-Making Criteria
   c. Develop Action Alternatives
   d. Evaluate Alternatives
   e. Decide on Action Plan
3. IMPLEMENT ACTION
   a. Check Trust Bond
   b. Define Responsibilities
   c. Set Up Implementation Schedule
   d. Establish Commitment
4. FOLLOW-THROUGH
   a. Check Trust Bond
   b. Establish Criteria for Success
   c. Determine How to Measure Performance
   d. Monitor Results
   e. Take Corrective Action

*All steps are done mutually by the manager and subordinate.

that the manager can help with. In interactive management, more time is spent on information gathering and diagnosis than on any other stage in the problem-solving process. The employee's problems or needs must be fully and accurately defined and understood in order to solve them effectively and progress to a better state of affairs. The rest of the problem-solving process must evolve from a solid, accurate informational base.

In technical management, this stage is limited. Much of the time is spent in presenting the organization's goals and how the employee must adjust. Little time is spent considering employees' feelings or defining their specific needs. In fact, the technical manager often *tells* employees their needs and problems and then moves quickly into the new action-planning process. Implicit assumptions are that the employee's needs aren't important and that the manager's new action plan is always best for both the employee and the organization. Of course, many people "manage" employees' problems this way. The foundation is weak, however, and the immediate loser is the employee. The later loser is the organization. When the interactive manager spends time helping the employee identify what is really necessary for doing the job better, both the employee and the organization can become winners. There doesn't have to be a loser.

ACTION PLANNING

In interactive management, new action plans are both custom-tailored and participative. Together, the employee and the manager generate as many alternatives as possible, decide on a workable solution, and formulate a new plan that relates to the specific needs or problems previously identified by the employee. As a result, employee interest tends to be high and tends to be maintained. After all, it is the employee's problem being tackled, and it is the solution that both manager and employee have created that is being prepared for implementation. This is in contrast to the usual negative results when a "canned" technical solution is "laid on" the employee from above without the worker being involved at all.

In interactive management, the action-planning process is participative. The employee takes an active part in generating alternatives, deciding on the solution, and designing a new action plan to meet specific needs. The interactive management approach encourages the employee to talk more and the manager to listen. Being involved and actively influencing one's own future on a cooperative basis generates trust and openness in the employee–manager relationship.

The technical manager, on the other hand, enters the new action-planning process with little specific information on the employee's feelings or personal needs. Even if the employee has been asked to provide a list of needs, they may be more concerned with what the employee thinks the manager wants to hear than with what is really the source of the problem. Technical management methods usually focus on the best organization solution and assume the employee's needs will be satisfied in the process. Usually the new action-planning process is "canned," disregarding individual differences in situations and personal needs. The employee tends to tune out the manager as a result. But if the employee doesn't listen or doesn't believe the solution is in his or her best interests, the new action plan will never be implemented, or at best, it will be carried out inaccurately and halfheartedly.

IMPLEMENTATION

No matter how good the potential of a solution, unless it is implemented properly, it won't be effective. Effective implementation of an action plan depends upon commitment by those involved to make it work.

The process in interactive management begins with the development of commitment to the agreed-upon solution. It occurs in an atmosphere of mutual trust and respect as opposed to the pressure of the technical approach. With employee problems, needs, and objectives mutually identified during the first stage of the problem-solving process; with solutions arrived at mutually; with the employee totally involved—the employee's commitment to the solution should be firm at the end of the new action-planning discussions. Because of the commitment process in interactive management, solution implementation becomes "when," not "if."

FOLLOW-THROUGH

Another difference between interactive management and the technical approach occurs in the follow-through process. At this point, the manager makes a commitment to the employee to monitor and assist that employee throughout the total implementation of the new action plan. In the first phase of follow-through, the interactive manager spends a lot of time establishing ways to be sure that the new action plan really works for each particular employee.

Technical managers handle their follow-through process differently. It tends to be more of a "control" process. They "smother" their employees to make sure they are doing their job the way it "should" be done. In the follow-through process, the technical manager plays the role of a critical parent or "Big Brother." Needless to say, this approach creates high levels of tension in the employees.

Many contemporary managers are turning toward the idea of better follow-up. The interactive management approach provides ways to do it well. After all, satisfied employees are a manager's greatest asset. They support their managers and usually have high productivity compared to less satisfied employees. Dissatisfied workers bide their time at best and look for ways to "get even" if they are so disposed. Interactive management depends on long-term, trust-bond relationships, and these are best accomplished through attentive managerial follow-through. A cooperative team atmosphere of mutual help is established, and people feel that they can depend on one another.

In the following chapters, we take a more detailed look at each phase of the interactive management problem-solving process.

REFERENCES

ELBING, A., *Behavioral Decisions in Organizations*, 2nd ed. (Glenview, Ill.: Scott, Foresman, 1978).

GIEGOLD, W. C., *Management by Objectives: A Self-Instructional Approach* (New York: McGraw-Hill, 1978).

MORRISEY, G. L., *Management by Objectives and Results for Business and Industry*, 2nd ed. (Reading, Mass.: Addison-Wesley, 1977).

15

Defining
the Problem

Accurate definition of an employee's problem is easier to assume
than to make. The employee's initial statements of the problem
are often vague and confused. Frequently, the employee is
unaware of the source of the problem or may be confused and
distracted. Other times the employee may intentionally try to
avoid discussing the problem because of not wanting to appear
foolish or to take responsibility for the situation.

To help solve a problem, the manager needs to understand
it from the employee's point of view and to figure out how it
prevents the person from adequately accomplishing desirable
goals. *Both* the manager and the employee must have a clear
understanding of the problem if it is to be solved.

When you interact with your employees in a problem-
solving process, follow the steps in Figure 15-1. Each step will
bring you closer to helping the employee to identify particular
needs and problems that you can help solve. As you go through
these steps, you will be faced with opportunities to take different
approaches based on your relationship with the employee and
the employee's behavioral, decision, and learning styles. What
follows is a step-by-step approach to fulfilling the goals of the
problem definition stage of interactive management.

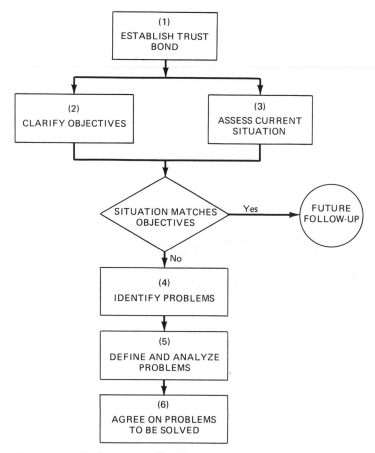

Figure 15-1 Defining the Problem

STEP 1: ESTABLISH TRUST BOND

The employee needs to feel understood and accepted and to believe that the problem can be resolved. The employee must feel secure enough in your presence to open up and discuss all aspects of how he sees the problem with you.

High trust and low tension—the name of the game in interactive management—are especially important at this point. Without all the relevant information to define the problem accurately, all remaining steps are useless.

You begin to establish trust by the initial impression you create—it should be one of confidence and interest in the employee. Think of the advice in the chapter on "image," and think of situations where you feel you made an immediate positive impression. What image factors helped? Think of a situation that seemed to have problems from the moment you came in contact with an employee. What image factors could have hindered the start of a good relationship? What vocal qualities might you have projected, and what did your body language "say" during this crucial initial stage?

Practice *flexibility*: treat employees the way they want to be treated. Establishing trust in the first stages of the problem-solving discussion is largely determined by how you interact with the "style" profiles of the employee. These initial interactions determine whether there will be a positive or negative progression in the manager–employee relationship. If you are skillful at this point, you will create the advantages of acceptance and trust. Remember, identify the employee's behavioral, learning, and decision styles; confirm them; and modify your own style preferences where they differ from those of the employee. It really isn't that hard to bite your tongue and refrain from telling the employee about the latest news story if she wants to get down to business. Nor is it impossible to listen to the employee's family vacation story for a while before getting to the meat of the problem-solving situation if doing so will help the process later. Your relationship with that employee may depend upon your "appropriate" responses. Remember the importance of good initial probes to get your employees to express thoughts and opinions and thereby to allow you to determine their style preferences more quickly.

Apply your active listening skills, too. With these, your employee immediately feels that you are listening because what is said is important. And it *is* important. Paraphrasing and clarifying as you go along not only make the employee feel understood; they also help elucidate all the ramifications of the problem situation.

With careful and skilled use of style flexibility and the communication skills, you not only establish trust but also build and maintain credibility throughout the relationship. Step 1, establishing a trust bond, is a separate step, but it uses procedures and skills that should never be put away.

As you progress through the problem-solving phases of interactive management, the first step of every process begins with checking the level of trust before you move from a previous step into the major portion of the new process. To do this, remember that in establishing and maintaining trust, you must always project to the employee—through both actions and words—that you are sincerely interested in helping solve the specific problems and in meeting the personal and professional needs of that employee.

STEP 2: CLARIFY OBJECTIVES

An objective is a desired state of affairs. It is the result you and your employee want to achieve. If you don't know what your objectives are, there is no way of knowing what your problems are. All you can conclude is that you don't know what you want to do. With most employees, in most cases, it is best to clarify your objectives first, before assessing the current situation. The reason for this is that if the situation is appraised first, there exists a very human propensity to state objectives in terms of what is already occurring. Such an approach may satisfy the required formalities, but in terms of results, it does little more than the old saying: "To be sure of hitting the target, shoot first, and whatever you shoot, call it the target."

Setting objectives accomplishes at least four purposes. First, it provides a clear, documented statement of what the employee intends to accomplish. Therefore it should be written. This way, the objective is both a form of acknowledgment and a means for commitment. Second, setting objectives establishes a basis for the *measurement* of performance in the current or future situation. Third, knowing what is expected and desired gives positive *motivation* to the employee. Finally, knowing where you're going is much more likely to allow you to get there than spinning your wheels without any direction. In other words, there is a higher probability of *better performance*.

When helping an employee set objectives, the manager should use the interactive skills of active listening, questioning, and behavioral flexibility to aid the employee in making sure that the objectives are accurately set and incorporate that person's *most important needs*. The tendency to seek approval by paraphrasing to the manager what the employee thinks the manager wants to hear should be avoided. To do this, the trust bond must be substantial, and some in-depth questions should be considered, such as the following:

"Who am I?"

"Why am I with this organization and in this job?"

"What do I want to contribute, and what do I want in return?"

The manager must also ensure that the objectives set by the individual are *supportive* of the overall organizational goals. If any real acceptance of and commitment to objectives suggested by the manager are expected, the reverse must be true also; organizational objectives must be supportive of the employee's personal goals.

Managers have the responsibility of coordinating the efforts of all subordinates. Consequently, the manager must make sure that the mutually established objectives for the employee *interlock*, or mesh, with those of other individuals who might be affected by them. In fact, to make sure that specific individual objectives do not have undesirable side effects on other employees, and also to avoid feelings of not being treated fairly with respect to other employees, it has been suggested that in some situations, the manager should conduct individual goal setting in team meetings, so that all vested parties can participate openly.

There is little motivational value in encouraging employees to set objectives that only require maintaining present levels of performance. On the other hand, objectives that are set too high, those that obviously are unattainable, can be demoralizing. In fact, it can be disastrous for the supervisor–subordinate relationship because it destroys trust and confidence. Consequently, objectives should not only be improvements over present performance but also must be clearly *achievable*.

STEP 3: ASSESS CURRENT SITUATION

In assessing the employee's current situation, the manager should be concerned with both the *what* and the *how* of the individual's performance. The situation should be viewed with an eye to the needs of both the organization and the employee.

The manager has the responsibility for knowing what to look for from the organization's perspective. If the manager can't confidently make such an assessment, an immediate need exists for the manager to clarify the important variables in this specific job with his or her own supervisor. Assuming that the manager is knowledgeable of the organization's concerns, these should be communicated to the employee so that they can appraise the situation together.

One problem with technical managers is that they only consider the organizational perspective. Even if they are concerned with employee growth and development, this emphasis contributes to differences in perception regarding what the employee's "real" needs are and what the worker's personal objectives "ought" to be. The resulting defensiveness and associated tension reduce the trust bond and inhibit a productive relationship because the employees *know* they are not understood and legitimately wonder if their manager even cares.

The interactive manager does care about how the employee perceives the situation. Both the organization and the employees must be winners for a long-term productive relationship to endure. Consequently, the interactive manager uses the appropriate skills to assess the employee's style profile and to react accordingly. Nonverbal skills are used to build and maintain the trust bond. Listening and questioning skills are engaged to help both the manager and the employee truly understand relevant perceptions and feelings.

To understand completely how the employee feels about the situation, it may be necessary to probe into such areas as how the individual feels about himself, or even about life. As the manager uses interactive skills to reflect back insights to the employee, not only does she feel understood and accepted, but both parties gain a better understanding of the meaning of the situation's appraisal.

Decision: Are Goals and Objectives Met by the Current Situation? Identifying the current situation, the goals, and the objectives may take many meetings; or you may need only one. If you have done your job, you will have a picture of the actual conditions of the current situation and the desired conditions as revealed in the goals and objectives. At this point, you need to contrast them. How do they compare?

When you have the two lists, you have a tool to help the employee work beyond assumptions. Mismatches and no-matches show up clearly. Sometimes, employees feel that the goals and objectives are being met when, in reality, they are not. Probing skills here help to determine with the employee whether the goals are too narrow, not far-reaching enough, or too far-reaching.

Similarly, the current situation can sometimes be overstated or taken for granted. How often have you asked an employee how her present plan of action was working and she replied that it was working satisfactorily? Employees often believe this when, in reality, it could be better. In problem solving, the manager is responsible for analyzing the current situation from all perspectives to make sure the situation is meeting the goals and objectives in the best way possible.

When the desired state of affairs (goals and objectives) and the actual state of affairs (situation) are fairly similar and working well, the employee should be commended for doing so well, and the situation can be marked for follow-up some time in the future. If both employee and organizational goals are satisfied, going further may be fruitless and a waste of time for you and your employee. On the other hand, you may have picked up hints that the employee has an even greater potential. If that is the case, it may be appropriate to arrange for a later meeting to determine how these strengths can be developed and applied. Additional training or greater job responsibilities might be called for to meet the employee's need for personal growth and to allow the organization to receive more benefits from the employee. If these growth needs are not recognized and dealt with accurately, future problems arising from boredom and frustration may develop, even though the current situation accurately matches the current desired objectives.

More often, the employee interview process will reveal some way in which you can be of genuine help to your employee in improving performance in the current situation. The careful information gathering done by the interactive manager helps both the employee and the manager identify, understand, and accept the existing situation. If there is a mutually agreed mismatch between the current and the desired situation, move on to the next step of identifying the problems. At this point, specify which problems are responsible for the mismatch.

STEP 4: IDENTIFY PROBLEMS

This step requires a total definition of the needs to be met or problems to be solved. It also necessitates gathering additional information so that all relevant factors can be analyzed to determine the exact problem that must be solved. Only then can you and your employee work together to generate a new action plan that will meet the employee's goals and objectives.

Look for root causes of problems. If instruction forms are constantly misinterpreted, are the forms incomplete or the information poorly supplied? Too often, a cause is assumed; look for all plausible alternatives before settling on the most probable cause(s).

Hasty assumptions also often result in symptoms being mistaken for sources of problems. If they are eliminated, both the employee and the manager may mistakenly assume that the problem is eliminated too. It is like controlling a skin rash with medication. The medication helps keep the problem out of sight; but the real assistance comes when you discover that the plant in the living room is the culprit, and all you need do is remove the plant to stop the itch without medication. Make sure you have identified correctly the basic reasons for the mismatch between the actual and desired state of affairs and not just associated symptoms.

Don't make the mistake of identifying a problem as such because it is an easy thing to solve. Although you may feel good about resolving an easy "problem," if it was only a symptom, you may end up more confused than before. Success as a problem solver includes the courage to face up to really difficult situations and things you may not want to hear, as well as the ability to generate effective solutions. Solving the wrong problem will only have negative consequences on your employee's trust and confidence in you; it will do little to improve the current situation.

Remember, accurate identification of the problem is much easier to assume than to make. This is why problem identification is often thought of as the most difficult and important step in the problem-solving process. The consequences of failure in this area can be severe; an innocent person may be convicted of a crime; a valuable employee may be fired; an important program may fail to meet its objectives.

STEP 5: DEFINE AND ANALYZE PROBLEMS

Checking to make sure that the problem is completely analyzed and accurately defined is a safeguard against incorrect assumptions, against treating symptoms only, and against incomplete understanding. Take some extra time and care to be certain you have all the information you need. Use your developmental, clarifying, and probing skills to ask the employee to provide more information on problems or needs identified, and to ask the employee to confirm or correct what you already understand of the problems. You might give new information to the employee in clarifying statements aimed at stimulating additional thoughts on the issues at hand. Continue until you and the employee are satisfied that you have identified and understood the cause of each problem under consideration.

Throughout this process, be aware of the employee's unique style mix, and react appropriately. Use all the skills you have to communicate interest, concern, and respect. Also develop your communications with sensitivity, and always try to sustain the trust bond.

Problem analysis should never be done in a hasty or flippant manner. Remember, no problem solution can be better than the quality of diagnosis on which it is built. Sound problem analyses should meet the following criteria:

1. They Differentiate Between Words and Facts. Although the words employees use to describe a situation are the manager's best clues to what really exists, they do not always convey the facts accurately. Nonverbal signals may indicate additional meanings that even the employee is not aware of. Providing feedback on what you "hear" in these communications can help clarify. Also keep in mind that the employee's words reflect only a personal perception and may reveal more about the person than about the actual situation. Both are important.

2. They Specify Causes Rather than Blame. Both the manager and the employee should strive to understand the situation and why it is this way, rather than to judge or evaluate it. Comparing desired to actual results is the function of the next stage in the problem definition process. At this point, the objective is to *gather valid information*, and evaluations tend to bias data. They contribute more to alleviating immediate emotional needs than to understanding thoroughly the situation that caused them.

3. They Specify Multiple Causality. Usually, a given situation is not caused by any one, single determinant. Interpersonal problems in organizations, for example, almost always involve behaviors and feelings of at least two people and quite often have contributions from various organizational factors. Using questioning and listening skills to determine the *whys* and *hows* can often draw out an interesting array of additional causes.

STEP 6: AGREE ON PROBLEMS TO BE SOLVED

You may have uncovered more than one problem, and you may have identified more than one factor contributing to the problem. Step 6 asks you to set priorities and make decisions as to which problems will be worked on first and which will be put aside temporarily or indefinitely. You may discover that some of the employee's problems are out of your domain, that others are not that serious, and that a few are both critical and within the range of your assistance. Make these evaluations with your employee. Apply your knowledge of the organization's perspective and your employee's knowledge of the specific situation and relevant personal attributes.

It is helpful to develop a priority list of problems, rank ordered according to how much their solutions will contribute to the employee's objectives. Some problems are clearly more important than others and should be dealt with first, even if their solutions seem more difficult. A basic criterion for developing priorities is to distinguish between *wants* and *needs*. You may *want* to solve a lot of problems, but take care of those you *need* to solve to meet important objectives first.

As you and your employee proceed, develop a priority set of problems that you can help solve. This leads to the second process, where you mutually generate a set of viable, new action plans.

REFERENCES

ELBING, A., "Step 2: The Diagnostic Process," Chapter 4 in *Behavioral Decisions in Organizations*, 2nd ed. (Glenview, Ill.: Scott, Foresman, 1978), pp. 74–83.

GIEGOLD, W. C., *Management by Objectives: A*

Self-Instructional Approach (New York: McGraw-Hill, 1978).

SPERRY, L., and HESS, L. R., "Guiding: Goal Setting," Chapter 5 in *Contact Counseling* (Reading, Mass.: Addison-Wesley, 1974), pp. 113–126.

16

Developing Action Plans

After information has been gathered, goals clarified, the situation assessed, and problem(s) identified, the next step is developing a particular course of action either to return the situation to the previous acceptable level or to bring it to a more desired place. The stress is on (1) working *with* the employee and (2) *improvements* to solve problems. Being *told* what to do is offensive to most people; yet it is a real temptation, once problems are defined, to rush in with the answers. Resist! Instead, help your employee as you solve the problem together.

There is usually more than one way to solve a problem. During this stage it is critical to keep an open mind to all possible solutions, so that several alternatives are available from which to select. Both the manager and the employee need to check preconceived ideas and preferences so that the best solution can be determined.

The steps identified in Figure 16-1 can facilitate the development of an action plan to solve the problem effectively. Remember that effective action planning can only take place after the problem has accurately been identified and understood. The most usual causes of failure in action planning are errors in clarifying objectives, assessing the current situation,

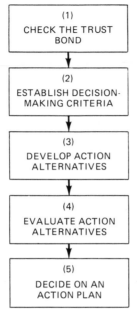

Figure 16-1 Developing an Action Plan

and defining the problem. If the problem definition stage has been completed effectively, the alternative solutions should stand out, and the choice of an action plan should not be that difficult.

STEP 1: CHECK THE TRUST BOND

The first step of this process is to check the trust bond. Remember that although maintaining trust is a continuing demand, you must pay special attention to the level of trust you have established before moving from one interactive management process to another. When trust is high, moving on to another process is easy. When trust has diminished, the employee is unprepared to make necessary decisions and is less willing to participate fully. The trust bond, like the marriage bond, needs constant work—or separation is likely.

STEP 2: ESTABLISH DECISION-MAKING CRITERIA

Decision-making criteria are statements that identify specific, measurable, attainable results that, when met, indicate the problem is solved or the goal accomplished. For example, the decision-making criteria could be: "I need to reduce scrap material waste by 10 percent, avoid a reduction in product quality, and increase production by 5 percent at a minimum." If the criteria for solving an employee's problem were always that specific, this part of the process would be very easy. If the criteria were "dream" figures, unreasonable, or very abstract and ambiguous, your help with making them more realistic and understandable would be needed to avoid the frustrations that would otherwise follow. Two of the features of an effective action plan are that the criteria can be attained and that you know when it happens.

Decision-making criteria should reflect the characteristics of good solution objectives. First, they should be *specific*. "I want to increase productivity by 5 percent," not just "I want to increase productivity." Second, they should be *measurable*. To say you want to increase employee morale is not as good a solution objective as saying that you want to increase employee morale and will recognize it by a 4 percent reduction in sick days taken over the next three months (if appropriate). Third, the criteria must be *attainable* if you really expect employees to try to accomplish them.

A fourth characteristic is that the set of objectives, or criteria, must be *complementary*. To achieve one should not eliminate achievement of any other. For example, if you wish to counsel your employees more effectively, you might try to achieve this by meeting with every employee daily for a few minutes and spending as much time as necessary with those who need more. This procedure, however, may prevent you from meeting another goal of writing more lengthy and exacting reports, which also would take a considerably greater amount of time. Although each goal may be attainable in itself, taken together, they are unlikely to be met because of limited time. Consequently, you should strive for complementary goals that can all be met when considered together.

A key criterion for accepting any action plan is that it not only solves the immediate problem but also *contributes to organizational goals*. Considering the quality of the solution with respect to overall organizational goals is the manager's responsibility. Both short-term and long-term objectives must be considered for the specific employee, other employees, the entire department, related departments, and the overall organization. The employee may understand the specific problem best, but if left alone, there is a good chance that any resulting action plans would overlook some criteria considered vital to other affected units.

On the other hand, the manager should not dominate the process or be so concerned with solution quality for the organization that the participation and consideration of the employee is diluted. Quality alone does not make a good decision. Even the highest-quality alternative may be a poor choice if the employee involved does not find it acceptable in view of personal goals or values. Another criterion for a good action plan is that it must be *acceptable* to the employee who is affected by it and who must implement it. In interactive management full participation by the employee in the joint problem-solving process is a safeguard against violating this criterion. In technical management, these criteria are often violated by managers who manipulate people just as they would any other resource. Interactive managers realize that unlike other resources such as money or material, people have feelings and care about how they are treated. It is important to use listening and probing skills to assess employee needs and preferences accurately. With this understanding, the best-quality technical decision may not be "the best" or even workable in this specific situation after acceptance is considered.

STEP 3: DEVELOP ACTION ALTERNATIVES

Armed with a good problem definition and decision-making criteria, you and the employee are ready to generate and explore potential action plans. These are direct responses to the decision-making criteria and should grow naturally out of the information discovered during the problem definition and analysis phase.

Whatever the process you and the employee use to generate new action plans and exchange ideas, you should view the alternatives in light of both the objectives and the criteria by which the objectives will be recognized as having been met. It is the matching of the results of the action plan to the needs of the employee. Notice that you match results, not just procedures of the new action plan. The procedures are basically the various parts that make up the action plan and the methods for their accomplishment. They answer the questions, "What is it?" and "How is it going to work?" On the other hand, a *result* is an outcome or product of the procedures that helps satisfy a specific need or problem on the part of the employee. The results are the most important part of the new action plan to know about. In reality, employees don't "buy" a new action plan; they are really concerned with what it will do to improve their situation. Employees are concerned with the *benefits* of an action plan first, and with the procedures for making it work second. New action plans are means to ends, not ends in themselves. For example, the employee does not view a movie theater as just a building, projector, and screen. It is a means toward the benefits of relaxation, pleasure, and social interaction.

The value of a new action plan is increased by involving the employee in the generation and analysis of alternatives. That way, the employee is allowed to discover personally the *benefits* received from implementing it. This means that you must be employee oriented. You must be sensitive to your employee's needs. Ask yourself: "If I were the employee, why would I want to implement this proposed action plan?" "How would it satisfy my needs?" "How would this action plan benefit me more than what I'm doing now or more than other action plans?" By having good, solid answers to these questions, and a thorough understanding of how the new action plan can truly benefit your employee, you will be well on your way toward consummating employee commitments to more productive personal and professional action plans.

Your employee's job in the suggestion process is twofold. As you suggest new action plans, the employee needs to respond and assist. Secondly, the employee should suggest new action plans of his own. Quite often it is better to solicit the employee's suggestions before you make your own. In this way, the employee is more involved and can take pride in new action plans that you might eventually have suggested yourself. If the action plans originate from the employee, there is a better chance for acceptance and effective implementation. Moreover, the employee may come up with a fresh, and even better, solution that would otherwise have been lost as you directed the effort down a different path.

You, as manager, have the same job of generating alternatives and analyzing their feasibility and benefits. Present your ideas briefly, and space their timing so that there is adequate opportunity for you both to think about each one. Present the procedures and benefits of any new action plan one at a time and in their order of importance. Try first to present the benefits that will have most personal or professional meaning to the employee. Before discussing the next most important result, solicit feedback to make sure the employee understands how the result will benefit her. This is actually the process of "testing acceptance." Feedback statements regarding procedures and results should take the form of open questions. For example: "How do you feel this will help you meet your objectives?" "What importance does this have to you (or your department)?" "What benefits do you think you might derive from this?" The feedback will give you some excellent clues about the readiness and willingness of your employee to make the necessary commitment.

View new action planning as a "discovery process" and not as a time for you to do all the talking. Presenting new action plan procedures and benefits one at a time, and getting feedback on each one before proceeding to the next, fosters the two-way communication process. To ask your employee how a specific aspect of the new action plan can provide personal benefits, add special meaning to the solution process by keeping the worker totally involved.

When you are satisfied that your employee fully understands, and accepts or rejects the importance of a given procedure or benefit in solving a problem, move on to the next procedure or benefit, going through the same process. Present as many new action plan details and benefits as necessary to determine comfortably whether or not your employee is ready and willing to make a commitment on implementing the new action.

Maintain the attitude that the solutions suggested are indeed "potential" and not "final." This avoids putting pressure on the employee and the problems associated with picking *the* solution prematurely and then discovering that it doesn't fit.

This stage, like all the others in interactive management, should be uniquely tailored to the specific needs of the individual employee. It has to be, for the benefits you present and the order in which you present them are dependent upon the information you received earlier and worked on with that individual worker. Each problem, each need, each employee, the influence of time, and each set of priorities is different; so is each new action plan.

Almost all problem situations have several alternatives for improvement. Generating alternatives is not a time for "either/ or" thinking. They may not be obvious, but alternatives can usually be found if the situation is approached with an open mind. As a manager, it is not enough to rely only on the solutions the employee suggests. As mentioned earlier, these may overlook criteria and consequences relevant to other people concerned. It is also your job, as manager, to stretch your mind and develop additional alternatives, even in the most discouraging situations. Even if none of the feasible alternatives are very desirable, at least there will be several to choose from, so that the least undesirable can be selected. At least there will be a choice.

STEP 4: EVALUATE ACTION ALTERNATIVES

Once the feasible set of action plans have been developed, it is time to evaluate them thoroughly with the decision-making criteria already developed to determine which one will provide the greatest amount of benefits and the least amount of unwanted consequences. Together, the manager and the subordinate should mentally test each alternative by imagining what would happen if the action plan were implemented. They should try to foresee potential difficulties in implementation and to appraise the probable consequences. Then they will be in a position to compare the relative desirability of each alternative and make a choice.

Several factors should be considered in evaluating the action plan alternatives. Perhaps the most important criterion in this regard is each alternative's probability of success and the degree of *risk* that negative consequences will occur. If the chances of failure are high, and the related costs great, it may not be worth it—even after considering the associated benefits—to try the alternative. Risks can be personal as well as economic, as in situations where an employee's reputation is on the line, or a performance review is coming up soon. Most employees cannot be expected to become enthusiastic about action plans that risk their job security or personal image.

Another factor is the question of *timing*. The amount of time required to implement the various action plans should be estimated and compared to the time available to carry them out. Another dimension of time is *economy of effort* associated with each alternative. The question here is which action alternative will give the greatest results for the least amount of effort.

Another critical question is, "How will the individuals involved and affected react?" Sometimes there are *reactions* to changes that create more problems than are solved. Sensitivity to emotional factors, personal values, and objectives is vital at this point. You should apply your interactive management skills of listening and questioning to find out as much as possible about how employees and others affected by the proposed action plan feel about it. The more accurate your understanding of the feelings of all involved, the better your chances of choosing a successful action plan.

As alternatives are evaluated according to these criteria, many will be clearly unsatisfactory and can be eliminated. Sometimes this evaluation will result in one alternative clearly being superior to the others, making the following decision step very easy. Other times, the evaluation of alternatives will determine that none of the alternatives is acceptable, and all of them should be eliminated. In this case, you must return to the process of developing new alternatives again. If several alter-

ALTERNATIVES		CRITERIA				
	Benefits	Probability of Success	Costs	Risks	Associated Consequence	Timing
Alternative A						
Alternative B						
Alternative C						

Figure 16-2 Decision-Making Grid

natives are evaluated as feasible and have different strengths and weaknesses, you are ready to move on to the decision-making stage. A decision-making grid like the one presented in Figure 16-2 is sometimes helpful in evaluating the various alternatives.

STEP 5: DECIDE ON AN ACTION PLAN

After the available alternatives have been thoroughly evaluated, it is time to select the best action plan for implementation. Although it is hardly ever possible to know for sure that the alternative selected will be precisely the best plan, following a systematic procedure, such as that suggested here, can help a lot. Going through the decision-making grid in Figure 16-2 in more detail may indicate which alternative will maximize benefits with minimum risks and costs. In deciding on an action plan, we are trying to find an optimum alternative for all considerations involved as opposed to maximizing any single objective without regard for associated consequences.

There are many factors that guide the manager in selecting an action plan to implement. Among them are experience, intuition, advice from others, experimentation, and management science.

Certain situations do reoccur. Although you should be open to variations in circumstances, the saying that "experience is the best teacher" does apply to a certain degree. Your own *experience*, or that of other managers, can provide important precedents for decision making in the current situation. Make sure that you don't follow past patterns blindly, however. Adapt your learnings to fit the nuances you are aware of in the present situation.

Intuition should also be recognized as a helpful force in making a decision. These inner feelings about what would be the best course of action usually emerge from a lot more effort than their seemingly magic appearance would indicate. They are usually the result of much unconscious activity on your part where many relevant variables (some of which may be unacceptable to public discussion, but important to you) concerning a particular action plan have been thoroughly analyzed. Consequently, there is also some truth and wisdom in the saying, "If it feels good, do it." The opposite sentiment should not be dismissed lightly, either. If it doesn't feel good, even though a formal analysis has indicated that a particular alternative is best, do not proceed too hastily.

Advice from others—whether they are managers, superiors, employees, or staff personnel—can provide valuable insights into which way to proceed. Suggestions from others are sometimes sought as a means of avoiding responsibility if the action plan fails. These excuses are usually in a form like, "Well, Charlie told me to do it this way." If this type of reaction occurs repeatedly, the manager soon will no longer have to worry about what others think, because the source will no longer be available. You still have to decide to accept the advice of others or not, and the responsibility for a decision can never be shifted.

If the time is available and the outcomes not too important, *experimentation*—or trying out several alternatives to see what happens—can be useful. Deciding how the new office furniture should be arranged, or which brand of typewriter to buy for the secretaries, could benefit from testing them out. Most often, however, the time and expense of experimentation make it prohibitive.

Management science consists of a sophisticated set of techniques designed to assist managers in making complex quantitative decisions. It consists of such techniques as linear programming, computer simulation, and operations research. For average operating problems, these techniques are not necessary. It is useful to be aware of their existence, however, if you should need expert assistance in the quantitative area.

If, after thoroughly going through all these procedures, several alternatives still seem equally important, do not get caught making the common assumption that the actions must be mutually exclusive. It may be possible to take the best from all of them in a combined action plan. In some situations the various courses of action can be arranged in an order of implementation and performed in sequence. It is useful to determine whether alternatives can be related to each other so that they can be integrated in a combined plan of action.

After the decision has been made, it is time actually to implement the action plan. Although the choice of an alternative surely included consideration for its implementation, this is a separate and vital step in the problem-solving process.

No matter how good the action plan decided upon, if it is not implemented properly, it will be useless.

REFERENCES

ELBING, A. O., "Selection of Human Decisions," Chapter 6 in *Behavioral Decisions in Organizations*, 2nd ed. (Glenview, Ill.: Scott, Foresman, 1978), pp. 132–153.

HAIMANN, T., and HILGERT, R. L., "Problem Solving and Decision Making," Chapter 5 in *Supervision*, 2nd ed. (Cincinnati: South-Western Publishing, 1977), pp. 59–78.

Implementing Action

Managers often go through the entire problem-solving process of defining problems, developing various alternative solutions, and deciding on an action plan to accomplish their objectives; and then nothing happens because no one does anything with the decision, or it is not implemented effectively. In many technical decisions it may not be necessary to give special consideration to implementation. If a decision has been made to install new air conditioning, a new computer, or new carpeting, it can be implemented simply by communicating what you want and having someone install it. In all decisions where people are affected, implementation may be the crucial factor.

The point is that making a choice between alternatives and deciding on an action plan is not the end of the problem-solving process. A decision and action plan are of little value unless they can be effectively implemented. This is often the most difficult step to accomplish. The important question is *"How?"* By what method is the action plan going to be accomplished? To omit this question from a problem-solving process is to divorce the decision from practical reality.

One of the most satisfying and relationship-enhancing experiences a supervisor and subordinate can have is to see their carefully thought-out plan of action being applied successfully. This doesn't happen by itself. It follows from a well-conceived implementation plan. Without such a strategy, an otherwise sound action plan can easily result in confusion, frustration, and the creation of more problems than it solves.

Most action plans require behavioral changes on the part of your employee, yourself, and other affected individuals in the organization. Since most people have a tendency to resist changes, it is vital to include a strategy for overcoming this human reaction in your implementation plan. The steps outlined in Figure 17-1 can help you avoid common pitfalls and implement your action plan successfully.

STEP 1: CHECK THE TRUST BOND

If the preceding steps in the problem-solving process have been done well, trust should be high at this point. You and your subordinate have openly explored the problem situation and jointly developed an action plan to solve it that meets both of your needs. Consequently, the subordinate should see the action plan as the best way to accomplish personal objectives in this situation and should strongly believe that you will support

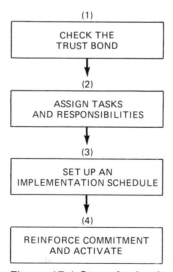

Figure 17-1 Steps for Implementing Actions Plans

and facilitate its implementation. At this stage, the question is not *if*, but *how* and *when*.

You should, as a matter of course, check the trust bond as your first step before actually moving into this new phase. If it is strong, get on with it. If it is weak for some reason, identify why, and spend some time reestablishing it. Is it because something was not fully cleared up? Is it because you began to respond less to the style preferences of the employee and more to your own preferences? It may be helpful to ask your subordinate. Summarize your previous decisions and considerations, and discuss again the possible effects of the decision on your subordinate's personal goals and job satisfaction. While you are listening to these responses, be aware of nonverbal messages, and look for indications of involvement or the lack of it. Tune up all your communication and flexibility skills. Check for thorough understanding of the processes on the employee's part. Only after trust and commitment are high should you move on to step 2 and outline each other's tasks and responsibilities.

STEP 2: ASSIGN TASKS AND RESPONSIBILITIES

Verbally clarify and confirm what each of you—the manager and the employee—will do to make the new action plan work. Follow this with a written agreement concerning who is to do what, by when, and how. To avoid misunderstandings and loss of trust, be sure to specify and solidify the details of the mutually accepted agreement. It is the manager's responsibility to do this—not the employee's.

This outlining of tasks and responsibilities is important with all styles, but be especially careful as you do it for Amiables and Expressives. These two behavioral styles are more prone toward relationships than tasks, and unless the tasks are put into writing with appropriate deadlines, the tasks may (unintentionally) not get done. Because of their typical lack of concern for details and tasks, they may forget or overlook things that are crucial for successful action plan implementation. Make sure to provide the structure that Expressives don't provide for themselves but need to ensure effective implementation.

With Amiables, be careful that you do not establish an

objective too quickly that may very well result in later hesitancy or change. When you do arrive at a decision, outline the tasks in realistic and concrete terms. Be very careful only to state what you can or are willing to do. By promising too much and not coming through, you may quickly destroy your trust bond with an Amiable. In addition, explore together potential areas for misunderstandings or dissatisfaction. An Amiable who is unhappy or dissatisfied will not readily talk about bad feelings in an effort to avoid conflict. When you explore areas of dissatisfaction and misunderstanding, as you outline tasks and responsibilities, keep in mind the different style characteristics so you recognize potentially detrimental situations.

As you outline the tasks and responsibilities, any time a conflict or problem arises in what you both understand, handle it then and there. Often, you will be able to negotiate mutually acceptable terms or redefine the tasks and responsibilities. At other times, the tasks or responsibilities, as understood by one of you, will remain unacceptable. If so, return to the beginning of the second process—finding new action plans. It will take extra time, but it is worth it. A potentially damaging problem has been uncovered early when it can be handled and defused.

STEP 3: SET UP AN IMPLEMENTATION SCHEDULE

With a mutually acceptable solution and a list of tasks and responsibilities drawn up mutually, you and your employee are ready to proceed to the last step of the implementation process. To do this, ask the employee an open question that requests direction, such as "When do we proceed?" Because of all the previous preparation, this question is an open, straightforward request. Since your employee has participated fully in the entire interactive management process and has had a major hand in arriving at the new action plan, you will generally be answered with a time, date, or other relevant reference. If there is something of concern, your employee will generally, by this time, feel comfortable and trusting enough to speak out. You are, after all, problem solvers working together.

Develop together a time schedule, in writing, for when each action step will be completed. One way to do this is to start at an end point (i.e., a date when the objective should be completed) and work back. Place the action implementation steps in priority order, and assign a time period within which they can reasonably be completed, starting with the last step before the objective is accomplished. If a completion date is not a necessity, as determined in the earlier problem definition stage, you may want to work forward in sequence to develop the time schedule. Either way, your implementation schedule should include the following two steps:

1. Break the action plan down into a sequential series of implementation steps.
2. Place a time estimate on each step.

STEP 4: REINFORCE COMMITMENT AND ACTIVATE

After the employee has committed to a specific sequence and time schedule, you are ready to put the plan into action. Begin by analyzing the current situation. Involvement in the problem-solving process may have distracted you from existing conditions that must be considered. Ask yourself: "Where are we now in relation to the problem?" "How will others involved react to our actions?" "What will motivate and activate the people involved?"

During this phase you will probably have the most difficult time with Amiables and Analytics. The Amiable style is slow-moving, risk avoiding, and security conscious. Amiables like guarantees that the new actions to be implemented involve a minimum of risk. Offer the Amiable employee your *personal* assurances that you will stand behind the actions agreed upon. This step will often take gentle, slow, but firmly directive action on your part to give the Amiable the confidence to follow through. If you handle your encouragement and prodding in a personal manner, the Amiable will generally go along with the plan. Remember, this prodding is not prodding an unwilling employee, but encouraging one who has gone through the entire process as a partner in problem solving.

The Analytic style also moves slowly and avoids risks. This style has a strong need to be right. Analytics are not as slow in implementing decisions as are Amiables *if* they are *sure* their actions cannot backfire. Provide the Analytic employee with tangible, factual guarantees that provide the needed assurance.

Drivers and Expressives generally provide neither resistance nor hesitation at this point. They usually want to get on with it, now that they have come this far.

Now that the action plan is being implemented, it would be easy to move on to something else and forget about it. Now that you have gone this far, however, it is important that no one drop the ball when you are so close to your goal. The next chapter describes how to follow through with the problem-solving process to ensure the desired results.

REFERENCES

BOYD, B. B., "Making Sound Decisions," Chapter 13 in *Management-Minded Supervision*, (New York: McGraw-Hill, 1968), pp. 274–293.

ELBING, A. O., "Implementation of the Solution," Chapter 7 in *Behavioral Decisions in Organizations*, 2nd ed. (Glenview, Ill.: Scott, Foresman, 1978), pp. 154–177.

18

Following Through

Even though, in developing the action plan and planning its implementation, you have done your best to anticipate anything that could go wrong, you can't send the employee off to implement action and then forget about it. As the old saying goes, "Even the best-laid plans go awry." You must follow closely the actions you have initiated to ensure the successful implementation of the action plan.

It is very important to develop and maintain a positive atmosphere with the employees during this stage and to give them plenty of positive reinforcement. Hopefully, this type of relationship has already been established through application of the interactive management attitudes and skills. If it is developing, however, do not attempt to transform the tone of the relationship overnight. A manager who has traditionally approached employees in an autocratic manner and suddenly changes to a folksy, personal style will probably be seen as manipulative, and the trust bond will be damaged. To avoid such a "credibility gap," apply the interactive management ideas over time, as they seem natural. In either case, keep the following suggestions in mind during the follow-through process:

First, to prevent problems, put yourself in your employee's position. The old adage, "Don't criticize a person until you have walked a mile in his shoes," certainly goes for employee relations. This frame of mind gives you a feeling for and an understanding of the employee's problems. The better you can get into your employee's "shoes," the better you can work together to solve future problems and meet additional or changing needs.

Second, develop an attitude of sincere friendship, respect, and concern. The more you give of these, the more you will receive from your employees. The working relationship that grows from this accepting approach to others is a strong one that resists destruction. Employees who return these feelings will be extremely faithful in implementing action plans they have agreed upon with you.

Third, provide your employee with thoughtful attention throughout the process. Following are some suggestions to consider:

1. Maintain frequent contact. This indicates that you care and are available if the need arises.
2. Always have a good reason for contacting employees. Dropping in on them is thoughtless, for they have schedules and demands on their time, too.
3. Check to see that your employees have the resources they should have when they should have them.
4. Periodically, inquire about the employee's experience with the action plan. Determine if help is required in any area in which you can be of service.
5. Determine how the employee is currently using the action plan, and suggest alternative uses where appropriate. Many times, employees are unaware of additional applications or benefits that the plan can supply.
6. Where possible, reasonable, and appropriate, supply your employees with suggestions to help them do a better job.
7. Inform your employees about new developments or requirements and any other factors that may be of assistance to them.

Plan your follow-through activities carefully. You will be respected and accepted. On this basis, you will enter a long, mutually profitable, personal and professional relationship with your employee. Both sides win! Some steps that can aid you during the follow-through stage are outlined in Figure 18-1.

STEP 1: CHECK THE TRUST BOND

The suggestions in the preceding paragraphs are all aimed at building a positive relationship with the employee. At this point, you should again check the trust bond and work at enhancing it. There is a dual payoff. Not only are the trust-building communication and flexibility skills practiced to enhance the follow-through, but the entire follow-through process itself helps you to maintain and enhance the trust bond with your employees. Many managers fail to follow through in the helpful spirit of the interactive management approach. This activity itself may set you apart as someone special.

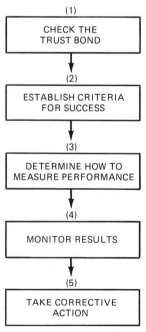

Figure 18-1 Follow-Through

STEP 2: ESTABLISH CRITERIA
FOR SUCCESS

After you are comfortable with the level of trust (or are consciously working at improving it), work with the employee to identify the criteria that will determine whether the results achieved by the new action plan were successful. These criteria are best considered with respect to the employee's overall goals. They usually are congruent with those criteria already developed in the action-planning stage for decision-making purposes. Be certain to include in the criteria the time and quantity elements developed for the implementation schedule. Is your employee seeking a 10 percent increase in productivity? A 25 percent decrease in absenteeism? A 6 percent increase in sales? Are the goals specific, measurable, attainable, and complementary? Further, when does your employee expect to achieve the results identified—in two months, six months, one year? These specifics will give you and your employee firm *benchmarks* by which to measure and compare actual results.

STEP 3: DETERMINE HOW TO
MEASURE PERFORMANCE

Once the criteria are firmly set, you can determine with your employee what and how to measure to see how well the criteria are met. Without common agreement, both you and your employee may assess different factors or measure the criteria differently. This can cause you to lose a common ground for discussion, improvement, and agreement. Whose figures indicate the success? If your figures are positive and your employee's are negative, how do you take corrective action, if you do at all? If your employee's figures are positive and yours are negative, you would be right in taking corrective action; but will your employee agree to a possible disruptive activity? If you never set down figures, will you even be able to communicate accurately with your employee about the "measured" results? Get your criteria (e.g., figures, times, and dates) specifically established in writing, and avoid all this potential conflict.

For example, when we sell a client a sales training program for a sales force, the client generally expects certain results from the training. These results are typically spelled out in the decision-making criteria that we derive. A typical client objective is to increase the sales of each attendee. How? Let's add the detail: Say that the increase of sales for each attendee is to rise 5 percent. OK? If we stopped here, we might assume the client wants that result within a year. Our client, however, wants it to happen within six months. Can you imagine what might result from this misunderstanding? It might be especially bad if the client's goals are truly reasonable *only* for the longer time span. Had we adequately communicated, we could have clarified the potential problem beforehand.

With clearly specified quantity and time criteria, we can now determine *how* and when to measure the actual new performance to see if it is successful or not. As several ways to do this are generally available, it is once again important to decide the specific procedures with your employee. In general, you will be engaged in gathering data on actual performance and determining if it matches up with our previously developed implementation schedule and other criteria for success.

If possible, you will want to use objective, numerical forms of measurement. There are times when these are not available, or you may wish to use specific subjective measures. What you finally decide upon depends on what best suits each specific situation and what both you and the employee are comfortable with.

Now, *when* do you apply the measures? This, too, needs to be decided mutually to avoid problems. Be sure to specify both *when* and *how often*. Be especially sure to document these if the employee is an Expressive. Otherwise, there is a good chance that details will be overlooked and parts of the measurement process will be left out. Analytics may create different problems by overdoing the measurement (either by measuring too often or too much). So get it down in writing with them, too. Confirm the process so that the chances of all going well are increased.

STEP 4: MONITOR RESULTS

Now you are ready to gather data on the results and compare them with the criteria established. If the new performance meets the criteria, take no other action than to continue to monitor and measure the new results on a continuing basis at a specified time as planned. If, on the other hand, the new results do not measure up, you need to determine why. You and the employee may want to ask such questions as: Is everything on schedule? Are results being measured properly and compared to valid criteria? Has new resistance to change developed? Are materials up to standard?

As you continue to assess feedback on results, it is important to recognize that you are now confronting a much different situation than existed before the action plan was implemented. The action-planning processes and changes—and even the time spent developing them—have created a new set of circumstances to deal with. Every implementation step may have altered the problem situation in ways you have not anticipated. Consequently, as you and the employee monitor results, constantly try to distinguish between the original problem and the situation that exists right now.

STEP 5: TAKE CORRECTIVE ACTION

In the first stage, defining the problem, if the current situation matched the goals and objectives, you did not need to come up with a new action plan. In the follow-through stage, if the new performance results match the success criteria, you are in a similar enviable position. Simply continue the scheduled follow-through process. But in the problem stage, if the employee's current situation did not match the desired goals and objectives, you went on to determine the problem(s) that caused the divergence. Likewise, in the follow-through process, if the new performance results fail to match the success criteria, you need to take corrective action by identifying the problem causing the divergence, finding another workable solution, and then implementing it. Sound familiar? It is. The problem-solving process is a closed-loop system. With a new corrective action plan, you again must establish new measures and schedules and gather fresh data to test against the criteria. If they match, continue to monitor and measure; if they fail to match, go back to the "define the problem" stage and start the whole process over again.

However, the second and subsequent times through the

problem-solving process with the same employee usually are not as time-consuming as the first effort, given a firm trust bond and the previous experience at arriving at the needed decisions.

Although we have reached the end of the problem-solving model, the process has no beginning or end. Managers must always monitor ongoing action plans and be alert for deviations from objectives. Breaking problem solving down into its various steps helps clarify the process, but to be optimally effective in interactive management, these procedures need to become automatic or continual. This outcome is the essence of interactive management.

It is similar to what Professor Alvar Elbing calls "preventive decision making." As you attempt to implement action plans and proceed to monitor results, you will become keenly aware of the importance of prevention. If you have gone through the entire problem-solving process thoroughly and effectively, you have a much better chance of preventing the need to take corrective action at the end, which would require you to invest additional time in another reiteration.

Go through the problem-solving process included at each phase, checking and building the trust bond. Preventive problem solving is the constructive process of building good relationships with your employees, so that problems don't occur in the first place. It *is* interactive management.

REFERENCES

ELBING, A. O., "Implementation of the Solution," Chapter 7 in *Behavioral Decisions in Organizations*, 2nd ed. (Glenview, Ill.: Scott, Foresman, 1978), pp. 154–177.

GEORGE, C. S., "How to Solve Problems and Make Decisions," Chapter 6 in *Supervi-sion in Action*, 2nd ed. (Reston, Va.: Reston, 1979), pp. 79–92.

MORRISEY, G. L., *Management by Objectives and Results for Business and Industry*, 2nd ed. (Reading, Mass.: Addison-Wesley, 1977).

19

What Do You Do with What You've Learned?

We have come a long way together since the first chapter. We initially set the stage for the interactive management philosophy and then introduced you to a number of ways to diagnose, understand, and relate to different personality styles. In this regard, we took a close look at the different ways people prefer to learn, and we suggested things that you could do to facilitate that process. We learned how to identify the different behavioral styles and how to relate to each style effectively and productively. In addition, we discovered methods for assessing individual decision styles and how to apply this knowledge in the problem-solving process. Last, transactional analysis was introduced to provide you with a simple and effective technique for improving your understanding of how and why people relate to each other the way they do.

After covering the foregoing material, we moved into interactive communication skills. Various questioning techniques and strategies were covered to give you a greater ability to uncover the problems and needs of your employees. Active listening was stressed so that you would be better able to be sensitive, attentive, and responsive with other people during the communications process. The full area of nonverbal communications was covered to provide you a deeper sensitivity to what other people are really communicating and how they are really feeling. In this regard, we covered the topics of image, vocal tones, body language, communicating with time, and communicating with space. The final chapter of the communications section dealt with the critical subject of feedback. This subject was stressed so that you could verify that you understand exactly what others are communicating to you and that they understand exactly what you are communicating to them.

The last section of this book covered the major processes of interactive management and how they relate to the problem-solving process. Each step of interactive management was covered in detail, and many of the concepts from the previous chapters were pragmatically discussed in terms of their effective usage during these four processes. Now we have arrived at the last chapter. Where do we go from here?

Where you go depends totally on you. You have just been exposed to a new experience and have seen a new way to look at, analyze, and conduct the managerial process. People generally respond to new experiences in one of five ways. First, a person might integrate the new experience with past experiences easily because the new experience was perceived as pleasant and compatible. Second, the new experience might be rejected totally because it was perceived as too threatening. Third, you can isolate the new experience from what you are presently accustomed to and thereby treat this experience as an exception to the rule. This allows a person to continue acting and thinking as he customarily has done. Fourth, the person might distort the new experience to make it "fit" her past experiences. Fifth, the person may perceive the experience as a new reality and change her old ways of thinking and acting to conform to her newly expanded or newly perceived reality.

The most productive of the five responses listed is the last one. By reacting in accordance with this response, you undergo a positive behavioral change. You do not just accept everything that you have read, of course. Instead, you take what makes sense to you and weave it into your current "reality." Nothing that you have seen in this book is cast in concrete. It works— part of it or all of it. What segments you use and how you use them will determine your personal and managerial effectiveness—now and in the future.

It would make us extremely pleased if, after reading this book, you went out and started practicing the interactive management philosophy and its processes. It won't be easy, though. It will take practice, some mistakes, and more practice to lead eventually to your successful implementation of interactive management. Can you remember back to the time when you first learned how to drive a car? Before you ever learned how, you were what we call an *unconscious incompetent*. That is, you didn't know how to drive the car, and you didn't even know why you didn't know how to drive it. When you first went out with one of your parents, a friend, or an instructor to learn how actually to drive the car, you became a *conscious incompetent*. You still couldn't drive the car; but because of your new awareness of the automobile and its parts, you were consciously aware of why you couldn't drive it. From this step, you at least had the awareness of what you had to do to acquire the competency to drive.

With some additional practice and guidance, you were able to become competent in driving the car. However, you had to be consciously aware of what you were doing with all the mechanical aspects of the car as well as with your body. You had to be consciously aware to turn on your blinker signals well before you executed a turn. You had to remember to monitor the traffic behind you in your rearview mirror. You kept both hands on the wheel and monitored your car's position relative to the centerline road divider. You were consciously aware of all these things as you "competently" drove.

Think of the last time you drove a car. Were you consciously aware of all the things we've just discussed? Of course not! Most of us, after having driven for a while, progress to a level of *unconscious competency*. This is the level where we can do something well and not even have to think about it. It comes somewhat naturally.

The foregoing example holds true for your use of interactive management. You must go through the competency processes in order to get to the highest level—the unconscious competence level. This is where you can manage others interactively and do it naturally and effectively. If you can get to that level, you should see an increase in your own managerial productivity, an increase in your employees' productivity, greater employee trust and respect, and more self-respect as well. However, you must pay a price to get to the level of unconscious competence in interactive management: Practice, practice, practice.

When you were learning to drive the car, you acquired your competency through practice. The same holds true for interactive management skills. For some of you, managing interactively may require a change of behavior from your present method of management. If this is the case, expect initially to see a decrease in your management productivity. This is a common occurrence in behavioral change. However, after persistence and practice—and as you approach the unconscious competency level of interactive management—your managerial productivity will increase beyond its previous level and form a new and higher plateau.

USE THE INTERACTIVE MANAGEMENT PROBLEM-SOLVING PROCESS TO IMPROVE YOUR INTERACTIVE MANAGEMENT SKILLS

So you've decided to accept the challenge of becoming an interactive manager. The payoffs are certainly well worth your efforts. Now you must meet the challenge. With so much to learn about the various style profiles, the interactive communication skills, and the steps of the interactive problem-solving process, you are probably confused as to where to start. How do you create an effective action plan that will meet your needs?

Our advice is that you first apply some of the interactive problem-solving processes to your own situation. Make sure that you clarify your objectives in becoming an interactive manager. Next, assess your current situation. How well do you practice style flexibility? How well do you probe? Listen? Read body language? Give and receive feedback? Communicate effectively with time and space? As you determine your current situation and compare it with your new objectives of becoming an interactive manager, you should identify those problem areas that need work. There may be a number of areas that need work, but take care to set priorities on problem areas according to how much attention they need. Work on those problem areas first that need the most help. As you become more competent in these areas, go on to the lower-priority problem areas. Specifically develop an action plan to improve those areas that will help you in your quest to become an interactive manager. Specifically define what must be done to accomplish your action plan. Set up an implementation schedule, and establish commitment to follow it through according to the scheduled completion times. Set goals and establish your criteria for success; determine how and when to measure your performance in improving your interactive management skills. Constantly monitor the results, and take corrective action where necessary. Through effective use of the interactive management problem-solving model, you can strategically and consistently improve your skills as an interactive manager.

Your new action plan might include further professional help in the form of seminars, books, or tapes. Keep informed of other learning devices that will help you improve any or all of the skills discussed in this book. Your plan may also include a more detailed review of relevant portions of this book when appropriate.

Whatever your goals and objectives, make sure you have an action plan with a specific implementation schedule and a method for tracking results. Otherwise, you may get too caught up in trying to do too much at one time and not really grow acceptably with any specific skill. This will undoubtedly lead to frustration on your part and the ultimate decision to quit your self-improvement program.

Correctly used, interactive management skills will allow you to interact with your employees and solve problems in an open, honest atmosphere of trust and helpfulness. Your employees will gain relevant solutions to their identified problems. You will gain support from your employees, who will be fully committed to solving their personal, professional, and organizational problems. Productivity for everyone involved in the interactive management process will increase dramatically. You will deservedly feel an increased pride in your new and successful management style—the *interactive management* style.

You needn't wait; you can start to apply interactive management skills immediately—on the job. The path has been mapped. Where do *you* go from here?

Index